DIVE

The Complete Book of
Skin Diving

DIVE

The Complete Book of Skin Diving

Rick & Barbara Carrier
Newly Revised by Charles Berlitz

Funk & Wagnalls / New York

Copyright © 1973 by Funk & Wagnalls, Inc.
Previous copyright 1955, 1963 by Wilfred Funk, Inc.

All rights reserved. Except for use in a review,
the reproduction or utilization of this work in
any form or by any electronic, mechanical, or
other means, now known or hereafter invented,
including xerography, photocopying, and recording, and in any information storage and retrieval
system is forbidden without the written permission
of the publisher. Published simultaneously in
Canada by Fitzhenry & Whiteside Limited, Toronto.

Manufactured in the United States of America

2   3   4   5   6   7   8   9   10

Library of Congress Cataloging in Publication Data

Carrier, Rick
    Dive: the complete book of skin diving.

    Bibliography: p.
    1. Skin diving. I. Carrier, Barbara, joint author.
II. Berlitz, Charles Frambach, 1913-   III. Title.
IV. Title: The complete book of skin diving.
GV840.S78C3   1973   797.2′3   73-4513
ISBN 0-308-10056-5

Photo by George Knoblach

To the sea from which we came and to which an increasing number of us have returned

Special Acknowledgments

The editor wishes to express his appreciation for the special help given in the preparation of this edition by the following:

Arnold Post, of Richards Aqualung Center and the New York Aqualung School, pioneer, designer, and developer of diving equipment, oceanographer, researcher, author of many articles and instruction manuals on diving and equipment, and an important early influence in convincing the U. S. Navy to change its training emphasis from "hard hat" to SCUBA diving. He has dived in most of the world's seas and oceans and has been notably active in the development of underwater safety devices.

Paul J. Tzimoulis, author and publisher of *Skin Diver* magazine, has covered half a million miles in his diving expeditions. He has distinguished himself as a writer, underwater photographer, commercial diver, SCUBA instructor, oceanographer, lecturer, and marine conservationalist. One of his remarkable pictures, showing a descent off the continental shelf in the Bahamas, is shown on the cover of this book.

Bob Schaefer and Ron Ribaudo, longtime divers, testers, and developers of underwater gear for freezing as well as tropical temperatures, have been especially helpful in furnishing pictures and information concerning underwater habitats and the most recent developments in underwater equipment.

Gene Parker, diver and photographer, author of the *Civil Defense Diver Manual*, who has made valuable contributions to the previous edition of *Dive*.

Contents

	Introduction IX
I	How It All Began 1
II	The Watery World 17
III	Physiological Problems of Diving 66
IV	Equipment and Its Uses 92
V	Build It Yourself 175
VI	The Techniques of Spearfishing 197
VII	SCUBA Clubs and Activities 218
VIII	Photography Under Water 232
IX	The Unexplored Sea 252
	Bibliography 271
	Acknowledgments 275
	Index 277

Introduction

For the thousands of years of civilized man's experience on earth, the sea has been an uncertain road for his travels as well as a dark, mysterious gulf which has swallowed ships and their cargoes, sailors, islands, cities, and perhaps entire continents. It is only within the last fifty years that man has been able to explore the other world which has always existed side by side with the one he was familiar with—the world under the sea. He can now explore a considerable part of the seven-eighths of the world's crust which lies below the waters of the earth. He is able to do so at present, not contained within diving bells or submarines, or shackled by heavy diving suits, but by swimming, free as a fish or a porpoise, on his own terms and, within certain limits, in any direction he wishes to travel.

A swimmer's first look at the underwater world through a face mask is an unforgettable experience. The water that before was covered by waves or ripples, or was blurry and opaque to the swimmer's unprotected eyes when seen from underwater, has suddenly changed. It has become transparent. Scenes that were invisible have suddenly materialized before the diver's eyes as if a light had been turned on in a darkened room. Fishes seem not so much to be swimming, but soaring through the element, as if their fins were wings;

and when the swimmer, aided by his fins, dives down to the now inviting sea bottom and then planes upward again, it seems to him that he is flying too. And when he is equipped with a lung or SCUBA (a self-contained underwater breathing apparatus) the illusion is even more remarkable. As he progresses along the sea bottom he soars over hills, canyons, valleys, and plains, landscapes of a new and incredible world where the trees (or algae) sway with the currents instead of the winds, where a whole creation of fish and marine life take on a new aspect when encountered under the water.

Besides the fascination of marine life, the skin or SCUBA diver can make his own way to historical or archaeological treasure. Ancient and modern wrecks still lie undiscovered on the sea bottom, undisturbed since they sunk hundreds or even thousands of years ago. Roads, causeways, temples, palaces, and even the remains of ancient cities lie beneath the sea where change of water levels or seismic disturbances have caused them to sink. SCUBA divers have frequently been rewarded by more material treasures, in the form of gold or valuable cargoes, which revert to the finder under maritime law. SCUBA diving is in one sense the key to the past, in that it can uncover undisturbed "encapsulated" history, the key to a new enjoyment of the earth's seas, lakes, and rivers for adventurous swimmers, and it eventually may be the key, through sea farming, to the future survival of the earth's population.

In the case of such a psychologically and often materially rewarding activity or sport, one may wonder why the number of its adherents has not grown even beyond the two million divers now in the United States, with a calculated increase, according to subscription figures of *Skin Diver* magazine, of ten thousand a month. Nevertheless, the ratio of skin divers to the general population is still less than one in two hundred.

This is perhaps due to a general misconception on the part of the public as to the difficulties of SCUBA diving, and because of the long preparation in lessons and practice that it seems to entail. This feeling has doubtless been augmented by the dangers attributed to SCUBA diving by so many movies, television programs, and personal, narrative stories published since SCUBA diving first became popular after World War II.

Dive was originally written in the early 50's, the first diving book not based on personal narrative but written for the purpose of telling the reader not only about diving but *how* to dive, how to use diving equipment, and what to expect and how to react underwater. *Dive* is still the most effective printed material and advice that the beginner has at his disposal, and the present edition, including as it does examples of the newest and most sophisticated diving equipment, as well as examples of the earlier "home made rigs," presents a complete survey as well as an important, informative guide to what the beginner should know about diving. It is based on the accumulative experience of SCUBA diving since the Cousteau-Gagnan Diving Lung was first made available to the public. And, most important for the beginning diver, *Dive* is written in simple, non-technical language that anyone can understand.

Long and expensive courses are not necessary to make one a proficient SCUBA diver. While it is certainly advisable to learn from experts how properly to use the lung and regulator and to understand and memorize the "do's" and "don'ts" relating to pressure changes, anyone in reasonably good health and possessing normal physical reflexes can learn the essentials of SCUBA diving in about one hour. But the aspirant diver must, of course, already feel "at home" in the water, and be able to cope with unexpected shifts in currents, waves, floating objects, and unexpected incidents. Otherwise, and especially if the person is basically afraid of the water, the amount of lessons one takes doesn't really matter. It frequently happens that much lesson time is taken in developing reflexes applicable to unexpected situations—changing masks under water—and taking off and putting on equipment in a pool. All this is important but comes under practice rather than basic information. This practice could better be accomplished in real undersea conditions, complete with tides, currents, waves, varying visibility, uneven sea bottom, algae forests and passing fish, instead of in a swimming pool, just as automobile driving lessons are given in city traffic instead of a controlled area. The dangers of SCUBA diving can, in a sense, be compared with the dangers of driving a car, which have been generally accepted and overcome by almost everyone, however lethal cars may have been considered in their early days. Like driving, SCUBA diving implies certain rules which must be followed to avoid accidents, just as certain procedures must be followed in driving to control the car and avoid accidents. If, for example, divers follow the basic information contained in this book, they will not only avoid diving mishaps, but will be, according to statistics, much safer than drivers or passengers in cars or on planes.

The analogy with driving can be further stated: you can't learn to drive without driving a car yourself: you can't learn to be a

SCUBA diver without diving on your own. A car is a machine dangerous to others and yourself: SCUBA equipment is potentially dangerous only to yourself and only if you disregard certain simple rules. Just as drivers who speed on the left side of the road are liable to accidents, divers who ignore or forget the down-up or descent-ascent rates of speed will encounter decompression difficulties. Nevertheless, since 98% of diving does not take place below a level of sixty feet, no decompression is involved at this level. The basic and easily remembered advice concerning ascent—come up no faster than your slowest bubbles and breathe normally at all times—will fully avoid the pressure problems so publicized in so many books on diving, which, after all, usually refer to specific dives of long duration. For the ordinary sport diver the information in this book on how to dive will serve as an invaluable aid to an activity which has progressed in a few years from a sport to an avocation with millions of adherents throughout the world.

Living on the earth and not having essayed a brief sojourn underwater—whether it be the ocean, bays, inland seas, lakes, or rivers—is like living in a spacious house but restricting oneself to visiting a few rooms only. The underwater world that we can *now* visit—the continental shelves, the underwater banks of surrounding oceanic islands and the inland waters constitute a considerable part, and a strangely beautiful one, of the earth's surface. Those who have visited there through SCUBA or skin diving have expanded their view of earth and nature and, in so doing, their own personality has been broadened as a result of what they have experienced.

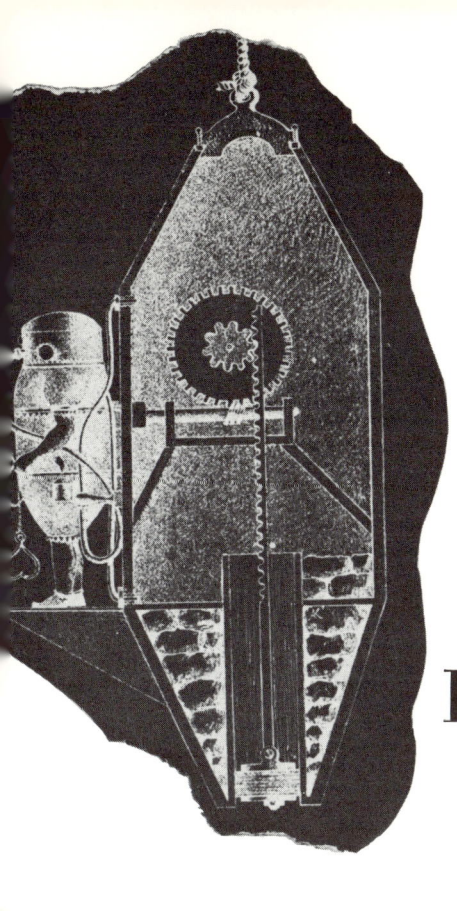

I

How It All Began

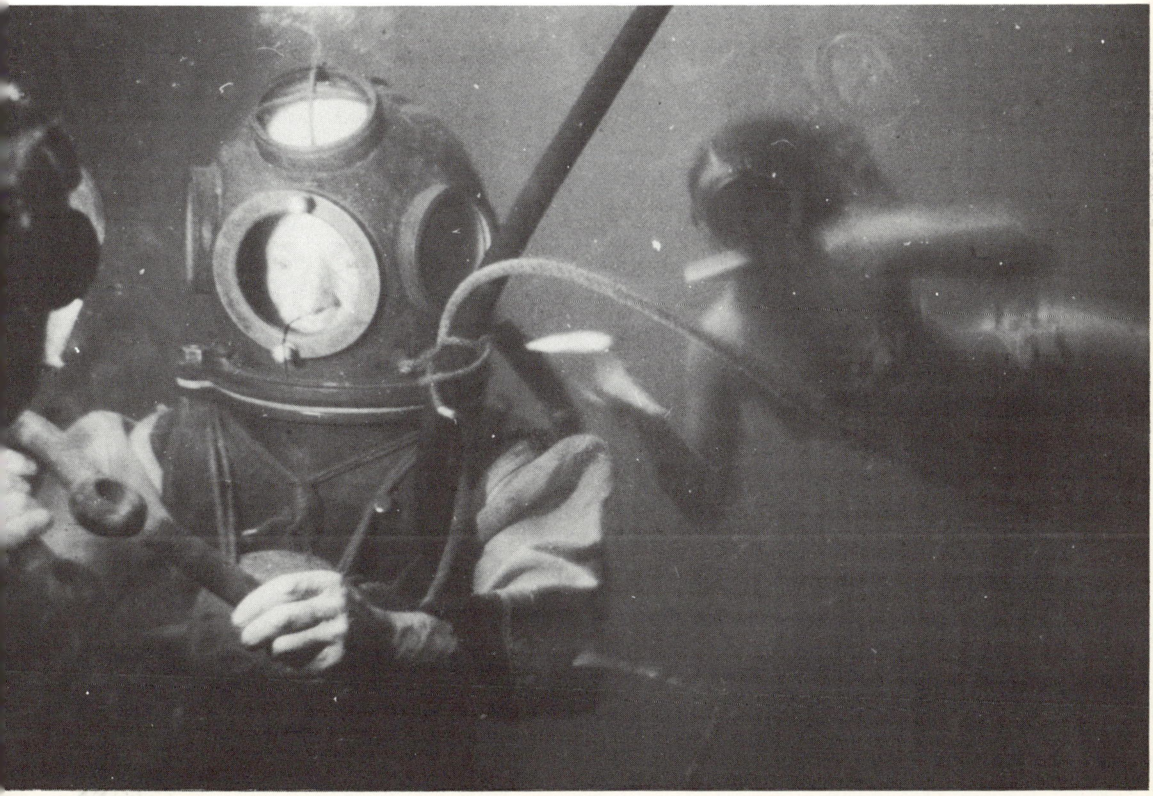

In recent summers, vacationists finding their favorite secluded beaches suddenly swarming with bronzed young men armed with knives, spears and carbon dioxide guns, or being startled during a quiet swim by the sudden appearance in the water beside them of a "man from Mars" complete with mask, flippers, and breathing apparatus, may have wondered what it is all about, and just how and why the sudden enthusiasm for skin diving developed.

Extended coverage of the sport by national magazines, television and Hollywood, the appearance of thousands of combination kits of mask and flippers on the counters of five and ten cent stores, and the spectacle of even three- and four-year old children standing bottoms up, intently peering into the water through junior-sized goggles and breathing noisily through red, yellow, and blue snorkel tubes are other indications of the development of a once fairly esoteric sport into the newest national fad.

The why of it all probably stems partly from the well-known American spirit of adventure and enthusiasm for anything new. During the 30's, sports divers, using no equipment other than diving masks and spears had been learning the pleasures of skin diving and spearfishing from the natives of Pacific islands, whose ancestors had been diving for pearls and sponges for centuries. These travelers, as well as servicemen later returning from Pacific war bases, helped to introduce the sport in warmer areas such as Florida and California. Later it spread to other sections of the United States.

In the Mediterranean in the meantime, where sponge divers had pursued their trade since the days of ancient civilizations, men such as Captain J. Y. Cousteau of France and Hans Hass of Germany had been exploring the possibilities of the sport and experimenting with new types of diving equipment. Their books, describing their experiences underwater in lyrical and evocative passages, communicated the excitement of a personal discovery, and created many new skin diving enthusiasts both in this country and in Europe. In addition, the exploits of the Navy frogmen during the war gave the whole thing an aura of heroism and daring that made it especially appealing to many boys. Today, there are over twelve million adults and children using mask, snorkel, and fins in this country. And many young adults are entering skin diving competitions.

Perhaps one of the more important reasons for the phenomenal growth of skin diving as a sport has been the rapid development in recent years of new and improved diving equipment. Well-designed masks, to allow the diver to see a world which would otherwise be

Fig. 1. Today more and more people set out to explore the underwater world. French girl diver with snorkel tucked jauntily in her bikini. *Photo by H. Broussard*

merely a watery blur, and foot flippers to give him more speed and greater downward propulsion on a dive, have become generally available at popular prices. For the more ambitious diver, the invention of safer, less cumbersome, and easier-to-operate self-contained underwater breathing apparatus (generally shortened to SCUBA) such as the Aqua-Lung, has made it possible to swim for long periods underwater, independent of the surface, with the freedom of a fish.

However before this degree of success in man's adaptation to the underwater world could be achieved, many centuries had to pass, many men had to attempt to solve the problem, with imagination and patient work and experimentation.

Natural diving, that is, diving without any equipment to supply air to the diver or counteract the effects of water pressure, has been practiced for thousands of years. Evidences such as ancient piles of oyster and other deep-water shells indicate that seacoast dwelling tribes in prehistoric times swam, dived, and got some of their food from the sea.

The early Cretan civilization (3000 B.C. to 1400 B.C.) built much of its economy and its art around the sea and its products—fish, sponges, and purple dye from murex shells.

References are found to divers being used several hundred years before Christ, in diving for sponges and mollusks, in the salvage of sunken vessels, as underwater saboteurs during wars, and in maintenance work on the hulls of ships. In Homer's *Iliad* (about 750 B.C.) one character derides a charioteer who has fallen, telling him he looked like a diver diving for seafood.

One of the earlier stories involving a diver taking part in naval warfare is the tale of Scyllias of Scione, as related by Herodotus (about 460 B.C.). Scyllias, a popular Greek diver to whom many heroic exploits were attributed, had been captured by the Persians under Xerxes and forced to work for them aboard a Persian ship. Learning that the Persians were planning a surprise attack on a fleet of Greek ships gathered at Artemisium, he jumped overboard during a storm, cut the cables of the Persian ships, rendering them uncontrollable in the storm, and swam to Artemisium ten miles away to warn the Greeks. Legends of the time credited him with swimming the entire distance underwater, an indication of the esteem in which he was held as a popular hero, virtually the "Superman" of his time.

A later, but equally colorful story of underwater attack on ships is the exploit of Byzantine divers who cut the cables of Roman ships which were blockading their harbor, and attached other cables by means of which the assembled populace of Byzantium hauled the ships to shore. This created great panic among the Roman sailors, who imagined the ships were deserting the fleet of their own accord.

In the first century A.D., the king of Sweden sent a fleet against the notorious Danish pirate Oddo, who had a reputation as a magician able to control the waters. Swedish divers soon punctured this myth by cutting holes in the bottom of his ships under cover of darkness. The next morning while Oddo and his men were frantically bailing them out, the crafty Swedes attacked and killed them all.

One would gather, from a story told by Plutarch about Antony and Cleopatra, that experienced divers were pretty generally available in those days. During a fishing contest held before Cleopatra, Antony, who wanted to make a big impression on her, secretly hired a diver to attach fish to his hook so that he would appear to be catching more than anyone else. His apparent skill seemed to impress Cleopatra, until the next day, having invited all her courtiers to be present, she had her own diver put a preserved, salted fish on Antony's hook. When he pulled up his "catch" she remarked that his calling seemed to be conquering countries rather than fishing.

During the Middle Ages the use of divers in naval warfare had become so common that sometimes enemy divers met underwater. This happened as late as 1565 at the siege of Malta, when Turkish and Maltese divers engaged in a bloody battle, hacking at each other with hatchets until the Turks were so badly injured that they had to retreat.

The invention of gunpowder minimized the diver's role in naval battles, and it was not until World War II that the frogmen, wearing self-contained underwater breathing apparatus, again made the diver important in naval warfare.

The last natural divers to be officially recognized were Louis XIII's *mourgons*, whose job was to maintain the hulls of ships. The Spanish still used unequipped divers as late as 1779, although some forms of diving equipment had come into general use by then.

Obviously, natural divers were limited both in the depths to which they could go and the length of time they could stay underwater. The average pearl and sponge diver does not go much deeper than 75 feet or stay submerged for more than a minute and a half. However there are many exceptions. Cousteau mentions a sixty-year-old Arab sponge diver he observed off Tunisia in 1939, who went to a depth of 130 feet in an immersion time of 2½ minutes. Professional

Fig. 2. Earliest known representation of an underwater breathing apparatus. From an Assyrian bas relief of about 900 B.C.

divers and performers have been able, as a stunt, to remain underwater without taking a breath for more than 4 minutes, one as long as 4 minutes, 46 seconds. However, these men were submerged in tanks at no great depth and were not involved in any work or activity.

To do any prolonged work underwater such as salvage or building or destroying harbor defenses, some form of diving equipment is necessary.

Also the human body is not built to take prolonged exposures to the pressures of deep water. Pearl and sponge divers are generally not long-lived people. They often suffer from divers' diseases such as the "bends," and frequently hemorrhage from the nose, ears and mouth. They often become deaf; many die from abnormal distension of the lungs.

Man having lost his embryonic gills, artificial means had to be devised to allow him to adapt himself again to the watery world his ancestors left so long ago. If men were to be able to explore the sea to any extent, equipment had to be developed to supply air to the diver and to counteract the effects of water pressure.

Early attempts at the development of diving equipment were crude and impracticable. One of the earliest indications of an air supply being provided for a diver is found in an Assyrian bas relief of about 900 B.C. (Fig. 2). This shows a man swimming, apparently underwater, with an air bladder (probably an inflated animal skin) held against his chest by a belt around his waist at one end and a tube held in his mouth at the other. However, the buoyancy of an air-filled skin of the size pictured would have made it impossible for one man to hold it underwater.

Aristotle described a diving appliance, apparently a form of diving bell, which was used by divers during the siege of Tyre by Alexander the Great in 333 B.C. Alexander himself featured in legends telling of his descent into the sea in some sort of diving bell. In old engravings it is variously pictured as resembling everything from an oversized beer barrel to a glass fish bowl (Fig. 6a).

Aristotle also mentioned divers drawing air through a tube from the surface, comparing this to elephants going through the water with their trunks held above water to take in air. Probably the earliest method of breathing underwater was through a hollow reed with its tip projecting above the water. Later divers often used tubes attached to a float at the surface, the float usually being made of cork (Fig. 4). However, this method was completely ineffective at depths greater than just below the surface, because of the immense effort needed to draw down air when the chest is compressed by the pressure of the surrounding water.

Many weird designs for diving gear can be found in early manuscripts. Some of them show completely enclosed helmets with no eye holes, apparently considering it unnecessary for the diver to be able to see his surroundings (Fig. 5).

Fig. 3. "Skin" divers: a. with air bladder—Vegetius, 1511 (or 1532); b. with tube to surface—Valentini, 1459. *Courtesy, New York Public Library*

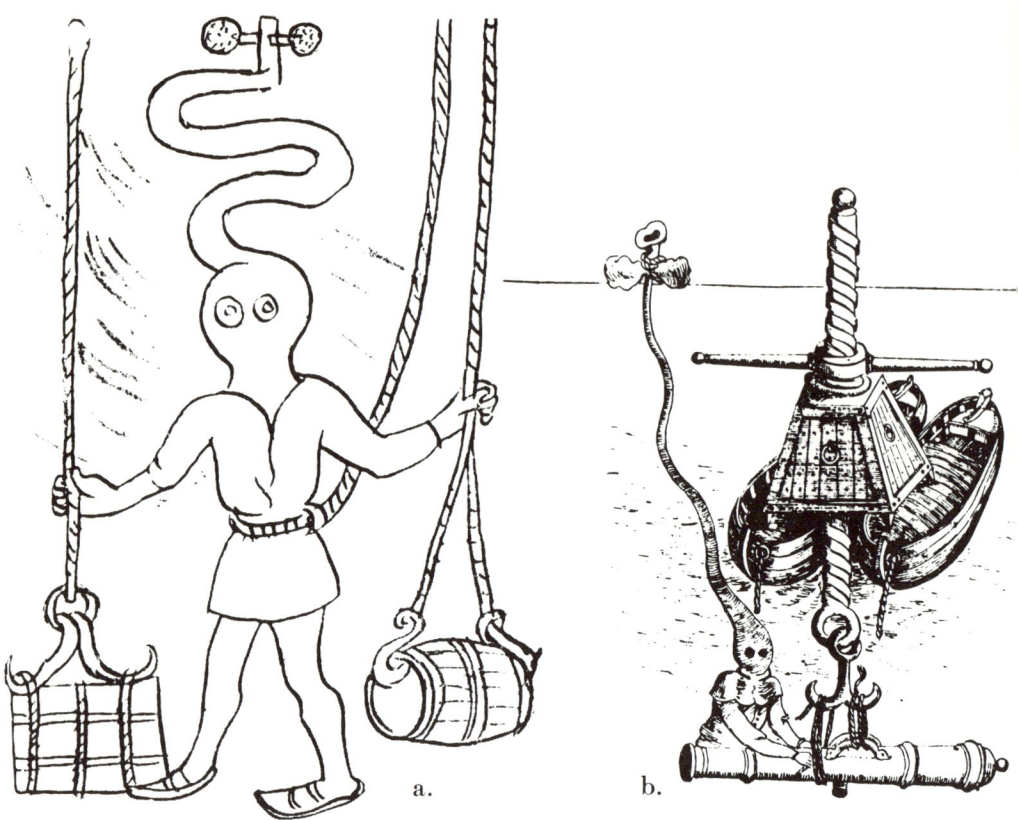

Fig. 4. Early prints of salvage divers using air tube and float: a. From manuscript of 1415; b. From Diego Ufano, 1613. *Courtesy, New York Public Library*

Leonardo da Vinci's notebooks show, among his designs for practically everything else, sketches of several types of diving apparatus. The designs range from simple tubes leading to floats at the surface to what is almost a complete self-contained diving suit, with a mask covering nose and mouth and connected to an air reservoir on the diver's chest, sandbags for ballast, and even an outlet for urination. He also showed a design for webbed swimming gloves, possibly an inspiration for the foot fins developed later.

Probably the first design for a re-circulating diving apparatus was that of Giovanni Borelli (Fig. 7a), an Italian astronomer and professor of mathematics, in 1680. His sketches show the diver's head inside a large air bag with a glass window, and a breathing pipe running first outside the air bag, through a small bag intended to trap moisture, and back into the air bag again. He felt that this water cooling would "purify" the exhaled air so that it could be re-

Fig. 5. Warrior ready for blind combat—Vegetius, 1511 (or 1532). *Courtesy, New York Public Library*

breathed. He also shows the diver carrying a rather involved cylinder and piston apparatus intended to regulate his displacement in the water. Of course his idea for regenerating the air was unworkable, but it is noteworthy as a first attempt at solving the problem of self-contained diving.

Not all of these early designs were completely unworkable. The diving bell principle seems to have had the most success, at this stage of the game. In Toledo, Spain, in 1538, two Greeks went to the bottom of the Tagus, using a large kettle for a diving bell, and returned to astound a waiting audience with dry clothes and a candle still burning.

Edmund Halley in 1716 developed a wooden bell in which the air was replenished by air sent down in barrels. This worked well enough for men to remain in it for over an hour and a half at a time. In 1715 an inventor named Becker stayed underwater for about an hour inside a stationary diving apparatus with an enormous breathing pipe similar to one used by Lorini in 1597 (Fig. 6b).

One of the first diving suits used to do real work underwater was a suit with leather pipes which were strengthened by brass wire leading to the surface. This was used in the attempted salvage of the ship-of-the-line *Royal George* in 1783; but due to the fatigue of

a.

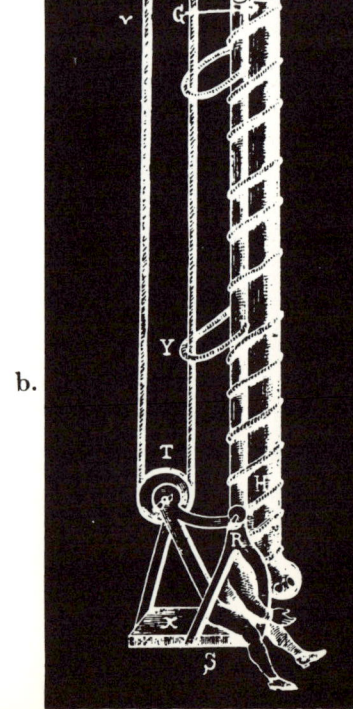

b.

Fig. 6. a. Alexander's diving bell—from a 15th century print; b. Lorini diver breathing through a large stationary pipe, 1597; c. Sturmius's diving bell, 1678; d. Early attempt at salvage of *Royal George*, 1783. Courtesy, New York Public Library

breathing with this arrangement, divers were able to remain submerged for only a short time.

Obviously it was necessary to pump the air down to the diver under pressure. Attempts had been made to do this using bellows, but with only limited success. One of the great milestones in diving history was the invention by Augustus Siebe of his "open dress" in 1819. Air was supplied under pressure to the helmet by means of a force pump and hose, and flowed out at the diver's waist.

The first self-contained diving suit to carry a supply of compressed air was one designed by W. H. James in 1825. The air was contained in an iron reservoir worn around the waist. The self-contained suit was not considered too important at that time, however, and in 1837, Siebe developed his closed suit which became the standard diving dress for about a century. This was an improvement over the open dress in that the diver could bend over without having water rush into the suit, and further, he was protected against the effects of external water pressure.

For years it was felt that Siebe's closed suit represented the ultimate in diving gear. Two Frenchmen, Rouquayrol and Denayrouze, added a compressed air tank, making it convertible into a self-contained apparatus, but since they retained the bulky suit and

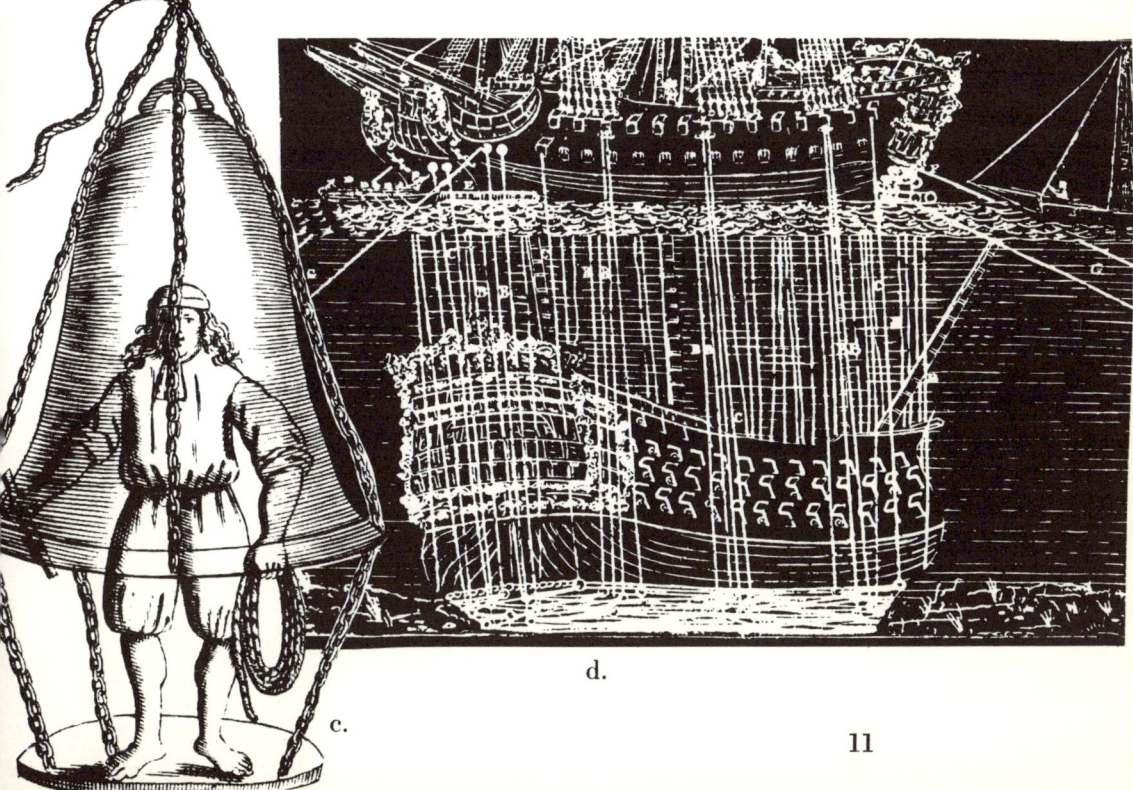

c.

d.

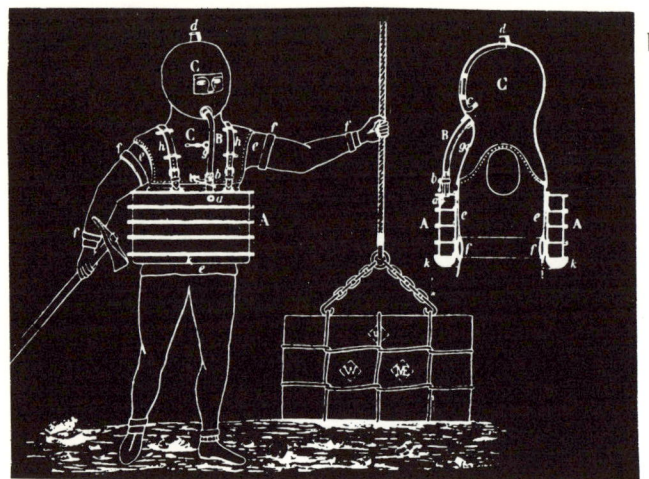

Fig. 7. Later attempts at self-contained underwater breathing apparatus: a. Borelli's "self-contained" breathing apparatus, 1582; b. James's self-contained breathing apparatus with compressed air reservoir at waist, 1825. *Courtesy, New York Public Library*

heavy foot-weights, self-contained diving did not become popular.

H. A. Fleuss of the British firm Siebe, Gorman & Company worked out an oxygen rebreathing apparatus using a solution of tow and caustic potash to absorb the exhaled carbon dioxide in 1878. In 1902, Sir R. H. Davis collaborated with Fleuss to improve the apparatus, using more effective carbon dioxide absorbents, steel cylinders for oxygen, and an automatic feed valve. This equipment was used during World War I for protection against poison gas and also as a submarine escape-device.

In 1925, a French naval officer, Commander Le Prieur, developed a self-contained device using compressed air rather than the oxygen of the Davis unit. This was an improvement over oxygen in that the diver could go to greater depths without the dangers of oxygen, which becomes poisonous under pressure, and cannot safely be used below about 35 feet. Also, the carbon dioxide absorbent had so far proved somewhat undependable, and several divers had had accidents using it. (Later improved CO_2 absorbents were devised.)

Le Prieur's apparatus carried a steel cylinder of compressed air, which was released in a continuous flow into a face mask, and the exhaled air flowed out into the water. The flow of air was regulated manually by the diver.

In 1943, Captain Cousteau, who had experimented with the idea for some years, introduced the Cousteau-Gagnan Aqua-Lung. This device also used cylinders of compressed air but had a regulator attached to adjust the air pressure automatically to the diver's needs. The diver breathed through a rubber mouthpiece clamped between the teeth, and the regulator automatically increased the air pressure to equalize pressures inside the body with increasing water pressure on the outside. This eliminated the need for a cumbersome pressurized suit.

Worn with the rubber foot flippers developed by Commander Le Corlieu and a diving mask, which was a direct descendant of the goggles and masks worn by native divers in the Pacific and in the Mediterranean for centuries, this apparatus allowed men to dive with new freedom and safety. The diver could turn, twist, swim in

Fig. 8. The Aqua-Lung self-contained underwater breathing apparatus which gives the diver the freedom and mobility of a fish. *Courtesy, Poseidon Systems USA*

any position, could move freely in the watery element as if he belonged there.

The achievement of this degree of freedom and mobility in a strange, beautiful, and largely unexplored world has had an intense psychological impact on sensitive men. Over and over in the books of divers like Cousteau, Philippe Tailliez, and Philippe Diolé, we find lyrical, almost ecstatic passages describing their reactions to the new experience.

In addition to the excitement of entering into and exploring a hitherto mysterious and hidden world, with its luminous effects of light and water, its brilliant corals and slow moving fish, there is the sheer physical joy of the experience.

The diver is freed from the strain of holding his body upright in air. Instead of balancing himself on the bones of his feet, which must support the weight of his entire body, he is supported evenly all over by a substance softer than any mattress. Not only does the water support him and keep him from falling but, with the addition of belt weights which paradoxically render him weightless, he is able to move through it, horizontally or vertically, with a freedom like that of a bird in air.

Cousteau mentions that he had frequently had dreams of flying through the air, using his arms as wings, but that after his first experience with the Aqua-lung, he never dreamed again of flying. He did not need to dream, the experience was his in reality. Diolé, in *The Undersea Adventure,* says also, "Perhaps it will be understood if I say that he (the diver) moves about the sea the way one flies in dreams."

He continues on, in the same theme: "I have perhaps lived a miracle, one which I want to talk about. I have traveled to another world in which 'action is sister to the dream.' I have swept away in the heart of the sea, at a depth of several fathoms, all my anxieties as a man. Worries of the moment, scientific curiosity, metaphysical doubts, have all been hurled into the sea and I do not regret it. Like many others I do not feel in perfect harmony with our age, and the solitude of diving lulls and stays a deeprooted dissatisfaction. Down below, where dream and action move silently forward, side by side, through the dense waters, man feels for a moment in tune with life!"

Perhaps this comment is the key to part of the appeal which skin diving seems to have for so many people today. Perhaps in a time so troubled and complex, when man has a sense of helplessness in the face of decisions and responsibilities which may involve the very survival or destruction of his world, more people than ever feel the need for some means of escape. Ours is an age so filled with anxiety that even the pastoral scenes which used to be escape and solace enough no longer seem to suffice. Even the trees seem to have gathered about them the miasma of our thoughts, associations, tensions. It may be that only in the cleansing freshness of the sea, where nothing is familiar to our eyes, can we still find peace.

Through diving one learns to slow down, to take time to observe his surroundings. In the underwater world he develops a sense of proportion about himself and his troubles, none of which seem after all as important as he had thought. The diver leaves something of his individual personality, his worries, tensions, preoccupations with self, behind him like an outer layer of clothing discarded on the beach. Gradually he begins to feel himself a part of the vast, slow, inevitable rhythms of nature, as he surrenders himself to the sea.

Fig. 9. The diver flies dream-like through a liquid luminous world of filtered light. *Photo Courtesy, Dmitri Rebikoff*

II

The Watery World

Courtesy, Ben Holder

Almost three quarters of the earth's surface is covered by water, and in the northern hemisphere there are about two square miles of ocean water for every square mile of land. We live in a water world which, if it were not for the irregularities of its surface, would be entirely submerged under water two and one-quarter miles deep.

Throughout the ages man has been deeply curious about the seas that wash his shores, mysterious and powerful; the sea in which he had his beginnings and whose mineral content is still reflected in the composition of his blood.

An element so powerful, so seemingly endless, was certain to instil fear. But gradually, through his courage, his innate curiosity and inventiveness, his need for food and transportation, and his restless resentment of nature's barriers, man learned to move upon the sea with some degree of freedom and safety and later, even to penetrate beneath it.

The diver, when he pierces the watery barrier, finds himself in a strange new world. Around him stretch mysterious undersea landscapes where seaweeds and plantlike animal forms move gently or are still. Slow fish swim past him, some inquisitive, some indifferent; others dart away, frightened. He feels himself to be an alien and an intruder here, where another quieter way of life, which has gone on like this for centuries, has been hidden from the eye of man.

Perhaps the diver stills his vague feeling of insecurity by attempting to create his own world here, as much like the one he left above in the sunlight as he can: diving with friends around him, for records, for sport; pursuing and spearing the fish he encounters; needing to conquer this new world and thus control it.

Or perhaps he is sensitive enough to realize that a new world of experience will be closed off forever from him if he is too quick to assert his dominance here. Perhaps he is content to be unassertive for a while, to be quiet, to be curious, to wait and look about him, and when he does spear fish to take only those which he needs for food.

There is so much to be learned about the sea and its life. Now that most of the land surface of the earth has been explored, the new frontier lies beneath the sea. The possibilities are limitless, for research and for development of new sources of food and power and natural resources, for new understanding of marine life and of the remains of ancient civilizations. But no one should attempt to explore even the fringes of the sea without some understanding of this alien environment and without a great deal of respect for it.

The part of the sea which is influenced by the tides is called the tidal zone. This area has its own characteristic forms of marine life that are so developed as to enable them to protect themselves against the effect of drying air as well as against the attacks of land animals.

From the tidal zone out to a depth of about six hundred feet is considered the continental shelf. The continental shelves are the part of the sea most important economically to man; most of the food he gets from the sea is found there; here lie oil and other natural resources which he is only beginning to utilize.

These shelves are caused by the silt washed down by rivers and sometimes by the sinking of land areas which were once above water. The width of the continental shelf off the United States varies considerably. Along the West Coast it is fairly narrow, not over 20 miles wide. On the East Coast it may be 100 or 150 miles wide in parts; off Florida, however, it is only a few miles wide. The widest shelves are found in the Arctic—up to 750 miles.

From a depth of about 600 feet, or from wherever the land begins to slope suddenly downward, to a depth of a mile or more is called the continental slope. The continental slope descends at an average angle of about three degrees. In some areas this slope continues downward to merge gradually with the vast sea bed. In other places it is cut abruptly by cliffs and marine canyons. Beyond the area where plant life can live, the slopes are more sparsely inhabited by marine animals than the thickly populated continental shelves. Here there is no seasonal change in temperature, no movement from surface waves. At the borderline of the continental shelf the strongest surface waves can move only tiny mud particles. Beyond a thousand feet, no light rays penetrate.

Below the continental slopes lies the abyss, the cold, dark, desolate, sparsely populated world which makes up most of the area covered by the sea. The abyss averages about three miles in depth but drops off to nearly seven miles in the Challenger Trench off the Mariana Islands. The deepest parts are found in the Pacific Ocean, greatest of seas, which occupies a huge gouge in the earth's surface, and whose floor is formed of basalt, the middle layer of the earth, rather than the granite covering which lies beneath the other oceans. However, off Puerto Rico in the Atlantic, the Puerto Rico Trench reaches a depth of almost six miles. These great gouges in the ocean floor are always found beside sharp upthrustings of the earth's crust, probably due to volcanic action. Some of these cavities may be the throats of long extinct volcanoes.

a.

The floor of the abyss is covered with the accumulated sediments of millions of years, in spots to a depth of 12,000 feet. The contours are irregular, with plains, valleys, and mountain ridges older, higher, and more sharply defined than those of the land, since once below the level of wave action there is nothing to wear them down. Recent soundings have revealed long river canyons along the floor of the abyss, and it has been suggested that the smooth abysmal plains are the result of accumulations of silt and sand carried down from the slopes of the continents and for unmeasurable miles along the bottom by powerful underocean rivers.

In spite of darkness, cold, and great pressures up to 7.96 tons per square inch, life does exist in the abyss. Much of it is deformed and distorted from the species with which we are familiar into creatures especially adapted to living at these great depths: strangely shaped, often luminescent, eyeless or with strange telescopic eyes.

But since the pressures inside the tissues of these animals correspond to outside water pressures, even seemingly fragile forms are

Fig. 10. Diving as a means for: a. Observing marine life in its natural habitat; b. Collecting shells, corals, and marine specimens; c. Archeological research. *Photos Courtesy, Poseidon Systems USA, Ben Holderness, and Dimitri Rebikoff*

able to exist here. There is enough oxygen for life, since colder water from the surface which has become mixed with oxygen due to wave action is constantly sinking because of its greater density and carrying down oxygen with it. Also, life in these icy depths is carried on at a much slower pace, and therefore animals need less oxygen.

In these abysmal depths the water, even near the equator, is close to the freezing point, and some parts of the sea are colder than the freezing point of fresh water. (When fresh water reaches 39° F. it expands and rises, so the bottom of a freshwater lake does not get as cold as the bottom of the sea.) Fish which live in ocean depths where the water temperature is less than 29° F. still swim and lead active lives, although if their blood is chilled experimentally it will freeze before reaching that temperature. Apparently the great pressures have the effect of lowering the water's freezing point, and this helps to keep the fish from freezing, although scientists feel that this is not the full explanation. There is still a vast amount that is not yet completely understood about the sea and its life, particularly in the inaccessible depths of the abyss.

Those areas which are specifically of concern to the skin diver are the tidal zone and the continental shelf. Divers, whether wearing self-contained breathing equipment or conventional diving suits, have yet to reach the six-hundred-foot drop-off line of the continental shelves, and it is felt that this depth is probably the limit reachable by individual divers, even with improved diving equipment and greater knowledge of physiology and safety measures. The blackness of the abyss beyond is penetrable only by diving bells and remote control cameras, armored and pressurized to resist the tremendous pressures of these depths.

The tidal zones and continental shelves contain the most abundant and most varied forms of marine life. The main reason for this is the availability of food. Almost nine-tenths of the ocean's food supply consists of one-celled microscopic plants called diatoms. Diatoms need silica to build their shells and, since this element is carried down to the ocean by rivers, these organisms are usually found within a few hundred miles of land. Diatoms, along with other microscopic organisms called dinoflagellates, animal larvae, and other small floating animals, which feed on the diatoms, are called plankton.

Many marine animals have equipment for straining the plankton out of the water flowing over their gills thus enabling them to feed without effort on their part. Even large sea animals such as whalebone whales and certain large sharks can feed directly on plankton and copepods (small crustaceans which feed on diatoms). Most large fish, however, are predatory, that is, they subsist on other, smaller fish. But these smaller fish are usually dependent on still smaller animals for their food supply; these in turn on still smaller ones that feed in their turn on diatoms. Thus these tiny plants are the original source of food on which all sea life is ultimately in some way dependent.

An important factor that determines the areas in which fish will be found is temperature. Fish, along with all forms of animal life apart from the mammals and birds, are unable to maintain a stable body temperature. Instead their temperature varies with their environment. In a cold-blooded land animal, being subjected to low temperatures causes its vital functions to slow down, often to the point where the animal becomes completely dormant (as in the case of frogs in the winter). Since temperatures on land may vary tremendously with the seasons, these animals can live only in certain areas and under certain conditions.

Water, however, has a fairly uniform temperature with nothing like the great temperature variations on land. The entire range of temperature in the sea is from 28.5° F. in the arctic depths to 85° F. at the surface in certain parts of the tropics. Three quarters of the sea's surface has a seasonal temperature change of less than 9° F.

But even small variations of temperature have an effect on sea life. Each form has a temperature range within which it can live, and anything above or below those levels may cause death. (Perhaps you have observed fish dying in tide pools exposed to the hot sun.) Therefore most forms of sea life are restricted by temperature to certain areas.

Ocean currents are also an important factor in the distribution of marine life, since they may affect the temperature or the salinity of the water and since they also aid in the distribution of larvae and serve as a carrier of food elements which diatoms and stationary marine life need.

In general, currents in the ocean, whether caused by prevailing winds, by the earth's rotation, or by tidal forces, tend to turn toward the right, or clockwise, in the Northern Hemisphere, and to the left, or counter-clockwise, in the Southern. This is due to the earth's rotation and to the fact that polar waters have a lesser distance to travel than those at the equator and therefore move more slowly. The most regular and constant currents are the Japan Current of the Pacific and the Gulf Stream of the Atlantic.

The Gulf Stream is a mile deep and an average of ninety-five miles wide, and flows with a velocity of about three knots. This warm current thus brings a variety of fish usually associated with warmer zones to the waters off Montauk Point, Long Island, New York, during the summer, and also is responsible for the tropical fish and coral reefs found east of the Florida Keys.

On the West Coast of the United States, the clockwise current and the prevailing winds from the north carry the surface waters of the coast out to sea and the cold waters of the depths well up to take their place, thus making the waters of the Pacific Coast colder in summer than those of the East Coast. The sea off Maine, for example, which most bathers think of as frigid, may have a surface temperature as high as 62° F. in the summer, while Monterey Bay below San Francisco has a seaonal range of between 52° F. and 59 °F. To the north, the warm waters of the Japan Current run close to shore, so that the water temperature is fairly uniform from Sitka, Alaska, down as far as Point Conception in California. Along this same stretch are also found both strong surf and great depths close to the shore, so that even the weather is similar, cool and foggy.

Surf along this stretch of unprotected coast in California is quite a bit more violent than on most of the East Coast and has been said to be among the strongest in the world. At Pacific Grove some years ago, strong surf swept four-hundred-pound boulders across the highway. In some areas it is said that any person standing within twenty feet of the water is risking his life, since so many people have been swept off rocks by unexpectedly large waves.

To be really large, waves must have traveled a great distance with a constant wind behind them and without obstruction. Most waves are not over twenty-five feet high at the greatest, but storm waves have been measured as high as one hundred and twelve feet. Since there is nothing to break the flow of the waves across the great expanse of the Pacific, some of the waves that reach the shores of California have come as far as six thousand miles. These waves can usually be distinguished from local waves, since they come into the surf zone as long regular swells, rather than wind-tossed peaks, which slow as they near shore, rear into a high majestic crest, and then crash with a booming roar. Due to prevailing westerly winds, the East Coast does not get swell from really distant storms.

The power of waves should never be underestimated. No diver should attempt to enter the surf if it is extremely rough and he has

Fig. 11. Storm surf, Montauk, L. I., New York. *Photo by George Knoblach*

any doubts about his ability to get through it, especially if he is carrying or wearing heavy equipment. At any time it is wise to observe the water carefully before going in, to try to locate a spot where the surf seems calmer, and also to judge the rhythm of the waves, since often a large wave will be followed by two or three smaller ones. A diver, if he times it right, can often get beyond the breaker zone before the next large wave.

As every swimmer knows, the best approach to large waves is to dive under them, swimming seaward, but apart from this, no real diving should be attempted until well outside the breaker line. It is best to allow a space between divers entering the surf together, since this way there will be no danger of collisions when carrying spears and equipment, and also if a diver gets into trouble in the surf, his companions are in a better position to come to his aid. (No one should attempt to dive in the ocean without first becoming a really good swimmer. Most skin diving clubs have swimming requirements an applicant must pass, and some wisely require some degree of training in life-saving techniques.)

Entering the surf from rock jetties or in a rocky area is particularly hazardous. Since rocks may be slippery with marine vegetation, it is necessary to maintain a firm hold at all times and to keep a weather eye on the waves in order to brace oneself whenever necessary. As soon as the water is deep enough, the diver can push off wherever the water seems calmest, riding high on his tube or float (see Chapter IV) in order to avoid underwater rocks and to have the best possible visibility of the surrounding water and thus avoid hazards such as rocks or patches of seaweed.

Once past the breaker line and submerged, the diver is still affected by the surge, the back and forth sweep of the water in response to the movement of surface waves. The only way to escape this is to go deeper if possible, or, if not, to utilize the surge moving in the desired direction and then cling to a rock or to kelp to resist the backward sweep of the water. If swept into a cave or crevice by surge (many abalone gatherers have been drowned this way in California), it is wisest not to fight it but to remain alert and keep from being wedged in a crack, and to keep calm and wait for the returning movement of the surge to carry you out again. Long rolling waves coming from great distances affect the water below the surface much more severely than do wind-tossed, choppy waves.

A major coastwise phenomenon which is not yet completely understood is rip currents, or currents flowing out to sea through surf, which have been responsible for many drownings. These currents seem to be caused by wind-driven receding surf setting up a regular flow through a groove or channel on the bottom. They can sometimes be spotted and thus avoided by observing that waves in one section seem slightly flattened or depressed with a higher peak on either side, or that a section of water looks duller and more turbid. If caught in a rip current, it is best not to fight it, but to seek calmer water or a shorebound flow to one side of it or at a different level,

Fig. 12. Entering rough water from rock ledge. Special care must be taken, when spearfishing or diving in rough water, not to lose or be struck by your own equipment when hit by a wave. When coming out of surf it is advisable to remove your fins as soon as you can stand and to carry them securely in your hand. *Photo by George Knoblach*

or, if unsuccessful in this, to wait until it swings back toward shore, as it will eventually do.

Tides also vary from one area to another. Tides are caused by the gravitational pull of the moon and, to a lesser degree, of the sun, during the rotation of the earth. But they vary considerably throughout the world, and even in places within a short distance of each other, due to the different patterns of oscillation of the basins they are in and the part of the basin in which they lie, whether near the center where the tidal forces originate or near the edges where the effects of the tides are stronger.

In certain areas, such as the Gulf of Mexico, the tidal rhythm is once every twenty-four hours instead of twice. In others the tides are a mixture of the two. This is the case on the Pacific Coast where the two high and low tides of the day vary considerably from each other, causing a high, high tide and a low, low tide, and a low high tide and a high low tide. Also here the tides are lower during midsummer and midwinter. Sometimes narrow passages cause tide waters to pile up and cause extremely high tides. The Bay of Fundy between Maine and Nova Scotia has tides running to 70 feet.

Due to the moon's revolution around the earth once every twenty-nine days, the times of high and low tide are about fifty minutes later each day. When the sun and moon are in line, the combined effect produces spring tides which rise higher and fall lower than ordinarily. When they are opposed, the rise and fall of the tides is less, and these are called neap tides. (In Tahiti the tides follow the sun only and occur at almost the same time each day.)

Tide tables for the entire year for various areas can be obtained for a slight fee from the United States Coast and Geodetic Survey district offices or by writing the Survey's offices at Washington 25, D.C. Tide tables available include those for the entire East or West Coast of the United States, and even for Europe, the West Coast of Africa, and for the Central and Western Pacific and Indian Oceans, in case anyone is planning a really ambitious skin diving trip.

The Survey also publishes annual current tables, which include daily predictions of the times of slack water, and the times and velocities or strength of flood and ebb currents for various areas. These also include methods for obtaining the velocity of current at any time, and the duration of slack coastal-tidal currents, wind currents, the combination of currents, etc. The current tables for the Atlantic Coast also include some information on the Gulf Stream.

Underwater visibility also varies considerably in different areas.

The distance to which light penetrates depends on the latitude and the clarity of the water. The longer rays of the spectrum fade out first. Beebe gave the following figures for the depths of penetration of various light rays in the waters off Bermuda: at 25 feet red is gone, at 150 feet orange disappears, at 300 feet yellow, at 400 feet blue, and at 700 feet violet. No light rays penetrate beyond 1,000 feet.

The clarity or turbidity of water near shore may depend on silt from rivers or on pollution, but in the open ocean it depends largely on the number of microscopic organisms present in the water. Most of the diatoms are found in the upper one hundred feet, but in the tropics they may extend below this. Diatoms are also found most abundantly in colder waters, since the cold water welling up from the depths is rich in nutrient salts. Off Oregon, skin divers report the water to be so thick with diatoms at times that visibility is only about one foot. At the other extreme, under exceptionally clear conditions in the Mediterranean, visibility may be up to forty to sixty yards or more according to Diolé.

Water transparency may vary from level to level in the same area, with alternate layers of clarity and cloudiness. Often, in spite of the diminishing intensity of light, visibility may be better at greater depths than near the surface, since the concentration of microscopic plant life, which needs light to grow, is greater at the surface. Choppy water also cuts down the penetration of light, and rain falling at the surface may cause temporary cloudiness of the upper few feet, since fresh and salt waters are of different densities and their mixing creates a blurring effect in the water.

Visibility also varies considerably in the same area according to the tide and the time of year. Often a changing tide will stir up sediment and impair visibility. The concentration of diatoms in most areas is greatest in the spring and to a lesser degree in the fall, so visibility may be limited then. Also at these seasons the sunlight is weaker than during the summer months, and so will not penetrate as deeply.

Since conditions of surf, sea life, currents, and visibility may vary so greatly from one area to another, a diver contemplating a trip to a new area would be well advised to get in touch with one of the local diving clubs upon arrival or, if it is farther removed from civilization, to check (whenever possible to do so), with others who have visited the area. Most clubs are happy to be of help to visiting divers.

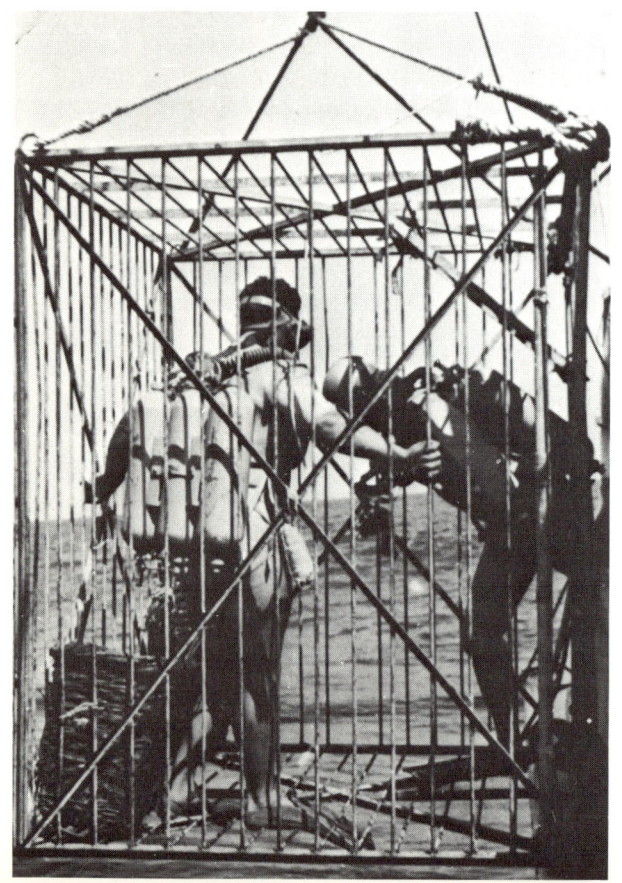

Fig. 13a. An effective way of dealing with too curious sharks is the Farallon CO_2 Shark Dart. It can be delivered by a sling spear. When it penetrates the central body area it immobilizes the shark through gas expansion within its body. As the operation is bloodless there is less danger of attracting other sharks. But if another one does appear, the dart can be reloaded within 30 seconds. *Courtesy, Farallon Industries*

Fig. 13b. Another effective measure for avoiding sharks, is the shark cage developed by Captain Jacques Cousteau for photographing sharks and their eating habits. *Établissement Cinématographique et Photographique des Armées*

They will point out the best diving areas and advise as to currents, underwater visibility, and other factors pertinent to safe and enjoyable diving. There are some facts that it is dangerous not to know, such as local surf and current conditions, hazards, poisonous or dangerous fish in the area, etc.

Perhaps the thing about exploring this strange underwater world which most worries the diver is the presence of hostile marine life, which may unexpectedly attack or injure him. Among the forms of sea life which most inspire fear are sharks, barracudas, moray eels, and poisonous underwater creatures.

Much has been written on the subject of sharks. Hardly a book on spearfishing and diving does not make some mention of them. Hans Hass has written an entire book on it, *Men and Sharks.*

The consensus seems to be that sharks are not the ferocious man-killers they were once considered to be. They are, of course, not to be lightly regarded. Incidents do happen of bathers', and even of a skin diver's, being attacked and killed by them. They seem to be most dangerous in certain areas, particularly off Australia. But if certain precautions are followed, these dangers can be minimized.

Hass discovered that generally the shark will chase a diver if he flees from it, but will turn to retreat itself if the diver swims toward it as if to attack; apparently the shark feels that any creature which dares attack it must be a formidable adversary indeed. He also found that he could scare off sharks by yelling under water, although others have not had complete success with this method. It also has been suggested that the bubbles from divers' suits or from the Aqua-Lung may frighten them.

Sharks have very sensitive olfactory organs consisting of many tiny folds over which water flows bringing them the scent or taste of the water around them. They are said to be attracted by the smell of blood, occasionally becoming so excited by it that they will bite each other, so it is wise to leave the water if you have a bleeding injury and also not to carry bleeding fish with you when swimming in waters known to be frequented by sharks.

Hans Hass believes that none of these factors is so important in explaining why sharks are attracted to or frightened away from something as the theory of underwater vibrations. Sharks, along with many other fish, have minute folds containing tiny sensitive hairs which pick up vibrations in the water about them. The flapping of a wounded fish will attract them from some distance, though attempts by divers to imitate these same movements will have no effect. Hass also believes it possible that the sharks were frightened off not by the actual shouting or bubbles but by the peculiar vibrations produced in the water by these actions.

Sharks apparently consider objects flapping about near the surface their legitimate prey, perhaps because they are used to finding injured fish there as well as garbage from ships. Therefore, the moments of entering and leaving the water are perhaps the most dangerous as far as attacks by sharks are concerned. Cupric acetate tablets strapped to leg and belt are supposed to be good as a shark repellent but there is some doubt as to their effectiveness. However, "sharkchaser" has proved effective in keeping the shark away from fishermen's nets, where other unprotected nets in the same area were attacked and torn.

Cousteau mentions making and carrying what he calls a "shark billy" for fending off possible attack by sharks. This he describes as a wooden staff about four feet long with nail tips at the end. The nails are simply to keep the staff from slipping off the shark and

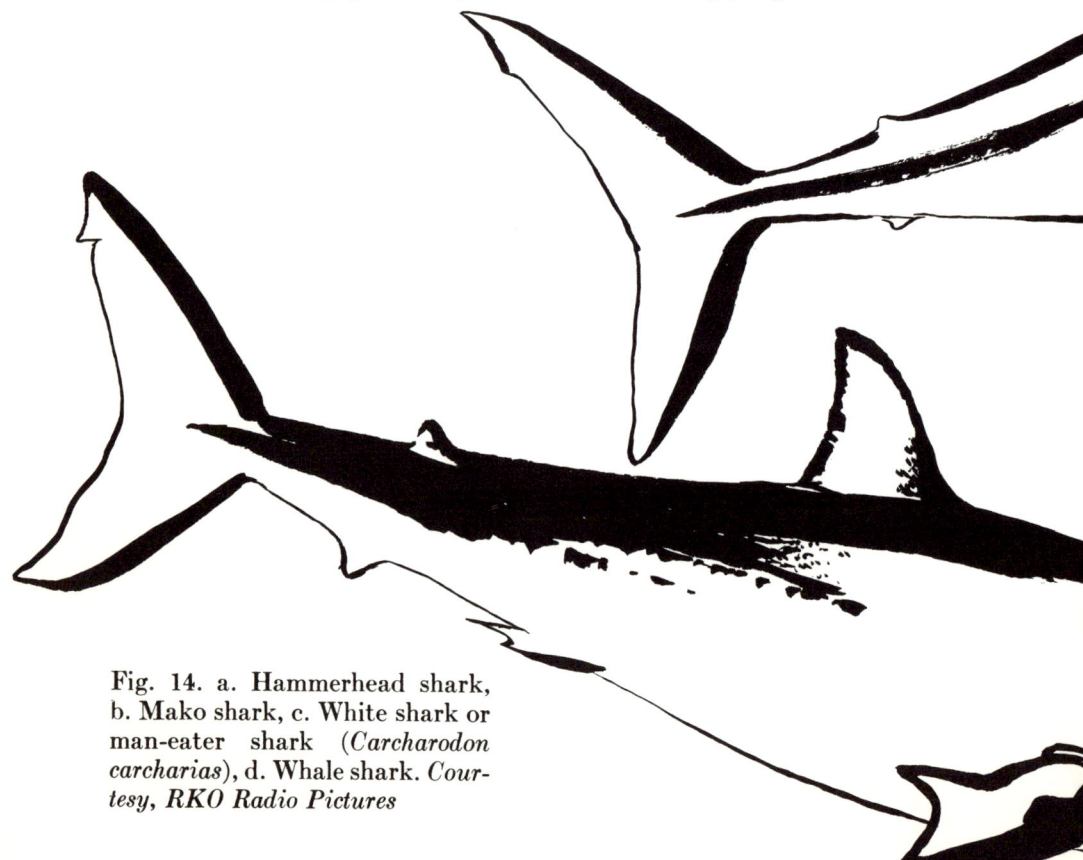

Fig. 14. a. Hammerhead shark, b. Mako shark, c. White shark or man-eater shark (*Carcharodon carcharias*), d. Whale shark. *Courtesy, RKO Radio Pictures*

not to injure it, and the billy is used solely for keeping sharks at a distance. As sharks have very tough hides, engaging in a knife fight with one is not recommended. Many sharks have been speared, however, and some of them make very good eating according to reports.

Culinary note. By report it is necessary to wash the meat well or to soak it in brine for 24 to 48 hours before eating since products of decomposition from the urea which is stored in the monster's flesh may otherwise give the meat an unpleasant odor and ammonia taste. But if correctly cooked, it is said to be as tender as chicken, with no difficulties with bones. Meat from the hammerhead shark is poisonous to eat should it be cooked in a metal container, but otherwise, apparently, it is all right.

Different species of shark show a great variety of characteristics. The largest are the whale shark and the basking shark. The basking shark is found in colder waters and may run to forty-five feet or more. The whale shark is found in warm seas and may be as large as sixty feet in length and weigh up to twenty tons. Neither of them, however, could eat a human being if it tried, since their teeth are minute and useless and they live by straining plankton and copepods out of the water.

The whale shark has markings of whitish spots and streaks and its mouth is at the front of its broad flat head. (See Figure 14.) The basking shark is mono-colored with a pointed nose.

The most common variety, the ground shark, is found in all warm seas. It varies in size from three or four feet to ten or twelve feet, and is found most often fairly close to shore and in bays or harbors. It is considered to be relatively harmless to man. This shark can be identified by the large triangular fin on its back and a smaller, but still conspicuous, unevenly lobed fin back toward the tail. Its shape is broader and stubbier than that of other species. It may be gray, brownish, or have a bluish tinge, and may have dark-tipped fins. Skin divers occasionally spear these sharks for sport.

Tiger sharks are somewhat similar but larger—up to thirty feet—and have a more tapered body with smaller fins. Young tiger sharks can be recognized by their stripes, which disappear as they get older. However, their teeth are distinctive, the same in upper and lower jaws, and triangular in shape with saw-toothed edges and a tip turned outward with an indentation below it. They are found in warm seas, farther from shore than the ground shark, though not generally in extremely deep water. This species is feared in the West Indies, but there are no authenticated accounts of attacks on man, and they are said to be rather lethargic except when aggravated.

The blue shark is actually a sea-going ground shark with a slenderer, pointed body and a deep blue coloring on its back. Its back fin is farther back than that of the ground shark, and its lower or breast fin is much longer and narrower. This species runs around twelve feet and is found in warm and temperate seas.

Weird-looking species of sharks are the hammerhead and the thresher shark. Hammerhead sharks are somewhat similar to the ground shark except for their peculiar, broadened head, with eyes at the end of two flat projections on the side. This odd head shape seems to act as a sort of bow rudder, enabling them to make turns more quickly when in pursuit of prey. They may run to over fifteen feet and are found in warm waters, usually near the coast. Occasionally hammerheads have been definitely known to have attacked bathers.

The thresher shark is a specialized offshoot of the mako shark and has an extremely elongated upper tail shaped like a scythe blade. They are rumored to "herd" schools of fish by swimming around them to group together so they will be easier to attack. These sharks are found in warm temperate seas.

The mako shark is the fastest-swimming and most streamlined of the sharks, sometimes feeding on the fastest sailfish. This shark has a pointed nose and long pointed teeth, and will leap out of the water when hooked, making it popular as a game fish. It grows to about twelve feet, and is found in warm seas, usually near the coast.

The most dangerous shark, and the one most often mentioned in connection with attacks on man, is the white shark, or man-eater shark (see illustration). It is a gigantic member of the mackerel shark family, which may be found as long as forty feet. Heavier and clumsier than the mako shark, it has flat, triangular, serrated teeth, and usually its upper part is dark and its belly white, although some larger ones are said to be all-white. These fortunately are a rare species, usually found only in deep water. However, in 1916 four people were killed in New York Bay and off the New Jersey shore, apparently by the same seven-and-one-half-foot man-eating shark, and two fifteen-foot sharks of this species were captured recently in the waters off Florida.

Formerly all known cases of shark attacks in coastal waters of the United States had been reported from the Atlantic Coast, but in October, 1950, a boy was attacked off the California coast, and in

December, 1952, another was attacked and killed by a shark, believed to be a man-eater, while swimming close to shore at Pacific Grove, California.

Reports show the sea at time of the attacks was murky, with a heavy surf running and the sky intermittently cloudy. These data are significant because many reports of attack by sharks seem to have occurred under similar conditions of cloudiness and low visibility under water. Certainly it would seem to indicate that divers should be particularly careful when swimming in murky water, especially when heavy surf or tidal currents might tend to bring closer to shore fish ordinarily found at greater depths.

Although it has been generally assumed that sharks will not attack submerged divers, a Royal Navy frogman was killed by one while searching for opium which was believed to have been dumped in Singapore Harbor. Since most harbor waters are not of the clearest or cleanest, to say the least, it is possible that visibility here was poor also and that it might have been a case of mistaken identity.

Even the nurse shark, considered the gentlest of creatures and often "ridden" in the water by small boys without harm, can be dangerous if threatened as two skin divers testified who had to have medical repairs after being attacked by one they had speared off Puerto Rico. However, the incident involved an injured animal fighting for its life and is not typical of the species. Most of the sharks shown in movies where the plot calls for a man to kill a shark singlehanded are really these harmless nurse sharks. They can be distinguished by the mouth, which is at the front of the head rather than underneath as in most sharks, and by a flap or projection of skin near the mouth and the deep grooves running from the nostrils to the mouth.

Sharks of today are living "fossils," descended with few changes from fish of millions of years ago. They are different from other fish in having a more primitive cartilaginous skeleton, and in having denticles rather than scales. Their teeth are really enlarged denticles, and they have several reserve sets of teeth in various stages of development beneath the other teeth. Sharks are related to skates and rays and have no air bladder, so must swim constantly or they will sink to the bottom.

Another fish which is greatly feared is the barracuda. The danger here as in the case of the shark is probably somewhat exaggerated. But instances have been known of people being attacked, and since they have large knife-sharp teeth and show a great deal of curiosity in regard to divers, barracuda are somewhat disconcerting to meet under water. They can grow to as large as eight to ten feet but most are only about four feet long. Apparently they usually do not attack men except in self-defense but they may strike out in a small light area or at a movement, such as the soles of kicking feet or glittering jewelry. They are usually found resting almost motionless just beneath the surface. As with many fish, their coloring changes with their mood or environment, and they are said to show dark stripes when asleep. They are found in warm waters and are prevalent off the coast of Florida.

Moray eels (see Figure 15) are long, slender, almost finless fish with quite formidable teeth. They may be greenish in color, or variously spotted and are notable for their extremely cold, malignant eyes. These eels stay mostly in holes in reefs with their ugly-looking heads sticking out, and since the head is small in proportion to the body, they may surprise the diver who thinks he has seen a small eel, and then when he tries to spear it discovers that it is a six-foot monster. The moray apparently does not attack man unless he reaches into its hole after it or tries to spear it. It is found in

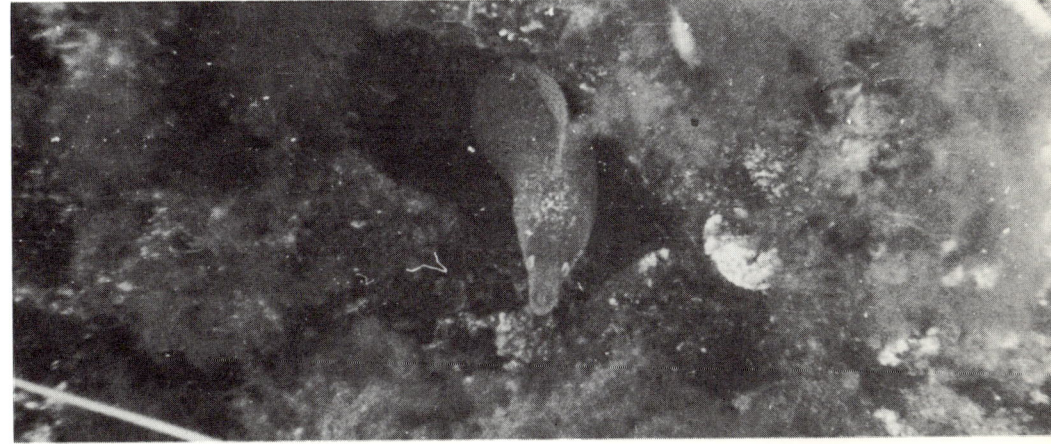

Fig. 15. A moray eel, camouflaged to match its surroundings. *Photo by J. Piroux*

Fig. 16. Brown moray eel in its hole. *Courtesy, American Museum of Natural History*

warm waters; many people have been bitten while looking for abalones in southern California. Vernon Brock, head of the Game and Fish Department of the Hawaiian Islands, had one, which he had speared, climb up the spear after him and inflict vicious bites that sent him to the hospital. When caught and dying, it will snap at anything, and if one is caught, its head should be crushed immediately. South Sea Island natives catch these eels by dangling bait in front of their holes and then catching them with a noose as they come out after it. Their natural food is the octopus, and an octopus in captivity will show signs of extreme fright if even squirted by water taken from near a moray eel. Therefore the diver should be careful about any motion of the arms and hands that might resemble than of an octopus.

Other dangers to the diver are stinging, poisonous or spiny undersea creatures. Most stinging undersea animals are coelenterates, which means they have only one body opening which is used to take in food as well as expel body wastes and eggs or sperm. This category includes jellyfish, sea anemones, most corals, and the Portuguese man-of-war. All are carnivorous and have stinging cells with which they paralyze their prey. They are often brilliantly colored and sometimes luminous, and are found attached to rocks, seaweed, and since they are delicate, in protected places.

The typical shape of jellyfish is a sort of bell or umbrella, usually translucent, with a mouth surrounded by a fringe of tentacles that hangs beneath it. They may vary in size from under an inch to as much as seven feet in diameter, but most are about a foot. Most of them are able to swim by contracting or pulsating the bell.

Corals and many hydroids form together in colonies with a common digestive system. The hydroids often look like seaweed and sometimes the only way to tell a plant from an animal is to see whether it moves when touched. The Portuguese man-of-war (Figure 17) is a colony of individuals formed into a translucent gas-filled bladder with a sail-like crest on top and hanging tentacles which can sting severely enough to send one to the hospital. Since sensitivity to its sting increases with repeated exposures, anyone who has been once stung may be seriously affected by later stinging. It is often beautifully colored in iridescent shades of scarlet, green, and violet and the "float" may be ten or twelve inches across with forty-foot tentacles. It is found in warm seas, particularly the west Atlantic.

Fig. 17. The beautiful but dangerous Portuguese man-of war. *Courtesy, American Museum of Natural History*

Fig. 18. A coral colony, *siderastrea radians*. Courtesy, American Museum of Natural History

Corals and the flowerlike sea anemones also feed by entrapping copepods and plankton in their tentacles and conveying them to the mouth. Most sea anemones can move by creeping slowly over the bottom, and some may live for a hundred years or more.

Some rather unusual relationships exist between stinging anemones and jellyfish and other sea creatures. The Portuguese man-of-war, which is dangerous to men, has a small fish called nomeus that lives unharmed among its tentacles and shares the food its host captures. Some hydroids have anemones living on them and certain anemones live on the shell of the hermit crab and even change shells when it does, although the anemones' usual food is crustaceans of the same family as the hermit crab.

Corals live in large colonies in warm seas, and secrete an exterior skeleton in order to protect the animal, and it is these structures which form decorative coral and even huge coral reefs, as more and more corals grow on the skeletons of dead corals. The Great Barrier Reef of Australia is 1,350 miles long and at some spots as far as ninety miles from the mainland. Scientists have been curious as to how these barrier reefs began, as coral cannot live below a certain depth, and have speculated that perhaps the level of the sea was much lower during the Ice Age and the corals built higher as the seas rose again. Coral stings are not usually harmful to man except for the fire coral which seems to bother some people though others are immune, in the same way as with poison ivy. However, unpleasant cuts can be received from sharp coral which take a while to heal.

Particularly dangerous forms of sea life are the sea snake and the various species of scorpion fish, especially the stonefish. Sea snakes are found in tropical waters and have attractively patterned bodies with flattened tails to aid in swimming. Although they have to come ashore to lay their eggs, they are sometimes found hundreds of miles from shore. They secrete a nerve poison which can kill a man very quickly, but they do not attack men except in self-defense. Dangerous scorpion fish such as the stonefish are found from Polynesia to the Red Sea and particularly along the Great Barrier Reef.

Fig. 19. Animals which look like flowers—the sea anemones, *metridium monginaltum*. Courtesy, American Museum of Natural History

The sharp spines of these ugly warty fish secrete a poison which causes severe agony and can be fatal to man. These fish are usually found lurking at the bottom among stones and vegetation, so the diver must be careful not to step on them. Apparently the best treatment if injured by one of their sharp spines is the same as that given for snake bite.

Painful and annoying but not a serious danger are the many species of sea urchin whose spiny bodies are quite unpleasant to step on (see Figure 20). These are related to the starfish and the sea cucumber and are found in all tropical waters, lying on the bottom or in the burrows they dig in rocks. There are three species found along the West Coast of the United States. The most usual is a purplish, thistlelike form which may grow as large as six or seven inches. Another type found in deeper water is the red sea urchin which may reach ten inches in diameter.

Another type found in deeper water off southern California is smaller but may have spines four or five inches long, and a whitish species living in the same area congregates in "herds" of hundreds at a time. Another species is the so-called heart urchin which has adapted itself to living on a muddy bottom and has become a bilaterally symmetrical animal which moves in one direction. A piece of shell broken off this creature and left in sea water will still respond for some time afterward by pointing its spines in the direction of the stimulus. Some tropical types have poison glands at the base of their spines which may make them more dangerous.

Rays and skates are a specialized branch-off of early sharks (see Figure 22, showing family tree). Some rays have stinging spines near the base of their tails which can inflict quite painful wounds that may become infected. But the ray will not attack man unless it is molested. If stepped on accidentally, however, it will lash its tail back hard, and the resulting wound may put the victim in the hospital. Sting-rays are found usually in quiet waters, often in quite shallow water, lying on the bottom, so it is wise to splash to give them warning when wading in waters where they are commonly found. The large, seven- or eight-foot, handsome, spotted whip ray is a species of ray evolved for free swimming which is found throughout the Pacific and in all warm seas. This ray has small spines on its tail but is not considered dangerous. A small spotted sting-ray a foot or two long is also found off the coast of California.

The manta ray or devilfish is a large free-swimming ray which

Fig. 20. Two common underwater menaces, a sting-ray and a sea-urchin. *Courtesy, Ben Holderness*

Fig. 21. Poison scorpion-fish

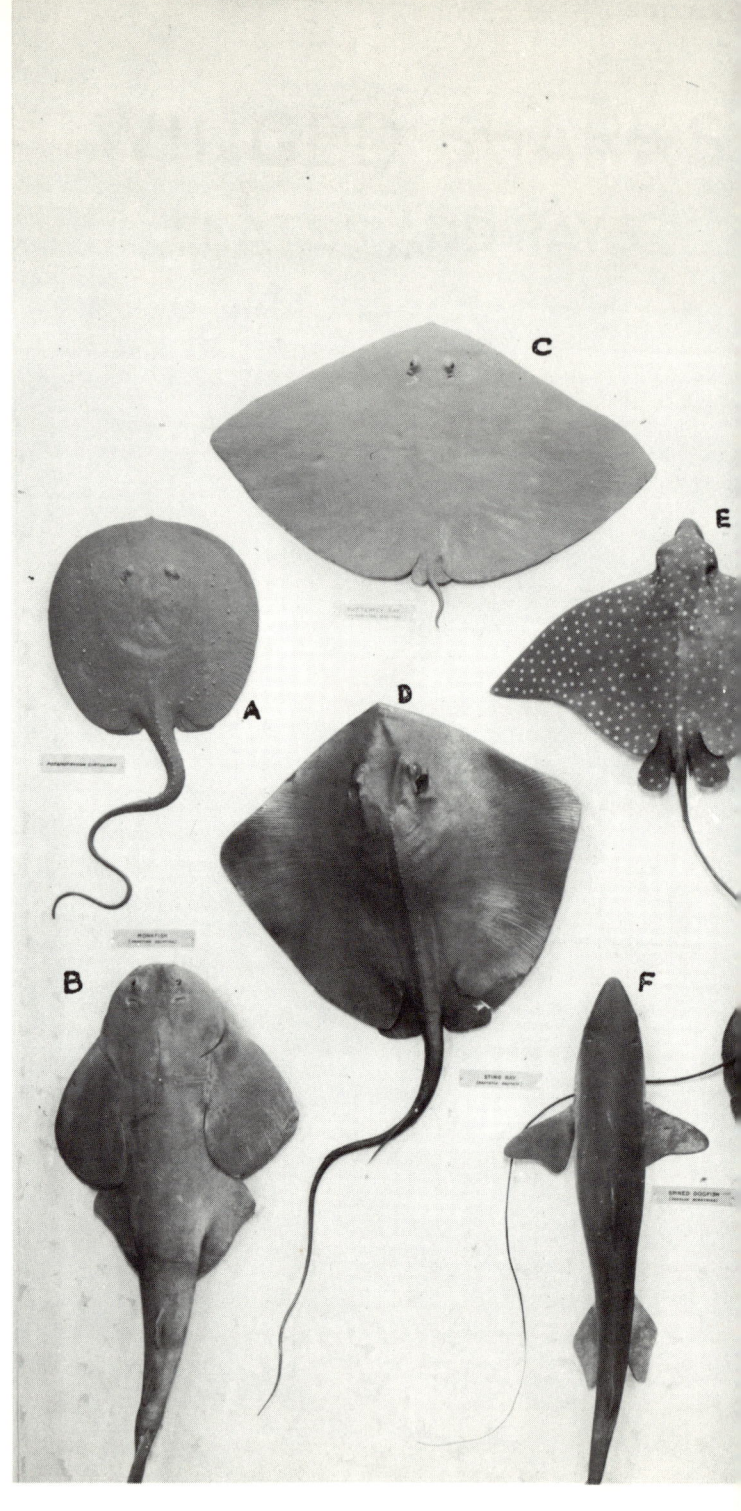

Fig. 22. Family tree of skates and rays: a. *Pomatrygon circularis*, b. Monkfish, c. Butterfly ray, d. Sting-ray, e. Spotted eagle ray, f. Spined dogfish,

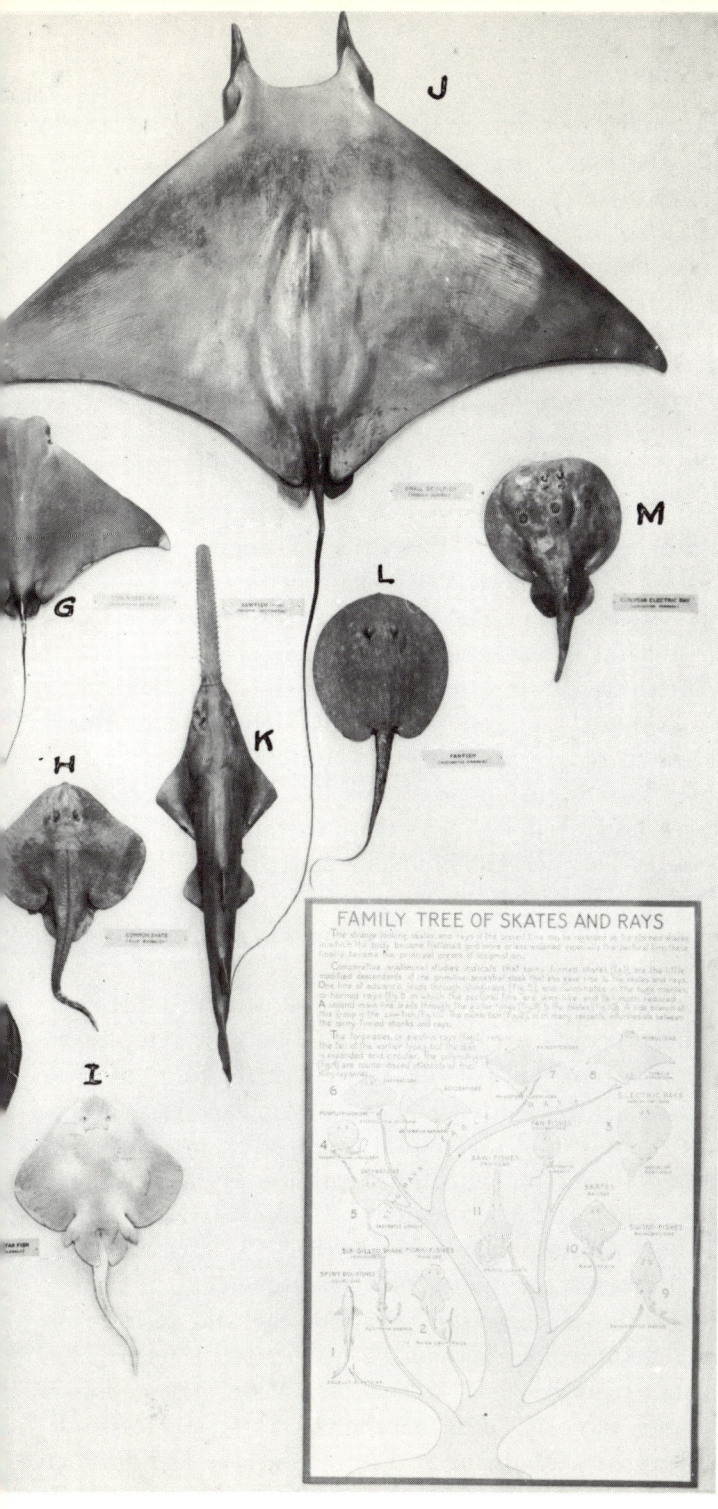

g. Cow-nose ray, h. Common skate, i. Japanese guitar-fish, j. Small devil-fish, k. Sawfish, l. Fanfish, m. European electric ray. *Courtesy, American Museum of Natural History*

may be as wide as twenty feet, but in spite of its menacing appearance, is not dangerous since it has no teeth or stingers and can eat only plankton.

Another species of bottom ray has an organ capable of giving an electric shock severe enough to stun a large fish. The severity of the shock varies according to the size of the ray. The electric organs are located only in certain areas of the fish which can be avoided when spearing the ray. A species of electric ray which grows to a size of about three feet is often found on sandy bottoms off northern California.

Fish which are poisonous to eat vary according to the locality and the season. Fish which are poisonous in some seas are considered safe food fish in others. Sometimes the poisonous part is removed and the rest eaten. In most, the poison seems to be concentrated in the intestines, and sometimes in the head, but it may spread to the rest of the fish after it has been dead awhile.

In the Pacific there are between one hundred and three hundred species of fish which may be considered as poisonous to eat. Most of these are found in tropical waters around coral reefs.

The species which is most often poisonous to eat is the swellfish or pufferfish. When confronted with an enemy these fish swell up by closing off the muscles between the stomach and the intestine and then swallowing water. Since they may swell to twice original size, and some, like the porcupine blowfish, are spiny, this discourages an enemy from trying to swallow it.

Cases of internal fish poisoning, or ichthyotoxism, will become more frequent as more people try spearfishing. The first symptoms appear anytime up to ten hours after eating, depending on the strength of the poison in the fish consumed, and generally include nausea, diarrhea, vomiting, and abdominal cramps. In more severe cases, however, other symptoms, such as numbness, paralysis, reversal of sensations of hot and cold, or of distinctions between light and heavy objects held in the hands, may appear.

Sickness may last from a few hours to several months, and may even prove fatal. Japanese scientists have isolated the pufferfish poison and discovered that in large enough quantities it paralyzes the nerve centers and causes death by suffocation. Very little definite data on fish poisoning have so far been compiled, but the School of Tropical and Preventive Medicine in California is investigating the subject and may eventually discover a positive cure. In the meantime, the best known treatment is to take a good emetic or to

Fig. 23. Twila Bratcher of the Sea Nymphs Club with a porcupine blowfish. *Photo by Lamar Boren*

induce vomiting by putting a finger down the throat, and then to get the victim to a doctor as quickly as possible.

Since species of fish which are poisonous to eat may vary from one area to another, or even from one season to another in the same place, it is sensible to check with local fishermen before eating any unfamiliar fish caught in tropical waters.

Another legendary terror of divers is the octopus, but the myth of its dangerousness has been pretty well exploded by now. They are timid, nocturnal creatures which will usually flee rather than attack human beings. However one or two incidents have been reported of their holding divers under water with their tentacles, so divers should be wary of disturbing large octopuses that are in a position to anchor themselves to some immovable object. They are, however, an interesting species, related to the squid, the cuttlefish, and the nautilus. Originally shellfish, the octopus evolved to the point where it now has only a vestigial internal skeletal structure to which its muscles are attached.

Fig. 24. An octopus. *Courtesy, Dmitri Rebikoff*

Octopuses seem to be one of the most intelligent of underwater species. Cousteau tells of seeing an octopus city where the octopuses actually constructed simple houses for themselves, using stones. A smallish species found along the coast of southern California makes a burrow for its body and piles debris in front of the opening which can be drawn up with a tentacle to hide itself. Diolé's descriptions of the octopus' courtship and mating would seem to indicate also, at least from our viewpoint, that it is a sensitive and "civilized" animal. Octopuses are not ordinarily found along the East Coast of the United States except around the Florida Keys, where they are often found in tidepools. Some of the largest, in the North Pacific, have a spread of twenty-eight feet, but most are no larger than five or six feet.

These animals move by a sort of jet-propulsion, taking in water through the mantle cavity and ejecting it through the siphon. They have a parrotlike beak which they use for cutting food and for de-

Fig. 25. Octopus propelling itself through the water. *Courtesy, Dmitri Rebikoff*

fense, but have never been known to bite humans, except in one recent instance of a skin diver who died following the bite of a small coral-reef species of octopus he was carrying on his shoulder. This species secretes a venom with which it paralyzes its prey, and apparently this particular diver had an unusual, allergic reaction to the venom.

When frightened, the octopus changes color, its surface becomes pebbly, and it ejects an inky fluid. The fluid from this ink sac was the sepia ink once used by artists. There are several theories about the exact function of this ejected inky blob. It had long been considered a sort of smokescreen, but the MacGinities in their *Natural History of Marine Animals*, say its function is to paralyze the olfactory sense of its enemies. They state that after being subjected to this discharge a moray eel, the traditional enemy of the octopus, will actually put its nose against an octopus without knowing that it is there. Cousteau mentions the theory that the long-tailed dark blob is a mock octopus shape to fool an enemy into attacking while the real octopus escapes.

Octopuses are considered delicious eating in many localities. Fishermen in the Orient and the Mediterranean used to utilize poison to bring octopuses out from under rocks until the practice was stopped. Copper sulphate bombs are used sometimes, but a handful of ordinary salt placed in their holes is said to be just as effective.

Squid are much faster than octopuses and also are capable of biting people severely with their beaks when bothered or caught. Unlike octopuses, which stay on the bottom, squids swim around, often in large schools. They have also a vestigial internal shell and have ten arms rather than the eight of the octopuses—eight short ones and two long ones with suckers.

Squid vary in size from one and a half inches to the fifty-five-foot or more giant squid (see Figure 185, in Chapter IX). What monster squid may lurk in the depths, we do not know. Giant sperm whales have been found with scars from tentacle suckers the size of saucers.

The depth-dwelling squid are often luminous. Cousteau speculates that the so-called "deep scattering layer," a mysterious layer of something, above the actual bottom of the sea, which rises to a higher level at night, might be caused by large schools of squid. A whale brought up from that level had thousands of squid in its stomach. However, recent photographs of vast shoals of small shrimplike crustaceans suggest that these might be the "deep scattering layer," though its actual composition is still not definitely known.

Luminescence in animals, a fascinating phenomenon, is caused either by luminescent bacteria or by luminescent organs on the animal. Decaying plants or flesh may appear luminous due to luminescent bacteria. Fireflies, some jellyfish and squid, and many deep-sea fish have organs controlled by the nervous system which produce luminescence. This light is so-called "cold light" since it produces light without heat (which is wasted energy), and thus is close to 100 percent efficient. If man could adapt the principles of this cold light for his own use, it would be much cheaper and more efficient than our present methods of producing artificial light.

Most luminous fish are found near the limit of light penetration but other marine animals, which live inside shells or burrows and thus would seem to have no need for it, also produce luminescence. In some animals, luminescence is connected with sexual activity, in others it may serve to help members of a species recognize each other.

Whatever its purposes, luminosity can be a strange and beautiful sight in the sea at night. Sailors have told of phosphorescent effects at night when the sea was streaked with flashes of fire, and glowing undulating spheres of light moved mysteriously through the dark waters. The authors, swimming in Long Island Sound in late summer, have seen nights when each stroke of a swimmer's arm trailed streams of luminescent bubbles through the water, the occasional touch of a fingertip to a tiny luminous jellyfish was like the sudden flash of an electric light bulb, and the splash of someone diving from a raft, a virtual fireworks display.

Marine animals have a strange variety of eyes or visual sense organs. Many are quite primitive, able only to distinguish degrees of light and dark. Some are sensitive to ultraviolet light beyond the human range of vision. The most highly developed eyes are found in squids and octopuses. Their eyes in some ways are more efficiently constructed than those of human beings, though they do not see as well as we do and, being adapted for seeing in dim light, are blinded by sudden bright lights.

Most fish are near-sighted, since there is no real need for them to see great distances. But in some fish and shrimp that live near the surface, the eye is divided into two parts, one for seeing in the air, one for seeing under water. A fish found in Mexican waters is called *Cuatros.Ojos* because of this strange construction which makes it appear that the fish has four eyes.

Barnacles, sponges, some coelenterates, and certain fish which live below the limit of light penetration are eyeless. A blind goby, which lives in the burrows of one species of shrimp, has completely functional eyes when it first hatches, but its eyes gradually become flesh-covered and useless. Certain bivalves also have eyes during the larval stage which later deteriorate to mere spots of color that are sensitive to light.

Flounders start out swimming like other fish, and with eyes on either side of the head. But gradually one eye shifts to the other side of the head, and the fish begins to live on the sea bottom lying on its blind side. In warm waters the left side usually faces up, in colder waters the right.

Almost all fish see separate images with each eye. Eugenie Clark describes experiments which indicated that some fish are unable to transfer knowledge acquired using one eye, so that it may have to be learned all over again when they are using the other eye.

Fig. 26. Diver pauses to view reef fish. *Photo by Paul Tzimoulis*

The most varied and colorful fish are the coral-reef fish. Some of the hundreds of different species are more brightly colored relatives of fish found elsewhere; others are species found only around coral reefs. The most characteristic are butterfly and angel-fish, wrasses, and parrot-fish. Most fish must necessarily be colored so as to blend with their environment. Although the coral reefs are not always as colorful as the fish around them, they provide so many hiding places that the fish have not so much need for protective camouflage. Since these fish are primarily decorative and inedible, it is a shame to spear them.

Many fish have the ability to change their colors and patterns according to their environment, their mood, or whether they are asleep or awake. Fish change color by expanding or contracting the differently pigmented areas of their "skin." Flounders and other fish change their marking to match the type of bottom they are on. Octopuses, when alarmed, may go through a series of rapid changes of color. Some tropical fish can change from one quite vivid color to another equally vivid, or change their markings from stripes to spots or triangles. These changes are usually seen when the fish is asleep, frightened, in mating or in death.

Many strange forms of life are found in the sea. One of the odder species of fish is the group to which the pipefish and the sea-horse belong. These fish swim in an upright position, and it is the male who has the babies. The female places the eggs in his pouch, and he then fertilizes them and later bears them with what appears to be some difficulty. Many of the strange elongated pipefish are almost indistinguishable from a blade of grass. Sea-horses wrap their tails around pieces of seaweed to anchor themselves, and there is an Australian species which has leaflike flaps and projections which exactly imitate the weed in which it lives.

Another odd-looking fish is the mola mola or ocean sunfish, a large, round, tailless fish which may weigh up to 2,700 pounds. It feeds on jellyfish and is related to the pufferfish, and therefore in some areas is considered poisonous to eat, although many claim to have eaten it without harm and say that the meat has the flavor and consistency of crab meat. It is found in warm, temperate waters, often off the Californian and Australian coasts, and also in the north Atlantic. One seen off Block Island recently was estimated to be twelve feet long and three feet thick.

The lungfish is another peculiar species. Distantly related to the ancestors of present-day amphibians, it has four paddlelike flippers which it uses to propel itself along on land (see Figure 27.); some species have long-trailing filaments instead. During the dry season it buries itself in the mud, enveloped in a hardened mucus that it secretes and with a hole left for breathing. It is able to live this way in a torpid state for months (experiments have indicated even for years), living off its own fat. Then when the rainy season comes, the water dissolves the mucus bag and the fish emerges. In one South American species, the male's hind flippers become enlarged during the mating season and are covered with a network of red blood vessels. This seems to serve as an accessory breathing organ so that the male does not have to leave the nest in order to breathe.

Another survival of the transition from marine life to amphibian is the coelacanth, until quite recently considered an extinct species.

Fig. 27. A lungfish. *Courtesy, American Museum of Natural History*

However, several of these strange fish have been brought up from the depths of the waters around Madagascar.

These fish have curious flipperlike fins from which the legs of reptiles and eventually of mammals, probably evolved. The capture of living specimens has excited great scientific interest; however, all of these caught so far have been either dead when found, due to exposure to air and to being battered and knifed when caught, or, as in the case of the most recent specimen, have died from the more intense light and decreased pressures of surface waters. Attempts are now being made to confine the next coelacanths captured in cages at a reasonable depth and bring them up only for brief study. The finding of living representatives of a species long considered extinct has provoked speculation as to what other strange forms of life may exist in the unexplored depths of the sea.

Another interesting species of sea life is the cetaceans, mammals whose ancestors left the sea and later returned to it.

The dugong is a sea-going mammal, the female of which nurses its young, clasping it to her with one flipper. For this reason, it is supposed to have been the source of the mermaid legends reported by sailors. Its flippers show traces of vestigial fingers, but in its present state it is not particularly human looking, having a long, smooth body tapering to a whalelike tail, and whiskers around its mouth. It is a vegetarian, and may have up to one hundred twenty feet of intestine. The dugong is found mostly in Australian waters and in the Orient.

Whales are the most completely aquatic of marine mammals. They are unable to breathe on land at all because their chest muscles are too weak to lift the great weight of their body in order to expand the lungs. Although they must breathe air, they are capable of diving and staying submerged for incredible lengths of time. Normally, they come up for air every three to five minutes, but instances have been recorded of whales staying under water for an hour and a quarter without coming up to breathe.

It has been a matter for speculation as to why whales do not have difficulties with the "bends" like divers, since they may go to depths of one-half mile or more and then rise rapidly to the surface. J. S.

Haldane discovered that there seemed to be some factor in the whale's body chemistry which prevented or inhibited the formation of nitrogen bubbles in the blood.

The gestation period for a whale is about a year, and the newborn whales are seven or eight feet long. Whale's milk is extremely rich, having a water content of only 55 percent as compared to 87 percent in cow's milk.

There are two groups of whales, the toothed whales and the whalebone whales. Whalebone whales have two blowholes, toothed whales one. The various species of toothed whales, which include the porpoise and the dolphin, feed mostly on fish, even on giant squid as in the case of the sperm whale.

The whalebone whales have a network of tiny bones through which they strain water to extract the plankton and small crustaceans. This whalebone or baleen was once sought after for its familiar use in corsets. These whales are limited to colder waters where the immense quantities of plankton which they need for food can be found.

The largest blue whales grow to about one hundred feet and weigh up to one hundred forty-five tons, making them the largest of earth's creatures. Possibly only an animal supported by water could grow to this size. Whales may live to be fifty to seventy-five years old.

A completely vicious species of toothed whale is the so-called killer whale. These are smaller and faster than other whales and have keener eyesight. They often force open the mouths of whalebone whales and tear out chunks of the thick spongy tongue. An incident was reported of a man having to flee over drifting ice while these whales pursued him, snapping at him with their vicious teeth. Fortunately, killer whales are ordinarily found only in deep water, although recently three were reported only three hundred yards off Redondo Beach in California. During World War II, packs of these killers terrorized the seas off Iceland, destroying so much fishing gear that American GI's stationed there were called on to shoot them.

Dolphins and porpoises are also fast swimmers, with keen eyesight, but are much better-natured than killer whales. Playful, gracefully leaping creatures, they have never been known to attack human beings, and in old sailors' legends, are even supposed to have helped to rescue people at sea.

Oddly enough, sharks are afraid of porpoises. Cousteau tells of harpooning a porpoise and watching sharks circle the helpless and dying animal, afraid to attack until it was dead. Porpoises are said to be able, working in groups, to surround a shark and batter it to death.

Among the most intriguing and mysterious of sea creatures are the palolo worm and the grunion, which inexplicably time their egg-laying activities to coincide exactly with certain phases of the moon and tides.

The palolo worm, which lives in coral formations in the waters near Samoa, modifies half of its body to carry eggs; then the egg-carrying half breaks off and comes to the surface to spawn at dawn on the day preceding that on which the moon is in its last quarter in October and November. On these days the water is covered with worms which the natives avidly gather for food. This behavior has been explained as being timed by the tides, but palolo worms confined in aquariums have spawned at the regular time, indicating some mysterious influence by the moon.

The grunion, a small silvery food fish found off Southern California, times its spawning to coincide with the peak of the high tide on the three nights just after the full moon during the spring months. Their timing is so exact that the spawning couples reach the highest point possible on the beach, lay their eggs, and return with the next outgoing wave. Subsequent waves do not reach as high a point, and thus the eggs are not washed away until the next spring tide ten days later, when the larvae are ready to hatch. The coming of the grunion is eagerly awaited by Southern Californians, who come from miles around to gather them and cook them over beach fires.

Of interest to the hungry diver looking for food which will not put up a fight is the mollusk family. (Details on game fish and their habitats will be found in the chapter on spearfishing techniques.)

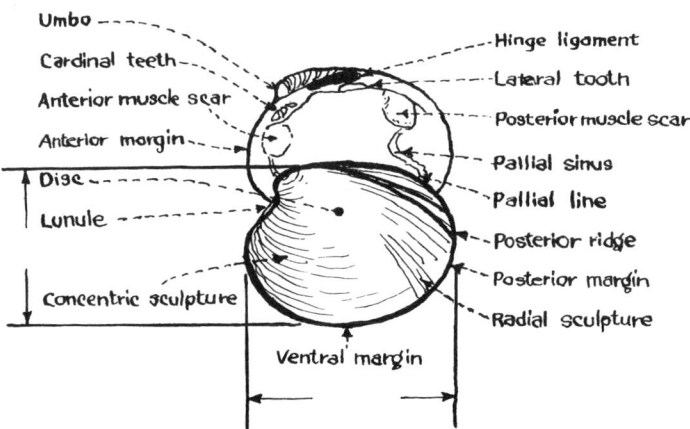

Fig. 28. The parts of a bivalve shell.

Mollusks include clams, mussels, oysters, snails, abalones, and even the octopus and squid, which have vestigial shells.

Mollusks are found all over the world, on land in the case of certain snails, and in all depths of the sea. They vary considerably in characteristics depending on their environment; on land, the kind of soil; in the sea, the type of bottom they live on, the amount of pressure, and the chemical content of the water.

Mollusk shells consist of three layers, an outer horny layer, a thick lusterless layer, and an inner nacreous or pearly layer. The insides of abalone shells are particularly lustrous and iridescent. This pearly substance is laid down in layers, and pearls are created by a grain of sand or other irritant becoming covered with layers of the pearly material. Pearls are created inside mussels, abalones and fresh-water clams as well as the familiar oyster.

The group, including clams, scallops, oysters, and mussels are known as bivalves, due to their hinged shells. The shell is closed by large muscles called adductor muscles, stretching from one half of the shell to the other. Most bivalve shells have interlocking teeth for tighter closure. They breathe and also feed by drawing water in through the in-going siphon and expelling it by the out-going siphon, extracting plankton from the water as it passes through. In the gaper clam the siphon is almost as large as the clam's body, and these clams can often be found by looking for the small holes in the sand created by their squirting or even feeling the spray of the water when crossing their beds at low tide. In one instance where erosion gradually caused a great deal of sand to pile up over them, these clams tried to reach the surface by stretching their siphons until they became as long as thirty inches!

Mussels and scallops have no visible siphons. The water enters and passes out through slits between their shells. In scallops, usually only the large adductor muscle is eaten. Scallops are the most alert of the group to which they belong, with keener vision and better swimming ability. This is necessary for protection, since they usually lie unprotected on the ocean bottom or on top of mud flats.

Mussels attach themselves in clusters to rocks or pilings by means of a sticky, threadlike secretion which hardens on contact with water and holds the animal firmly. Many of them make delicious eating, with a bit more taste than clams. Some of their shells have a beautiful luster on the inside. They vary in size according to the amount of food they are able to obtain; off Oregon they may grow as large as fourteen inches, but off Southern California about seven inches is the largest.

There are many species of clams. Most of them dig down into mud or sand, but others can actually burrow into solid rock. Another species of clam is the shipworm which bores into wood and feeds on it, causing a great deal of damage to ships and wharves. These normally are about six inches long, but one South Pacific specimen was found which was twenty-six feet long. Some clams live to be seventeen or eighteen years old. Clams are one of the few forms of marine life which are able to live on sandy beaches. The Pismo clam actually needs strong surf in order to live and has a fine network across the opening of its siphon to screen out sand. This species has been so popular as food in California that it is in danger of becoming extinct.

Clams vary in size from well under an inch to the ten- or twelve-pound geoducks and the giant Tridacna, which may be over a yard long and weigh up to five hundred pounds. These giant clams actually live on algae which live in their tissues, and they even see to it that the algae get enough sunlight to grow. Despite a common misconception, a diver would have to be exceedingly careless to get his foot caught inside of one of these clams. It normally takes three to seven seconds for the Tridacna to close its shell.

Oysters are the most important marine crop today and, except for the herring, the seafood most used by man. Oysters live attached to rocks or debris, and cannot live in waters where the sediment prevents a free flow of water in and out of their shells. However, they can adjust to greater quantities of fresh water than most other marine animals.

Many fish and shore birds, as well as people, prey upon bivalves.

Fig. 29. French girl diver with pinna clam, a throwback to prehistoric times. It is usually found buried in the sand with only the upper part of the lip showing, and is rather rare. *Photo by H. Broussard*

Pollution and starfish have both been seriously depleting the bivalve population recently. Groups of skin divers have made club projects of diving to collect the starfish that prey upon these animals.

Abalones are a species of snail which have large lovely shells, and are commonly eaten in California. Local laws prevent the export outside the state of shells or meat, and those laws govern the size and number which may be taken. They are pried off rocks with an iron prier known as an "ab iron." Only the large foot muscle is edible, and this should be thin sliced and pounded to tenderize it. Abalone has a delicious, distinctive taste all its own.

Another group of sea life which makes delicious eating is the crustacean, which includes lobsters, shrimp and crabs, and which are characterized by jointed legs and a hard external skeleton. They shed their skeletons periodically as they grow, having a new one already developed in a soft state underneath. Some of them actually have teeth inside their stomachs which help digest their food. Barnacles are also considered to be crustaceans. Shrimp, lobsters, crayfish, and crabs all have ten legs, a pair with claws, and four pairs for walking.

There are various species of shrimp, including such odd kinds as the brine shrimp which can live in water with almost any concentration of salt, the pistol shrimp which makes loud snapping noises and is capable of breaking a glass jar or paralyzing its prey with its large snapper claw, a shrimp which is almost a perfect copy of a lobster and which lives inside the abalone, a transparent shrimp whose insides can be seen through its shell, and a species which is male at birth and changes to female after two years.

Some species of shrimp are found in tide pools or mud flats, but the species usually caught for food are found only at twenty- to twenty-five-foot depths or greater. Shrimp fishing is carried on from North Carolina through the Gulf of Mexico on the East Coast, and for a different species of shrimp, from Alaska to San Diego on the West Coast.

The West Coast shrimp average about three inches, and those of the East Coast six or seven inches. These latter are found in bays and creeks when they are young and migrate to deeper water as they mature.

The East Coast or American lobster, is found from Labrador to North Carolina. Usually they are found in deep water in autumn and winter, and shallower water during the summer. These lobsters may run up to thirty-five or forty pounds, and have large claws which often weigh one half as much as the lobster itself.

Lobsters swim near the surface when young, then settle on the bottom, usually among rocks or grass. They molt periodically, as do crabs, frequently during the first year, and at longer intervals from then on. A lobster molts about twenty-five times up to the time it is five years old and about ten inches long.

The West Coast lobster is quite a bit different in appearance from the East Coast variety. It has spines on its body for defense rather than claws and has very long antennae. These lobsters are able to make a peculiar grating noise by rubbing together parts at the base of their antennae, probably to scare off attacking fish. Like the East Coast lobster, they settle on the bottom as they mature, usually among eel grass, where they find the small snails they are fond of. These lobsters are found off southern California, and another similar spiny lobster is found near Florida and the West Indies. Both these

Fig. 30. A spiny lobster. *Courtesy, Sons of the Beaches*

species make delicious eating, although the large-clawed New England type is considered a bit better.

Crabs vary in size from the tiny pea crabs found in clam and oyster shells to the giant spider crabs of Japan which may have legs as long as five feet. They include the amusing little hermit crab which lives in discarded snail shells and often carries a shell containing a female crab with him for days, waiting for her to shed her body shell so he can fertilize her, and as well as many descendants of hermit crabs which no longer live inside shells but show traces of a similar shape. There are also the coconut crabs which have learned to live on land but show their hermit crab inheritance by trying to hide themselves in coconut shells; the tiny sand crabs that can be seen by the hundreds digging frantically into the sand after a wave; and the decorator crabs which drape themselves with growing pieces of seaweed or sponge for camouflage, as well as many others.

The main edible crabs are the blue swimming crab on the East Coast, and the cancer crabs, especially the *Cancer magister*, on the West Coast. The blue swimming crab is found from New England to the Gulf states, and the majority of cancer crabs from San Francisco and northward. Other smaller species are also eaten, but are harder to pick the meat out of.

An odd species of crab is the King crab or horseshoe crab found on the East Coast of the United States. This crab is not actually a crab or crustacean, but is a close relative of the spider. Its armored, tanklike appearance makes it resemble a creature left over from a more primitive age, which indeed it is. These creatures are large, up to a foot long, not counting the long, projecting spine, but are not edible. The authors have seen beaches on Long Island Sound lined with hundreds of these strange crabs which had apparently come out of the water to lay their eggs.

In addition to the more obvious and commonly eaten items of seafood, the sea has many other possibilities as a source of food. It has been calculated that nearly nine times as much vegetation grows in the sea as on land. A single quart of water may hold thousands of diatoms, and somewhere around five and one-half tons per acre are produced in the English Channel alone. Theoretically this is enough vegetable matter to more than feed the entire population of the world. As land areas become overcrowded and farm lands depleted, we may well look to the sea for much of our food. Eventually sea pastures may be farmed in as systematic a way as those on land. Even the fish and other seafood we do extract today are only a small percentage of what is potentially available.

There are at least seventy kinds of edible seaweed which are eaten in the Orient today. Horses fed on dried seaweed in an experiment gained over forty pounds in fifteen days. Seaweed has also been found to have antibiotic properties.

The investigation and development of the immense resources of the sea has only just begun. Practically every known element is contained in the sea, some in minute quantities. According to researchers at the Dow Chemical Company, a cubic mile of sea water contains 175 million tons of dissolved chemicals worth 5 billion dollars. Included are several tons of uranium and gold, about 25 tons of copper, zinc, lead, and manganese, and 300,000 tons of bromine (which is used for gasoline anti-knock compounds). All of the magnesium made (among its uses is to make aluminum stronger and lighter, especially valuable for airplanes) in the United States today comes from the sea.

Recently skin divers have been employed to look for information that will aid in locating underwater oil pools. It has been estimated that there are forty billion barrels of petroleum off the coast of

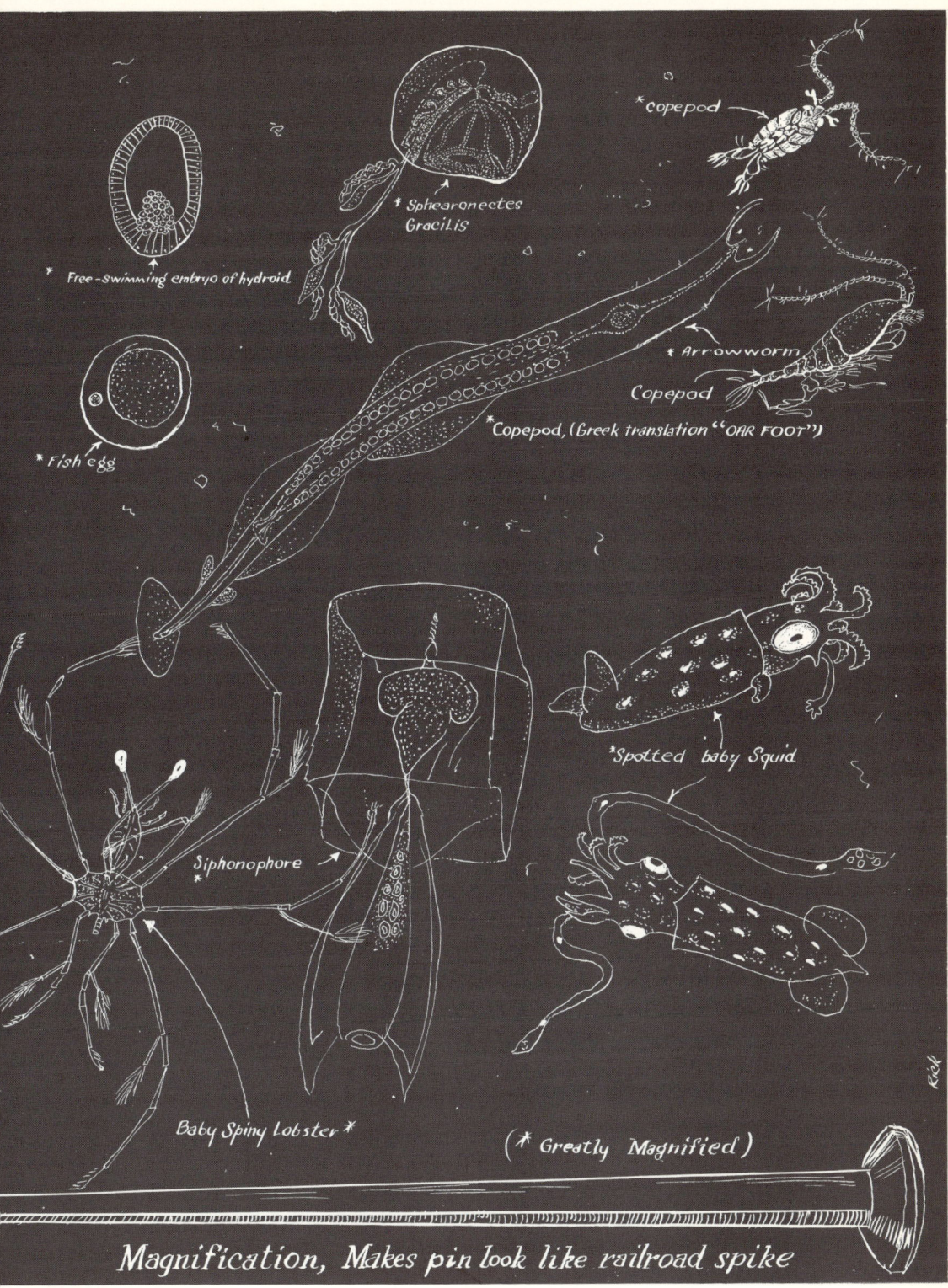

Fig. 31. The varied composition of plankton, the principal food source of the sea.

Southern California alone. Skin divers in the Gulf of Mexico have been gathering samples of sediments and sea creatures, investigating marine vegetation, and trapping bubbles of natural gas, since all of these help indicate buried limestone formations or dome rock which may contain oil. Oil wells have been drilled on many portions of the continental shelf off California and the Gulf of Mexico.

The sea is also a great potential source of power. According to *Time* magazine: "Scientists have said that the energy of fusion of light elements can be turned from destructive to peaceful uses. In 1950, all of man's needs required about 10^{17} B.T.U. of energy. The hydrogen in 1600 tons of water, if turned into helium, will give roughly this quantity. Since there are 15 by 10^{17} tons of water in the ocean, the world's stock of hydrogen can keep man supplied with energy at the 1950 rate for more than 900 thousand billion years."(Courtesy *Time, Inc.*, copyright 1954.)

The potential of the sea is enormous and is only beginning to be tapped. Skin divers will become more and more necessary in the research and development of the sea's resources, since most of the areas to be developed will be contained within the continental shelves of the various countries. Already many ichthyologists, oceanographers, etc. have learned that they must become skin divers in order to investigate the sea and its life at first hand. Beneath the sea lies an exciting and productive new world to be explored and developed, and the skin diver will be among the first to penetrate it, the man of the future.

Fig. 32a. Divers at bottom of this and following page are oil company divers searching for oil under the sea floor. Such divers are also employed to maintain rigs, and to check pipelines for leakage and pollution. *Courtesy, Socony Mobil Oil Co., Inc.*

Fig. 32b. Working under the sea. The diver is repairing a valve on an air chamber at the Perry Oceanographic Hydrolab Habitat. The airspace inside the chamber enables divers to rest without using up their air. The rear structure is an undersea lab, serving among other things, for the study of the effects of nitrogen supersaturation on divers. *Courtesy Poseidon Systems USA*

III

Physiological Problems of Diving

We live on the earth as though at the bottom of an ocean of air. Although we are not conscious of feeling its weight upon us, every square inch of our bodies is regularly subjected to a pressure of 14.7 pounds. This is called atmospheric pressure. Because this pressure is exerted equally from all directions and since the human body has adjusted itself to it, there are no difficulties encountered in everyday living.

However, whenever man attempts to enter a different "air" environment—the greater pressures under water or the diminished pressure of the upper atmosphere, for example—problems of adjustment arise. Even at the bottom of a coal mine the air pressure is perceptibly greater, and at the top of Mount Everest the air exerts a pressure of only 4.6 pounds per square inch, making it necessary for the men who climbed it to use oxygen flasks as they neared the summit.

In diving, the main problem is that of adjusting to the greatly increased pressure on the body caused by the weight of the water in addition to the pressure of the atmosphere above. Fresh water weighs approximately 62.4 pounds and salt water about 64 pounds per cubic foot. Therefore, at a depth of 33 feet in salt water, the pressure which the water exerts on the bottom would be about 2112 pounds per square foot, which is equal to 14.7 pounds per square inch or 1 atmosphere of pressure. (In fresh water, the pressure at a given depth would be about 3 percent less than in salt water.) The added weight of the atmosphere above the surface would give a total pressure on a body submerged at that depth of 29.4 pounds per square inch, or 2 atmospheres.

There are two methods of measuring pressure. One disregards the normal atmospheric pressure of 14.7 pounds per square inch and only measures pressures over and above it. This is known as "positive pressure" or "gage pressure." However, in order to calculate the amount of air needed by a diver at various depths, it is necessary to add the atmospheric pressure to the gage pressure. This total or true pressure is called "absolute pressure."

It is a remarkable phenomenon that the human body can adjust to pressures equivalent to a depth of 1,000 feet, or about 455 pounds per square inch, as long as the air under equal pressure has free access to all body surfaces, including internal air spaces. This is possible because the entire body, with the exception of the respiratory system, middle ear spaces, and sinuses, is composed of fluids and solids, which are practically incompressible.

Fig. 33. Comparison of pressures on the body: a. At the top of Mt. Everest; b. At sea level; c. At a depth of 100 feet.

However, if for any reason the increased pressure is not applied equally to all body surfaces, pain and distortion may result.

A diver is subjected to an increased pressure on his body of .445 pounds a square inch for every foot in depth. Thus a diver with a chest area of, say, 120 square inches to be expanded, who tries to breathe through a snorkel (see Chapter IV) from only one foot under the water is breathing against an increased pressure on his chest of over 53 pounds. At a depth of only three or four feet, it becomes impossible to breathe through a tube from the surface, since the effort required to expand the chest is too great. This is the reason the early designers of diving helmets with air hoses leading from the surface found them ineffective until it was realized that air must be pumped down under pressure to the diver.

Pressure on a diver increases about one atmosphere (14.7 pounds per square inch) for every thirty-three feet of depth. Therefore, at a depth of only one hundred feet, the total or absolute pressure (including normal atmospheric pressure) on a diver's body is about 58.8 pounds per square inch, or, with a body area of approximately 2500 square inches, he is being subjected to a total pressure of 147,000 pounds. At this depth a skin diver who dives by taking a gulp of air and then holding his breath has the twelve pints or so of air which was in his lungs on the surface compressed to one quarter its volume, or about three pints—Boyle's Law states that at a constant temperature the volume of a gas varies inversely as the absolute pressure varies, while the density varies directly as the pressure varies—that is about the amount of residual air in the lungs, or that which remains after the most forceful expiration.

If the diver goes down much farther, the additional pressure, unable to compress the chest walls or raise the diaphragm further without injury, will force blood and tissue fluids into the lung air spaces. This condition is known as the "squeeze" and if not relieved may cause severe lung damage and eventually death. If the diver descends further, his chest walls may be crushed in like a sealed tin can lowered into the water. This obviously has limited the depths to which skin divers wearing no breathing apparatus may go. The official record now stands at about 170 feet.

However, even with a method figured out to supply the diver with compressed air at a pressure equal to the outside water pressure, there still remain other problems of adjustment. Inside the human body are several natural air spaces, notably the sinuses and the middle ear spaces. When the outside of the eardrum is subjected to pressure, the inside air pressure must be equal or the drum may rupture inward. Normally this equalization of pressure is accomplished by the passage of air through the Eustachian tube which leads from the throat to the middle ear space. However, if this tube is blocked

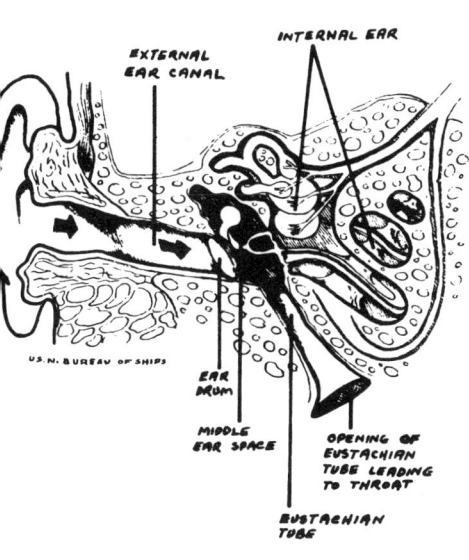

Fig. 34. Diagram of the inner ear.

Fig. 35. Effects of unequal pressures on the ear drum.

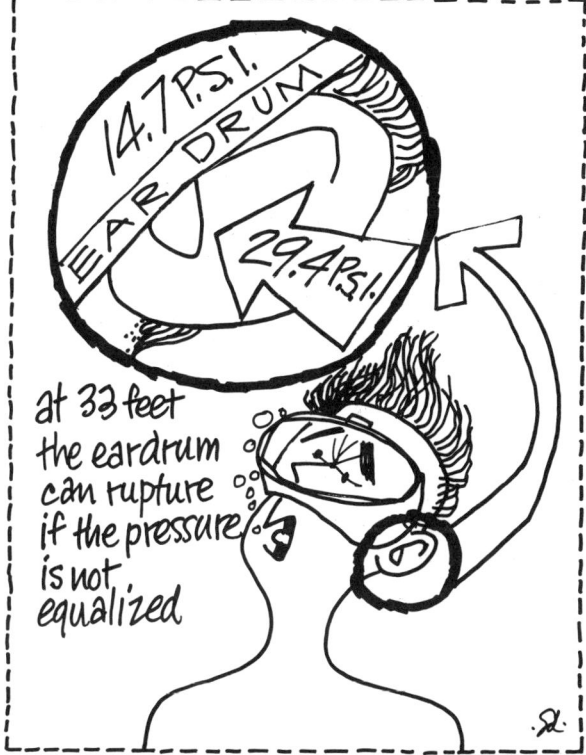

with mucus due to a cold or hay fever, this equalization cannot take place and the drum may burst. For this reason it is not advisable to dive when suffering from a cold, and if at any time during a dive there is any feeling of pain in the ears, the diver should rise slightly and try to clear the ears by swallowing, yawning, or snorting into the mask while pressing it against his nostrils, until a pop and then a hissing sound in the ear indicates that the tube has been cleared.

It is dangerous to use ear plugs while diving, since they may be forced deep into the ear by external pressures or, when the diver is breathing compressed air, the eardrum may rupture outward because the pressure on the inside of the drum is greater than in the space between it and the ear plug.

Other natural air spaces, the nasal accessory sinuses, are located within the hollow spaces of the skull bones and are connected with the nasal cavity by passages called ostia. The frontal sinuses are located on the forehead above the eyes, the maxillary sinuses on either side of the nose under the eyes, and the ethmoidal air cells and the sphenoid sinus form tiny air spaces between the nasal air space and the brain. Obstruction of any of these sinuses by mucus will cause pain when diving, since pressures cannot be equalized, and under enough pressure hemorrhage of the mucus membrane lining may result. As with the ears, returning to normal pressures will relieve the problem, or sometimes a slow descent will allow the air to seep in and gradually equalize the pressures.

Another characteristic of water, in addition to its pressure, which the diver must overcome, is its buoyant effect. Archimedes' principle states that "any object wholly or partly immersed in a liquid is buoyed by a force equal to the weight of the liquid it displaces." Therefore, a skin diver weighing, say, 180 pounds, and having a body surface area of about 2500 square inches would displace about 2.89 cubic feet of water. Since salt water weighs approximately 64 pounds per cubic foot, the total weight displaced would amount to about 185 pounds, 5 pounds more than the diver's own weight. In order to offset this 5 pounds of positive buoyancy, the diver might wear a weight belt to allow him to submerge more quickly and easily. Early pearl and sponge divers used a stone and later an iron weight gripped in the hand for the same purpose; divers in conventional suits wear weighted shoes in addition to a weight belt.

Other difficulties are presented by the nature of air itself, the physiology of breathing, and the laws of the behavior of gases under pressure.

The air we breathe is a mixture of gases, the principal ones being nitrogen (approximately 79 percent), oxygen (approximately 20.94 percent), and carbon dioxide, CO_2, (about .03 percent). The air we exhale contains about 79.7 percent nitrogen, 16.3 percent oxygen, and 4.0 percent carbon dioxide. The change takes place within the alveolar air spaces of air sacs of the lungs, where carbon dioxide given off by body cells as a waste product is eliminated from the blood and oxygen is absorbed by the blood to replace that which was consumed by the body cells. The air we exhale is a mixture of alveolar and inspired air.

The human body consumes about 300 cubic centimeters of oxygen per minute when at rest, 900 cc. when performing moderate work, and about 2100 cc. during heavy labor. This need for oxygen limits

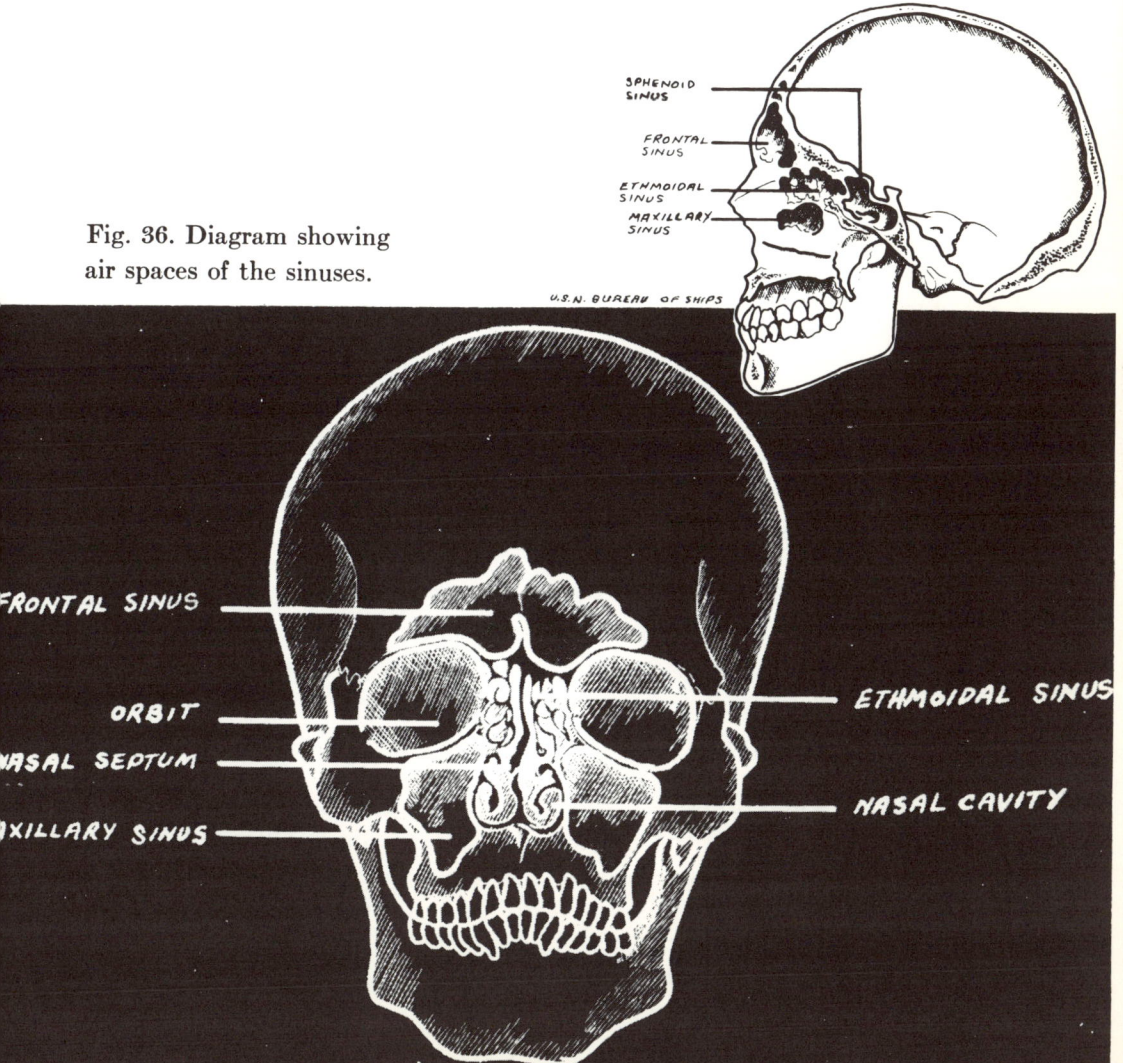

Fig. 36. Diagram showing air spaces of the sinuses.

Fig. 37. A body immersed in water is buoyed up by a force equal to the weight of the water it displaces. *Courtesy, Fran Gaar—Aqualung School of New York*

the time natural divers, using no breathing equipment, can stay submerged. Some natural divers, with training, can go to fairly great depths and perform work in a condition of anoxia, or oxygen deficiency.

The Ama, the female divers of Japan, are able to stay submerged and work for $2\frac{1}{2}$ minutes at a time, under pressures of $3\frac{1}{2}$ atmospheres. Studies of air exhaled upon surfacing have shown a percentage of oxygen of only 3.3 percent, and an oxygen consumption of only 2 to 3 cc. per second after the first minute, which is amazingly low.

As the Amas prepare to dive, low whistling sounds are heard across the water, all over the fishery. Whistling is done to test body response to cold. (If lips are cold, a person cannot whistle.) The Amas expel as much air as possible from the lungs, and then take a light but deep breath before submerging. The theory is that the light breath does not fatigue the respiratory muscles, and the breath can be held longer since the lungs are thoroughly ventilated and enough CO_2 is given off and enough oxygen taken in. Medical investigation revealed that the content of CO_2 in the alveolar air did not increase with the length of the dive, but rather the CO_2 accumulated in the tissues and blood, thus slowing up the absorption of oxygen by the blood and lowering the rate of consumption.

Many skin divers diving without breathing equipment have found that they can increase the duration of a dive by first breathing in and out deeply several times to build up the oxygen saturation of the blood, thus enabling them to hold their breath longer. Experiments with subjects breathing pure oxygen for an interval have shown that it is possible to hold the breath up to fifteen minutes at a stretch afterward. However, no diver should attempt to prolong a dive beyond his endurance, since anoxia can cause a sudden blackout with no warning.

In order to understand other physiological problems of diving such as CO_2 poisoning, the toxic effects of breathing pure oxygen under pressure, nitrogen narcosis, and "the bends," or compressed air illness, some understanding of the laws of the behavior of gases is necessary.

According to Dalton's Law, the total pressure exerted by a mixture of gases may be considered to be the sum of the pressures that would be exerted by each of the gases if it alone were present and

Fig. 38. Diagram showing water displacement of a submerged body.

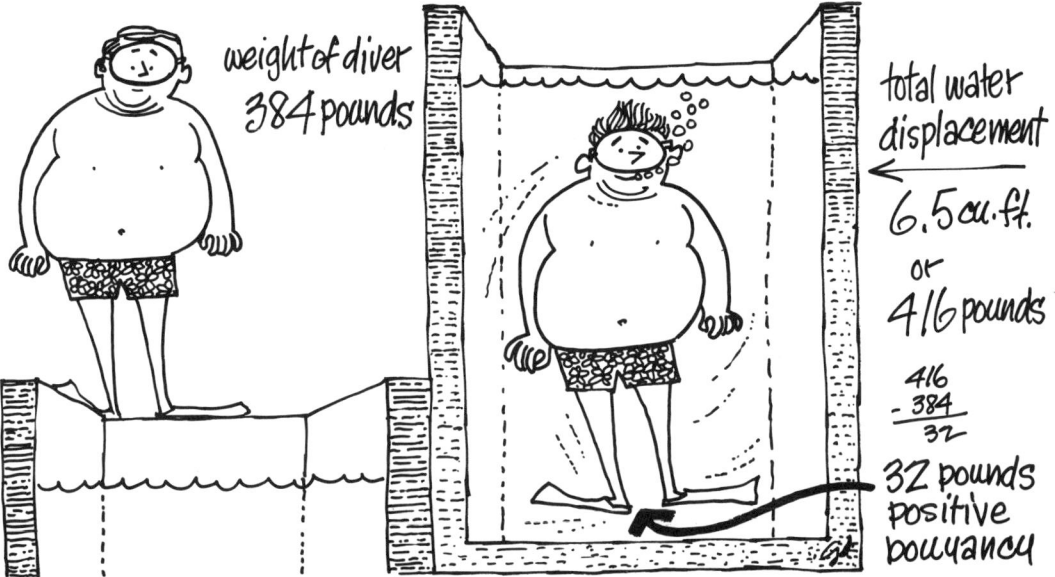

occupied the total volume. Henry's Law states, "With temperature constant, the quantity of a gas which goes into solution of any given liquid is in direct proportion to the partial pressure of the gas." Boyle's Law, as mentioned previously, states that at a constant temperature, the volume of a gas varies inversely as the absolute pressure, while the density varies directly as the pressure. Thus, if the pressure on a gas in doubled, the density also is doubled, but the volume is decreased to one half of the original volume.

Therefore air, being a mixture of gases, decreases in volume as the diver goes deeper, but the partial pressures of all its components increase proportionately. Thus, if air at normal atmospheric pressure is about 20 percent oxygen and 80 percent nitrogen by volume, the oxygen exerts 20 percent of the total pressure or 2.94 pounds per square inch, and the nitrogen exerts 80 percent of the total pressure, or 11.76 pounds p.s.i. If a diver goes to a depth of 132 feet, where he is subjected to a pressure of 5 atmospheres, or 73.5 p.s.i. absolute pressure, the partial pressure exerted by the oxygen would still be 20 percent, or 14.7 p.s.i. absolute (or 1 atmosphere of pressure). The partial pressure of the nitrogen, at 80 percent, would now be 58.8 p.s.i. absolute. At 462 feet, or 15 atmospheres of abso-

Fig. 39. Diagram illustrating Boyle's Law.

lute pressure, the partial pressure of oxygen would now amount to 44.1 p.s.i. or 3 atmospheres, and the partial pressure of the nitrogen 176.4 p.s.i. absolute.

Since, according to Henry's Law, the quantity of a gas which goes in solution of any given liquid is in direct proportion to the partial pressure of the gas, more of all the gases present in air will be diffusing into the blood at greater depths. Thus a seemingly insignificant percentage of one gas in a mixture at atmospheric pressure becomes increasingly important as pressures increase, since the respiratory function is adapted to coping with certain saturations of these gases only.

In breathing air at atmospheric pressure, for instance, the partial pressure of oxygen in the alveolar air is sufficient to saturate the hemoglobin contained in our red blood cells to within 95.5 percent of full saturation. In breathing pure oxygen at a pressure of 3 atmospheres, however, such a high partial pressure of oxygen is created in the alveoli that besides fully saturating the hemoglobin, a great deal of oxygen is dissolved within the blood fluids. In the blood's passage though the body, the dissolved oxygen is sufficient to meet the needs of body tissues, and the oxygen which is chemically com-

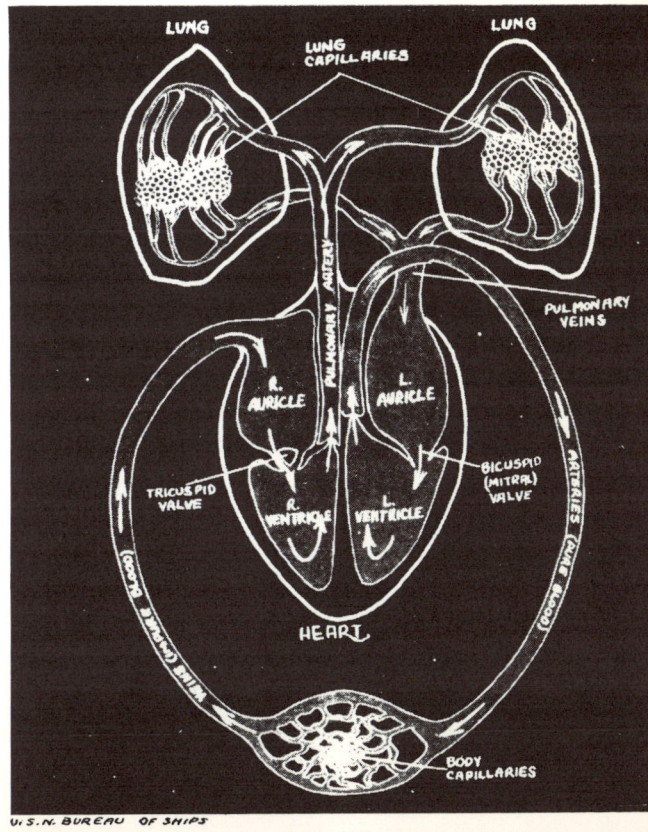

Fig. 40. Diagram showing the principles of the circulation of the blood.

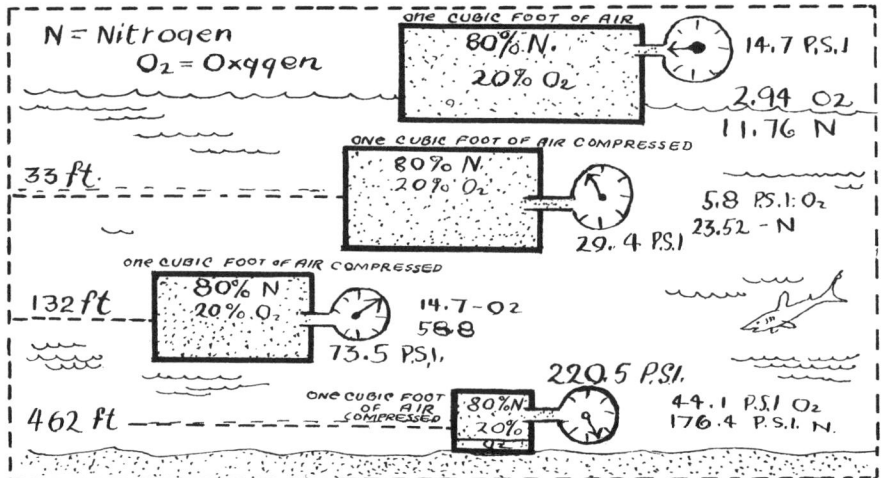

Fig. 41. The principle of increased partial pressures of gases at greater depths.

bined with the hemoglobin is not used as it normally would be. The result is that the reflexes which control the breathing cycle permit a build-up of CO_2 without stimulating faster breathing to remove it, and the symptoms of oxygen poisoning, nausea and dizziness, muscular twitching, convulsions and eventual unconsciousness occur.

For this reason it is not safe to use a breathing device using pure oxygen below a depth of about 35 feet, or for prolonged periods of time. (See Chapter IV for further discussion of oxygen-recirculating equipment.) If oxygen poisoning should occur, the best treatment is a return to atmospheric air, and if breathing has stopped, the administration of artificial respiration.

Carbon dioxide poisoning can result from insufficient ventilation of a diving helmet or from using a re-circulating breathing apparatus in which the CO_2 absorbent is not functioning properly. This hazard also increases with depth, and a slight increase in the percentage of CO_2 in the air breathed, say to 1 percent, which could not be noticeable on the surface would at a depth of 66 feet be equivalent to a pressure of 3 percent CO_2 because of the increased partial pressure of the gas. This concentration is sufficient for breathing to become noticeably more rapid; a concentration of 6 percent will cause distress and symptoms of fogging of the face plate, shortness of breath, headache and fatigue, and a concentration of 10 percent or more results in unconsciousness and eventually death. Thus it becomes increasingly important with greater depths that the concentration of CO_2 be kept extremely low.

Carbon monoxide poisoning also becomes more of a hazard under

PERCENTAGE AND PARTIAL PRESSURES OF GASES IN THE AIR OF THE LUNGS			
Gas (barometer 760 mm. Hg.)	Partial pressure		
	Inspired* air	Expired air	Alveolar air
	mm. Hg.	mm. Hg.	mm. Hg.
Oxygen	156.30	116.2	101.2
Carbon dioxide	0.20	28.5	40.0
Nitrogen	588.50	568.3	571.8
Water vapor	*15.00	47.0	47.0
Total	760.00	760.0	760.0

*Variable, according to humidity and temperature of inspired air.

PARTIAL PRESSURES OF GASES DISSOLVED IN ARTERIAL AND VENOUS BLOOD		
Gas	Gas tension or partial pressure	
	Arterial blood	Venous blood
	mm. Hg.	mm. Hg.
Oxygen	100	40
Carbon dioxide	40	46
Water vapor	47	47
Nitrogen	570	570
Total	757	703

U. S. N. BUREAU OF SHIPS

Fig. 42.

increased pressures. When using a SCUBA unit, carbon monoxide may contaminate the air supply if the exhaust outlet of a gasoline-driven air compressor is too close to the intake manifold of the compressor. It can also occur from oil flashing in the compressor when oil of too low a flashing point is used for lubrication. The symptoms of asphyxia, or suffocation, from anoxia, carbon dioxide poisoning, or carbon monoxide poisoning can be detected in a diver by the following symptoms: respiration absent or present only as an occasional gasp, muscles either limp or rigidly contracted, face blue or deep red, eyes as a rule bloodshot, rapid or irregular pulse, body cold and clammy, and unconsciousness or semiconsciousness. The treatment here is essentially the same, whatever the cause—returning the victim to fresh air and applying artificial respiration if breathing has stopped.

With the increasing pressures of the depths, the ordinarily innocuous gaseous nitrogen in the air breathed has curious effects on the mental processes, similar to alcoholic intoxication. Divers describe the sensation as a euphoria in which the instinct for self-preservation disappears. Cousteau mentions having to battle an impulse to hand his Aqua-Lung mouthpiece expansively to a passing fish, to offer him a drink of air. This nitrogen narcosis or "rapture of the depths" as it has been called, seems to have varying effects on different types of people. According to the United States Navy's experiences with its divers, as well as Cousteau's, stable phlegmatic personalities tend to react to the phenomenon by increased vigor and effort which may result in eventual loss of consciousness, while less stable or more nervous and imaginative intellectuals experience vivid attacks on all senses and are incapable of purposeful effort throughout the dive.

Fig. 43. For safety's sake, never dive alone or stray too far from the group. *Photo by H. Broussard*

Fig. 44. The most important rule when using a SCUBA: To avoid air embolism *never* hold the breath while ascending and never rise faster than 60 feet per minute. *Courtesy, RKO Radio Pictures*

The depth at which these effects will be felt also varies with the individual. Some people experience the symptoms of nitrogen narcosis at only one hundred feet or so, while others may go to three hundred feet before being affected. From about one hundred fifty to two hundred feet is the usual danger point, and since several experienced divers have died from this cause, while attempting to reach record depths, no diver should attempt to go this deep except an expert diver, under proper supervision and preferably breathing a helium-oxygen mixture. The recent seven hundred and twenty-eight foot record dive by Hans Keller of Switzerland was made while breathing a special gas mixture. Before this every diver using self-contained equipment who had gone below three hundred thirty feet had died in the attempt.

Just why helium, in contrast to nitrogen, does not produce these narcotic effects is not yet completely understood. Apparently it has something to do with the relative solubility of the two gases in water and oil, the oil-water solubility ratio of helium being one third that

Fig. 45. Possible diving accidents: a. Air embolism; b. Spontaneous pneumothorax; c. Overexpansion of intestinal organs; d. Cuts from sharp equipment or fish spines.

of nitrogen and of argon, a minor component of air, which, though inert like helium, is also narcotic under high pressures. It is also being investigated whether or not the molecular weight of helium, which is much less than that of nitrogen or argon, may have something to do with the absence of a narcotic effect. Experiments with mixtures using hydrogen which, although of a lower molecular weight than helium, has a higher solubility coefficient in oil may shed more light on the question. The Swedish engineer, Arne Zetterstrom, was successful in reaching a depth of 465 feet using a hydrogen-oxygen mixture, but died when a faulty winch caused him to be raised too rapidly.

Experiments with helium-oxygen mixtures were begun in 1924 at the Bureau of Mines Experimental Station at Pittsburgh, Pennsylvania, and later continued by the Navy's Experimental Diving Unit at Washington, D.C. It was discovered that helium not only does not produce the narcotic effects of nitrogen, but also that it is eliminated from body tissues more quickly, thus shortening decompression time. Diving with helium-oxygen mixtures is impracticable in depths less than one hundred fifty feet, since complicated special equipment is needed to provide enough ventilation and to prevent a carbon dioxide build-up. Since, in addition to special equipment, special training is required, this type of diving is definitely not for the non-professional diver, so it will not be gone into in detail here.

"The bends," also called caisson disease or decompression sickness, and probably the most common diving disorder, is also due to the effects of nitrogen under pressure. Nitrogen, unlike oxygen, does not combine chemically with the blood but goes into solution in the blood and is carried to all the body tissues, which then assume the same partial pressure of nitrogen as in the alveolar air. Therefore a certain amount of nitrogen is always present in a dissolved state throughout all body tissues.

When a diver breathes compressed air under pressure, the partial pressure of nitrogen in the alveolar air increases and gradually, in a period of eight to twelve hours, all body tissues would come in equilibrium with the increased partial pressure of nitrogen in the lungs. Thus the saturation of the tissues with nitrogen increases with the length of the dive.

As the diver begins to ascend, the partial pressure of nitrogen in the alveoli decreases, and when the denitrogenated blood leaves the lungs and becomes exposed to the various body tissues, which contain dissolved nitrogen at a higher partial pressure, there is an escape of the gaseous nitrogen from the tissues into the blood. The blood then carries it to the lungs and eliminates it, and with each round of circulation more nitrogen is taken from the tissues and expelled in this manner. Because fat is capable of holding over five times as much dissolved nitrogen as the water of the blood and tissues, it naturally takes longer to desaturate this type of tissue. Nitrogen elimination from fully saturated tissues, like nitrogen absorption, takes a period of 9 to 12 hours to complete itself. This process is called decompression.

However, if decompression is too rapid, the blood and tissues accumulate more dissolved gas than they are capable of holding in solution. Since this load of dissolved gas cannot be carried to and eliminated via the lungs quickly enough, the gas liberates itself in the form of bubbles which appear within the blood and tissues, as when a bottle of carbonated water is opened and a flurry of small bubbles rushes to the surface. The bubbles of gas released from solution may cause symptoms of suffocation and chokes (if trapped in blood vessels of the lungs or heart), pain or paralysis (bubbles trapped in nerves, brain or spinal cord), stiffness and pain in joints and muscles, and itch or rash of the skin.

Before the principle of the bubble theory was proposed, many divers and caisson workers were crippled or killed from attacks of the bends. A French physiologist named Paul Bert was the first to investigate the causes of this illness, and he recommended a system of gradual decompression or slow return to normal pressures, to prevent the formation of bubbles. From this it was discovered that returning to the original pressure when illness occurred would relieve the symptoms, and this led to the development of the recompression chamber.

This study resulted in the drawing up of standard stage decompression tables, which recently have been replaced with the repetitive dive table now used by the U. S. Navy.

The 1952 Navy Standard Decompression Table provided for decompression from a single dive. Decompression for subsequent dives on the same day was difficult to figure. A residual amount of nitrogen could be expected to remain in the blood after a long, deep dive, gradually being dissipated over a certain number of hours and minutes. This meant that in order to be safe, the next dive would have to be severely limited.

In cases of poor weather or water conditions, or in emergencies, decompression using a recompression chamber is sometimes resorted to, but since these chambers are not generally available to the sport diver, only the first method will be covered here. No diver who is not thoroughly experienced, and in the company of responsible companions including a timekeeper, should ever attempt a dive of a depth or duration requiring decompression; and then the new Navy Air Decompression Tables (pages 83 through 83f) should be rigidly adhered to. It is, in fact, better, provided the diver has plenty of air, to allow a bit more time at each stop, to give a margin of safety.

As can be noted, the decompression table on page 83a lists the required decompression for depths of 40 to 190 feet for various times of exposure. (Page 83e contains a table for depths to 300 feet, and a table for extreme exposures.) The second column, Bottom Time, includes the time spent between leaving the surface and beginning the ascent. When the duration of a dive exceeds the time shown on the table, the next greater time listed should be used. For instance, when diving to 120 feet for 22 minutes, the figures used would be those for a dive to 120 feet for 25 minutes. Also, when the exact depth of a dive is not tabulated, the next greater depth should be used. Thus a dive to 125 feet would be calculated as for a dive to 130 feet for the same length of time. Optimum times, that is, the length of time at each depth which represents the best balance between the length of work period and amount of useful work for the average diver, are indicated for all tabulated depths. These exposure times should not be exceeded.

GENERAL INSTRUCTIONS FOR AIR DIVING

Need for Decompression

A quantity of nitrogen is taken up by the body during every dive. The amount absorbed depends upon the depth of the dive and the exposure (bottom) time. If the quantity of nitrogen dissolved in the body tissues exceeds a certain critical amount, the ascent must be delayed to allow the body tissue to remove the excess nitrogen. Decompression sickness results from failure to delay the ascent and to allow this process of gradual desaturation. A specified time at a specific depth for purposes of desaturation is called a decompression stop.

"No Decompression" Schedules

Dives that are not long or deep enough to require decompression stops are "no decompression" dives. Dives to 33 feet or less do not require decompression stops. As the depth increases, the allowable bottom time for "no decompression" dives decreases. Five minutes at 190 feet is the shortest and deepest "no decompression" schedule. These dives are all listed in the No Decompression Limits and Repetitive Group Designation Table for "No Decompression" Dives, ("No Decompression Table" (table 1-6)) and only require compliance with the 60 feet per minute rate of ascent.

Schedules That Require Decompression Stops

All dives beyond the limits of the "No Decompression Table" require decompression stops. These dives are listed in the Navy Standard Air Decompression Table (table 1-5). Comply exactly with instructions except as modified by surface decompression procedures.

Variations in Rate of Ascent

Ascend from all dives at the rate of 60 feet per minute.
In the event you exceed the 60 feet per minute rate:
(1) If no decompression stops are required, but the bottom time places you within 10 minutes of a schedule that does require decompression; stop at 10 feet for the time that you should have taken in ascent at 60 feet per minute.
(2) If decompression is required; stop 10 feet below the first listed decompression depth for the time that you should have taken in ascent at 60 feet per minute.
In the event you are unable to maintain the 60 feet per minute rate of ascent:
(1) If the delay was at or near the bottom; add to the bottom time, the additional time used in ascent. Decompress according to the requirements of the total bottom time. This is the safer procedure.
(2) If the delay was near the surface; increase the first stop by the difference between the time consumed in ascent and the time that should have been consumed at 60 feet per minute.

Repetitive Dive Procedure

A dive performed within 12 hours of surfacing from a previous dive is a repetitive dive. The period between dives is the surface interval. Excess nitrogen requires 12 hours to effectively be lost from the body. These tables are designed to protect the diver from the effects of this residual nitrogen. Allow a minimum surface interval of 10 minutes between all dives. Specific instructions are given for the use of each table in the following order:
(1) The "No Decompression Table" or the Navy Standard Air Decompression Table gives the repetitive group designation for all schedules which may preceed a repetitive dive.
(2) The Surface Interval Credit Table gives credit for the desaturation occurring during the surface interval.
(3) The Repetitive Dive Timetable gives the number of minutes or residual nitrogen time to add to the actual bottom time of the repetitive dive in order to obtain decompression for the residual nitrogen.
(4) The "No Decompression Table" or the Navy Standard Air Decompression Table gives the decompression required for the repetitive dive.

U.S. NAVY STANDARD AIR DECOMPRESSION TABLE

INSTRUCTIONS FOR USE

Time of decompression stops in the table is in minutes.
Enter the table at the exact or the next greater depth than the maximum depth attained during the dive. Select the listed bottom time that is exactly equal to or is next greater than the bottom time of the dive. Maintain the diver's chest as close as possible to each decompression depth for the number of minutes listed. The rate of ascent between stops is not critical. Commence timing each stop on arrival at the decompression depth and resume ascent when the specified time has lapsed.
For example – a dive to 82 feet for 36 minutes. To determine the proper decompression procedure: The next greater depth listed in this table is 90 feet. The next greater bottom time listed opposite 90 feet is 40. Stop 7 minutes at 10 feet in accordance with the 90/40 schedule.
For example – a dive to 110 feet for 30 minutes. It is known that the depth did not exceed 110 feet. To determine the proper decompression schedule: The exact depth of 110 feet is listed. The exact bottom time of 30 minutes is listed opposite 110 feet. Decompress according to the 110/30 schedule unless the dive was particularly cold or arduous. In that case, go to the 110/40, the 120/30, or the 120/40 at your own discretion.

Fig. 46. U.S. Navy Repetitive Decompression Tables (through p. 83f). Table 1-4. Decompression procedures. Courtesy of the Department of the Navy Bureau of Ships.

DEPTH (ft)	BOTTOM TIME (mins)	TIME TO FIRST STOP	DECOMPRESSION STOPS 50	40	30	20	10	TOTAL ASCENT TIME	REPET GROUP
40	200						0	0.7	*
	210	0.5					2	2.5	N
	230	0.5					7	7.5	N
	250	0.5					11	11.5	O
	270	0.5					15	15.5	O
	300	0.5					19	19.5	Z
50	100						0	0.8	*
	110	0.7					3	3.7	L
	120	0.7					5	5.7	M
	140	0.7					10	10.7	M
	160	0.7					21	21.7	N
	180	0.7					29	29.7	O
	200	0.7					35	35.7	O
	220	0.7					40	40.7	Z
	240	0.7					47	47.7	Z
60	60						0	1.0	*
	70	0.8					2	2.8	K
	80	0.8					7	7.8	L
	100	0.8					14	14.8	M
	120	0.8					26	26.8	N
	140	0.8					39	39.8	O
	160	0.8					48	48.8	Z
	180	0.8					56	56.8	Z
	200	0.6					69	70.6	Z
70	50						0	1.2	*
	60	1.0					8	9.0	K
	70	1.0					14	15.0	L
	80	1.0					18	19.0	M
	90	1.0					23	24.0	N
	100	1.0					33	34.0	N
	110	0.8				2	41	43.8	O
	120	0.8				4	47	51.8	O
	130	0.8				6	52	58.8	O
	140	0.8				8	56	64.8	Z
	150	0.8				9	61	70.8	Z
	160	0.8				13	72	85.8	Z
	170	0.8				19	79	98.8	Z
80	40						0	1.3	*
	50	1.2					10	11.2	K
	60	1.2					17	18.2	L
	70	1.2					23	24.2	M
	80	1.0				2	31	34.0	N
	90	1.0				7	39	47.0	N
	100	1.0				11	46	58.0	O
	110	1.0				13	53	67.0	O
	120	1.0				17	56	74.0	Z
	130	1.0				19	63	83.0	Z
	140	1.0				26	69	96.0	Z
	150	1.0				32	77	110.0	Z
90	30						0	1.5	*
	40	1.3					7	8.3	J
	50	1.3					18	19.3	L
	60	1.3					25	26.3	M
	70	1.2				7	30	38.2	N
	80	1.2				13	40	54.2	N
	90	1.2				18	48	67.2	O
	100	1.2				21	54	76.2	Z
	110	1.2				24	61	86.2	Z
	120	1.2				32	68	101.2	Z
	130	1.0			5	36	74	116.0	Z
100	25						0	1.7	*
	30	1.5					3	4.5	I
	40	1.5					15	16.5	K
	50	1.3				2	24	27.3	L
	60	1.3				9	28	38.3	N
	70	1.3				17	39	57.3	O
	80	1.3				23	48	72.3	O
	90	1.2			3	23	57	84.2	Z
	100	1.2			7	23	66	97.2	Z
	110	1.2			10	34	72	117.2	Z
	120	1.2			12	41	78	132.2	Z
110	20						0	1.8	*
	25	1.7					3	4.7	H
	30	1.7					7	8.7	J
	40	1.5				2	21	24.5	L
	50	1.5				8	26	35.5	M
	60	1.5				18	36	55.5	N
	70	1.3			1	23	48	73.3	O
	80	1.3			7	23	57	88.3	Z
	90	1.3			12	30	64	107.3	Z
	100	1.3			15	37	72	125.3	Z
120	15						0	2.0	*
	20	1.8					2	3.8	H
	25	1.8					6	7.8	I
	30	1.8					14	15.8	J
	40	1.7				5	25	31.7	L
	50	1.7				15	31	47.7	N
	60	1.5			2	22	45	70.5	O
	70	1.5			9	23	55	88.5	O
	80	1.5			15	27	63	106.5	Z
	90	1.5			19	37	74	131.5	Z
	100	1.5			23	45	80	149.5	Z
130	10						0	2.2	*
	15	2.0					1	3.0	F
	20	2.0					4	6.0	H
	25	2.0					10	12.0	J
	30	1.8				3	18	22.8	M
	40	1.8				10	25	36.8	N
	50	1.7			3	21	37	62.7	O
	60	1.7			9	23	52	85.7	Z
	70	1.7			16	24	61	102.7	Z
	80	1.5		3	19	35	72	130.5	Z
	90	1.5		8	19	45	80	153.5	Z
140	10						0	2.3	*
	15	2.2					2	4.2	G
	20	2.2					6	8.2	I
	25	2.0				2	14	18.0	J
	30	2.0				5	21	28.0	K
	40	1.8			2	16	26	45.8	N
	50	1.8			6	24	44	75.8	O
	60	1.8			16	23	56	96.8	Z
	70	1.7		4	19	32	68	124.7	Z
	80	1.7		10	23	41	79	154.7	Z
150	5						0	2.5	C
	10	2.3					1	3.3	E
	15	2.3					3	5.3	G
	20	2.2				2	7	11.2	H
	25	2.2				4	17	23.2	K
	30	2.2				8	24	34.2	L
	40	2.0			5	19	33	59.0	O
	50	2.0			12	23	51	88.0	O
	60	1.8		3	19	26	62	111.8	Z
	70	1.8		11	19	39	75	145.8	Z
	80	1.7	1	17	19	50	84	172.7	Z
160	5						0	2.7	D
	10	2.5					1	3.5	F
	15	2.3				1	4	7.3	H
	20	2.3				3	11	16.3	J
	25	2.3				7	20	29.3	K
	30	2.2			2	11	25	40.2	N
	40	2.2			7	23	39	71.2	N
	50	2.0		2	16	23	55	98.0	Z
	60	2.0		9	19	33	69	132.0	Z
	70	1.8	1	17	22	44	80	165.8	Z
170	5						0	2.8	D
	10	2.7					2	4.7	F
	15	2.5				2	5	9.5	H
	20	2.5				4	15	21.5	J
	25	2.3			2	7	23	34.3	L
	30	2.3			4	13	26	45.3	M
	40	2.2			5	18	23	45	81.2	O
	50	2.2			5	18	23	61	109.2	Z
	60	2.0	2	15	22	37	74	152.0	Z
	70	2.0	8	17	19	51	86	183.0	Z
180	5						0	3.0	D
	10	2.8					3	5.8	F
	15	2.7				3	6	11.7	H
	20	2.5				5	17	25.5	K
	25	2.5			3	10	24	39.5	L
	30	2.5			6	17	27	52.5	N
	40	2.3		5	14	23	50	92.3	O
	50	2.2	2	9	19	30	65	127.2	Z
	60	2.2	5	16	19	44	81	167.2	Z
190	5						0	3.2	D
	10	2.8					3	6.8	G
	15	2.8				4	7	13.8	I
	20	2.7			2	6	20	30.7	K
	25	2.7			5	11	25	43.7	M
	30	2.5		1	8	19	32	62.5	N
	40	2.5		8	14	23	55	102.5	O
	50	2.3	4	13	22	33	72	146.3	Z
	60	2.3	10	17	19	50	84	182.3	Z

Fig. 46a. Table 1-5. U.S. Navy standard air decompression table. Times in above table are given in minutes and tenths of minutes. It should be remembered that while a longer than necessary decompression stop is always allowable, *never* make a shorter stop than the one indicated.

DEPTH (ft.)	NO DECOM-PRESSION LIMITS (Min.)	REPETITIVE GROUPS													
		A	B	C	D	E	F	G	H	I	J	K	L	M	N	O
10	–	60	120	210	300											
15	–	35	70	110	160	225	350									
20	–	25	50	75	100	135	180	240	325							
25	–	20	35	55	75	100	125	160	195	245	315					
30	–	15	30	45	60	75	95	120	145	170	205	250	310			
35	310	5	15	25	40	50	60	80	100	120	140	160	190	220	270	310
40	200	5	15	25	30	40	50	70	80	100	110	130	150	170	200	
50	100	–	10	15	25	30	40	50	60	70	80	90	100			
60	60	–	10	15	20	25	30	40	50	55	60					
70	50	–	5	10	15	20	30	35	40	45	50					
80	40	–	5	10	15	20	25	30	35	40						
90	30	–	5	10	12	15	20	25	30							
100	25	–	5	7	10	15	20	22	25							
110	20	–	–	5	10	13	15	20								
120	15	–	–	5	10	12	15									
130	10	–	–	5	8	10										
140	10	–	–	5	7	10										
150	5	–	–	5												
160	5	–	–	–	5											
170	5	–	–	–	5											
180	5	–	–	–	5											
190	5	–	–	–	5											

INSTRUCTIONS FOR USE

I. "No decompression" limits
   This column shows at various depths greater than 30 feet the allowable diving times (in minutes) which permit surfacing directly at 60 ft. a minute with no decompression stops. Longer exposure times require the use of the Standard Air Decompression Table (Table 1-5).

II. Repetitive group designation table
   The tabulated exposure times (or bottom times) are in minutes. The times at the various depths in each vertical column are the maximum exposures during which a diver will remain within the group listed at the head of the column.
   To find the repetitive group designation at surfacing for dives involving exposures up to and including the "no decompression limits": Enter the table on the <u>exact or next greater depth</u> than that to which exposed and select the listed exposure time <u>exact or next greater</u> than the actual exposure time. The repetitive group designation is indicated by the letter at the head of the vertical column where the selected exposure time is listed.
   For example: A dive was to 32 feet for 45 minutes. Enter the table along the 35 ft. depth line since it is next greater than 32 ft. The table shows that since group "D" is left after 40 minutes exposure and group "E" after 50 minutes, group "E" (at the head of the column where the 50 min. exposure is listed) is the proper selection.
   Exposure times for depths less than 40 ft. are listed only up to approximately five hours since this is considered to be beyond field requirements for this table.

Fig. 46b. Table 1-6. "No decompression" limits and repetitive group designation table for "no decompression" dives.

REPETITIVE GROUP AT THE END OF THE SURFACE INTERVAL

	Z	O	N	M	L	K	J	I	H	G	F	E	D	C	B	A
Z	0:10-0:22	0:34	0:48	1:02	1:18	1:36	1:55	2:17	2:42	3:10	3:45	4:29	5:27	6:56	10:05	12:00*
O		0:10-0:23	0:36	0:51	1:07	1:24	1:43	2:04	2:29	2:59	3:33	4:17	5:16	6:44	9:54	12:00*
N			0:10-0:24	0:39	0:54	1:11	1:30	1:53	2:18	2:47	3:22	4:04	5:03	6:32	9:43	12:00
M				0:10-0:25	0:42	0:59	1:18	1:39	2:05	2:34	3:08	3:52	4:49	6:18	9:28	12:00*
L					0:10-0:26	0:45	1:04	1:25	1:49	2:19	2:53	3:36	4:35	6:02	9:12	12:00*
K						0:10-0:28	0:49	1:11	1:35	2:03	2:38	3:21	4:19	5:48	8:58	12:00*
J							0:10-0:31	0:54	1:19	1:47	2:20	3:04	4:02	5:40	8:40	12:00*
I								0:10-0:33	0:59	1:29	2:02	2:44	3:43	5:12	8:21	12:00*
H									0:10-0:36	1:06	1:41	2:23	3:20	4:49	7:59	12:00*
G										0:10-0:40	1:15	1:59	2:58	4:25	7:35	12:00*
F											0:10-0:45	1:29	2:28	3:57	7:05	12:00*
E												0:10-0:54	1:57	3:22	6:32	12:00*
D													0:10-1:09	2:38	5:48	12:00
C														0:10-1:39	2:49	12:00*
B															0:10-2:10	12:00*
A																0:10-12:00*

REPETITIVE GROUP AT THE BEGINNING OF SURFACE INTERVAL (FROM PREVIOUS DIVE)

INSTRUCTIONS FOR USE

Surface interval time in the table is in <u>hours</u> and <u>minutes</u> ("7:59" means 7 hours and 59 minutes). The surface interval must be at least 10 minutes.

Find the <u>repetitive group designation letter</u> (from the <u>previous dive schedule</u>) on the diagonal slope. Enter the table horizontally to select the listed surface interval time that is exactly or <u>next greater</u> than the actual surface interval time. The repetitive group designation for the <u>end</u> of the surface interval is at the head of the vertical column where the selected surface interval time is listed. For example — a previous dive was to 110 ft. for 30 minutes. The diver remains on the surface 1 hour and 30 minutes and wishes to find the new repetitive group designation: The repetitive group from the last column of the 110/30 schedule in the Standard Air Decompression Tables is "J". Enter the surface interval credit table along the horizontal line labeled "J". The 1 hour and 47 min. listed surface interval time is <u>next greater</u> than the actual 1 hour and 30 minutes surface interval time. Therefore, the diver <u>has lost</u> sufficient inert gas to place him in group "G" (at the head of the vertical column selected).

*NOTE: Dives following surface intervals of <u>more</u> than 12 hours are not considered repetitive dives. <u>Actual</u> bottom times in the Standard Air Decompression Tables may be used in computing decompression for such dives.

Fig. 46c. Table 1–7. Surface interval credit table.

REPET. GROUPS	REPETITIVE DIVE DEPTH (Ft.)															
	40	50	60	70	80	90	100	110	120	130	140	150	160	170	180	190
A	7	6	5	4	4	3	3	3	3	3	2	2	2	2	2	2
B	17	13	11	9	8	7	7	6	6	6	5	5	4	4	4	4
C	25	21	17	15	13	11	10	10	9	8	7	7	6	6	6	6
D	37	29	24	20	18	16	14	13	12	11	10	9	9	8	8	8
E	49	38	30	26	23	20	18	16	15	13	12	12	11	10	10	10
F	61	47	36	31	28	24	22	20	18	16	15	14	13	13	12	11
G	73	56	44	37	32	29	26	24	21	19	18	17	16	15	14	13
H ✓	87	66	52	43	38	33	30	27	25	22	20	19	18	17	16	15
I	101	76	61	50	43	38	34	31	28	25	23	22	20	19	18	17
J	116	87	70	57	48	43	38	34	32	28	26	24	23	22	20	19
K	138	99	79	64	54	47	43	38	35	31	29	27	26	24	22	21
L	161	111	88	72	61	53	48	42	39	35	32	30	28	26	25	24
M	187	124	97	80	68	58	52	47	43	38	35	32	31	29	27	26
N	213	142	107	87	73	64	57	51	46	40	38	35	33	31	29	28
O	241	160	117	96	80	70	62	55	50	44	40	38	36	34	31	30
Z	257	169	122	100	84	73	64	57	52	46	42	40	37	35	32	31

INSTRUCTIONS FOR USE

The bottom times listed in this table are called "residual nitrogen times" and are the times a diver is to consider he has **already** spent on bottom when he **starts** a repetitive dive to a specific depth. They are in minutes.

Enter the table horizontally with the repetitive group designation from the Surface Interval Credit Table. The time in each vertical column is the number of minutes that would be required (at the depth listed at the head of the column) to saturate to the particular group.

For example — the final group designation from the Surface Interval Credit Table, on the basis of a previous dive and surface interval, is "H". To plan a dive to 110 feet, determine the "residual nitrogen time" for this depth required by the repetitive group designation: Enter this table along the horizontal line labeled "H". The table shows that one must **start** a dive to 110 feet as though he had already been on the bottom for 27 minutes. This information can then be applied to the Standard Air Decompression table or "No Decompression" Table in a number of ways:

(1) Assuming a diver is going to finish a job and take whatever decompression is required, he must add 27 minutes to his actual bottom time and be prepared to take decompression according to the 110 foot schedules for the sum or equivalent single dive time.

(2) Assuming one wishes to make a quick inspection dive for the minimum decompression, he will decompress according to the 110/30 schedule for a dive of 3 minutes or less (27 + 3 = 30). For a dive of over 3 minutes but less than 13, he will decompress according to the 110/40 schedule (27 + 13 = 40).

(3) Assuming that one does not want to exceed the 110/50 schedule and the amount of decompression it requires, he will have to start ascent before 23 minutes of actual bottom time (50 - 27 = 23).

(4) Assuming that a diver has air for approximately 45 minutes bottom time and decompression stops, the possible dives can be computed: A dive of 13 minutes will require 23 minutes of decompression (110/40 schedule), for a total submerged time of 36 minutes. A dive of 13 to 23 minutes will require 34 minutes of decompression (110/50 schedule), for a total submerged time of 47 to 57 minutes. Therefore, to be safe, the diver will have to start ascent before 13 minutes or a standby air source will have to be provided.

Fig. 46d. Table 1-8. Repetitive dive timetable.

DEPTH (ft.)	BOTTOM TIME (Min.)	TIME TO FIRST STOP	DECOMPRESSION STOPS												TOTAL ASCENT TIME
			130	120	110	100	90	80	70	60	50	40	30	20	10	
40	360	0.5													23	24
	480	0.5													41	42
	720	0.5													69	70
60	240	0.7												2	79	82
	360	0.7												20	110	140
	480	0.7												44	148	193
	720	0.7												78	187	266
80	180	1.0												35	85	121
	240	0.8											6	52	120	179
	360	0.8											29	90	160	280
	480	0.8											59	107	187	354
	720	0.7											17	108	142	187	455
100	180	1.0										1	29	53	118	202
	240	1.0										14	42	84	142	283
	360	0.8									2	42	73	111	187	416
	480	0.8									21	61	91	142	187	502
	720	0.8									55	106	122	142	187	613
120	120	1.3									10	19	47	98	176
	180	1.2								5	27	37	76	137	283
	240	1.2								23	35	60	97	179	395
	360	1.0							18	45	64	93	142	187	550
	480	0.8						3	41	64	93	122	142	187	653
	720	0.8						32	74	100	114	122	142	187	772
140	90	1.5									2	14	18	42	88	166
	120	1.5									12	14	36	56	120	240
	180	1.3									10	26	32	54	94	168	386
	240	1.2								8	28	34	50	78	124	187	511
	360	1.0							9	32	42	64	84	122	142	187	683
	480	1.0						31	44	50	100	114	122	142	187	800
	720	0.8					16	56	88	97	100	114	122	142	187	923
170	90	1.8								12	12	14	34	52	120	232
	120	1.5						2	10	12	18	32	42	82	156	356
	180	1.3					4	10	22	28	34	50	78	120	187	535
	240	1.3					18	24	30	42	50	70	116	142	187	681
	360	1.2				22	34	40	52	60	98	114	122	142	187	873
	480	1.0			14	40	42	56	91	97	100	114	122	142	187	1006
200	5	3.2													1	5
	10	3.0												1	4	8
	15	2.8											1	4	10	18
	20	2.8											3	7	27	40
	25	2.8											7	14	25	49
	30	2.7										2	9	22	37	73
	40	2.5									2	5	17	23	59	112
	50	2.5									6	16	22	39	75	161
	60	2.3								2	18	17	24	51	89	199
	90	1.8							1	10	10	12	30	38	74	134	323
	120	1.7						6	10	10	24	28	40	64	98	180	472
	180	1.3				1	10	10	18	24	24	42	48	70	106	142	187	684
	240	1.3				6	20	24	24	36	42	54	68	114	122	142	187	841
	360	1.2			12	22	36	40	44	56	82	98	100	114	122	142	187	1057
210	5	3.3													1	5
	10	3.2												2	4	10
	15	3.0											1	5	13	22
	20	3.0											4	10	23	40
	25	2.8										2	7	17	27	56
	30	2.8										4	9	24	41	81
	40	2.7									4	9	19	26	63	124
	50	2.5									1	9	17	19	45	80	174
220	5	3.5													2	6
	10	3.3												2	5	11
	15	3.2											2	5	16	27
	20	3.0										1	3	11	24	43
	25	3.0										3	8	19	33	66
	30	2.8									1	7	10	23	47	91
	40	2.8									6	12	22	29	68	140
	50	2.7									3	12	17	18	51	86	190

DEPTH (ft.)	BOTTOM TIME (Min.)	TIME TO FIRST STOP	DECOMPRESSION STOPS												TOTAL ASCENT TIME
			130	120	110	100	90	80	70	60	50	40	30	20	10	
230	5	3.7													2	6
	10	3.5												1	2	6	13
	15	3.5												3	6	18	31
	20	3.2											2	5	12	26	49
	25	3.2											4	8	22	37	75
	30	3.0										2	8	12	23	51	99
	40	2.8									1	7	15	22	34	74	156
	50	2.8									5	14	16	24	51	89	202
240	5	3.8													2	6
	10	3.5											1	3	6	14
	15	3.5											4	6	21	35
	20	3.3										3	6	18	26	63
	25	3.2										1	4	9	24	40	82
	30	3.2										4	8	15	22	56	109
	40	3.0									3	7	17	22	39	75	166
	50	2.8								1	8	15	16	29	51	94	217
250	5	3.8													1	2	7
	10	3.7												1	4	7	16
	15	3.5											1	4	7	22	38
	20	3.5											4	7	17	27	59
	25	3.3										2	7	10	24	45	92
	30	3.3										6	7	17	23	59	116
	40	3.2									5	9	17	19	45	79	178
	60	2.7								4	10	10	10	22	28	64	126	297
	90	2.2						8	10	10	10	10	28	28	44	68	98	186	513
	120						(SEE EXTREME EXPOSURES BELOW)										
	180																
	240																
260	5	4.0													1	2	7
	10	3.8												2	4	9	19
	15	3.7											2	4	10	22	42
	20	3.5											1	4	7	20	31	67
	25	3.5											3	8	11	23	50	99
	30	3.3										2	6	8	19	26	61	128
	40	3.2									1	6	11	16	19	49	84	190
270	5	4.2													1	3	9
	10	4.0												2	5	11	22
	15	3.8											3	4	11	24	46
	20	3.7											2	3	9	21	35	74
	25	3.5										2	3	8	13	23	53	106
	30	3.5										3	6	12	22	27	64	138
	40	3.3									5	6	11	17	22	51	88	204
280	5	4.3													2	2	9
	10	4.0												1	2	5	13	25
	15	3.8											1	3	4	11	26	49
	20	3.8											3	4	8	23	39	81
	25	3.7										2	5	7	16	23	56	113
	30	3.5										1	3	7	13	22	30	70	160
	40	3.3									1	6	6	13	17	27	51	93	218
290	5	4.5													2	3	10
	10	4.2												1	3	5	16	30
	15	4.0											1	3	6	12	26	52
	20	4.0											3	7	9	23	43	89
	25	3.8											3	5	8	17	23	60	120
	30	3.7										1	5	6	16	22	36	72	162
	40	3.5										5	7	15	16	32	51	95	234
300	5	4.7													3	3	11
	10	4.3												1	3	6	17	32
	15	4.2											2	3	6	15	26	56
	20	4.0											2	3	7	10	23	47	104
	25	3.8										1	3	6	8	19	26	61	128
	30	3.8										2	5	7	17	22	39	75	171
	40	3.7									4	6	9	15	17	34	51	90	234
	60	3.0								4	10	10	10	10	14	28	32	50	90	187	455
	90																	
	120					(SEE EXTREME EXPOSURES BELOW)											
	180																

EXTREME EXPOSURES – 250 AND 300 FT.

DEPTH (ft.)	BOTTOM TIME (Min.)	TIME TO FIRST STOP	DECOMPRESSION STOPS															TOTAL ASCENT TIME
			200	190	180	170	160	150	140	130	120	110	100	90	80	70	60	50	40	30	20	10	
250	120	1.8							5	10	10	10	10	16	24	36	48	64	94	142	187	662
	180	1.5					4	8	8	10	22	24	24	32	42	44	60	84	114	122	142	187	929
	240	1.5				9	14	21	22	22	40	40	42	56	76	98	100	114	122	142	187	1107
300	90	2.3				3	8	8	10	10	10	16	24	24	34	48	64	90	142	187	691
	120	2.0			3	4	8	8	8	10	14	24	24	24	34	52	66	102	122	142	187	887
	180	1.7	6	8	8	8	14	20	21	21	28	40	40	48	56	82	98	100	114	122	142	187	1165

Fig. 46e. Table 1–9. U.S. Navy standard air decompression table for exceptional exposures.

I. PREVIOUS DIVE:

24 minutes } see table 1-5 or 1-6 for } Group K
160 feet   } repetitive group designation }

II. SURFACE INTERVAL:

1 hour 28 minutes on surface } see table 1-7 } Group H
Group K (from I.)   } for new group }

III. RESIDUAL NITROGEN TIME:

110 feet (depth of repetitive dive) } see table } 14 minutes
Group H (from II.)   } 1-8   }

IV. EQUIVALENT SINGLE DIVE TIME:

       27 minutes (residual nitrogen time from III.)
(add) 14 minutes (actual bottom time of repetitive dive)
(sum) 41 minutes

V. DECOMPRESSION FOR REPETITIVE DIVE:

41 minutes (equivalent single dive } see table }
    time from IV.)   } 1-5 or 1-6 }
110 feet (depth of repetitive dive) }

☐ No decompression required
    or
Decompression stops: 20 feet 8 minutes
                      10 feet 26 minutes
                      ____feet____minutes
                      ____feet____minutes

Fig. 46f. Repetitive Dive Worksheet.

Column 3 of the table lists the stops—feet from the surface and minutes to be spent at each stop. The rate of ascent from the bottom to the first stop, or any ascent in a dive using SCUBA, should not exceed 60 feet per minute. This is faster than the speed at which bubbles from an Aqua-Lung rise. Column 4 indicates the Decompression Stops. A dive to 120 feet for 40 minutes requires that the diver stop at 20 feet for five minutes, and at 10 feet for 25 minutes before surfacing. Column 5 lists the Total Ascent Time, which is the sum of times spent at various stops, plus the time required for ascent at a rate of 60 feet per minute to the first stop. Column 6 shows the code letter for the Repetitive Group. This letter indicates the excess amount of nitrogen in the body after a dive.

Value "A" means that no significant amount of nitrogen has been retained from the previous dive. Value "B" shows that there is a small amount of residual nitrogen in the body. And so on to "Z" which indicates that there is a larger amount of excess nitrogen remaining even after decompression.

To best understand the workings of the tables, try a hypothetical problem: (see page 83f for worksheet). The diver has made a previous dive of 24 minutes to 160 feet. Jot down these figures under "I. Previous Dive." Look at Table 1–5 (page 83a). Twenty-five minutes is the next largest number greater than 24 minutes. Read horizontally across the page to find the repetitive group value "K." Write "K" in space indicating "Group." The diver has been out of the water for one hour and 28 minutes. On the work sheet where it says "II. Surface Interval" write the figures 1 and 28 in the appropriate space. Place the letter "K" in the space indicating Group (from I). Turn to table 1–7 (page 83c). On the slanting column indicating "Repetitive Group at the Beginning of Surface Interval" find "K." Read horizontally to locate the number equal to, or next largest to, 1 hour and 28 minutes. You will find "1:35" which means 1 hour and 35 minutes. Follow this column upward vertically to locate the "Repetitive Group at the End of the Surface Interval." This letter is "H." Write "H" in "Group" on worksheet.

The diver then makes a second dive, this time to 110 feet for 14 minutes. Write this information in "III. Residual Nitrogen Time." Turn to table 1–8 (page 83d). Under Repetitive Groups go to "H." Read horizontally across page to find the number 110 (110 is at top of page). The number is "27." This means that 27 must be added to the 14 minutes of the second dive. In other words, he must *start* the

Fig. 47. SCUBA divers entering surf in a group dive. Upper right-hand picture shows method of slipping directly into the surf from rocks, while lower-right demonstrates importance of maintaining distance from other divers when waves are prevalent near the shore. *Courtesy, Hartford Gillmen*

second dive as though he had been on the bottom for 27 minutes. Go back to table 1–5 (page 83a) and compute the dive as though it were for 41 minutes at 110 feet (from worksheet "IV. Equivalent Single Dive Time"). Forty-one minutes at 110 feet indicates decompression stops of 8 minutes at 20 feet, and 26 minutes at 10 feet. Enter these figures on the worksheet under "V. Decompression for Repetitive Dive."

A timekeeper should be designated to keep an accurate record of the time required for the diver to reach the bottom, the time spent on the bottom (signals should be prearranged to indicate when to begin the ascent), and the time spent at each stop during the ascent. Since accidents can happen, divers should check the location of the nearest recompression chamber before attempting any deep dives, and should be able to recognize the symptoms of compressed air illness.

The most common symptom seems to be pain, described as of a deep boring character, in the bones or joints, particularly of the arms and legs.

Dizziness, or "the staggers," usually accompanied by ringing of the ears, is less common, and the more severe symptoms such as paralysis, difficulty in breathing, extreme fatigue, asphyxia and collapse, though of infrequent occurrence, are so dramatic in nature that they are immediately recognized. In cases where there is any doubt, the diver should be treated as though suffering from compressed air illness, taken back down to the depth at which all pain is relieved and then decompressed according to treatment tables, or to a recompression chamber with trained personnel, if one is in the vicinity.

If proper precautions are followed, no sport diver should experience any real difficulty with this problem. No one should dive who is not in top physical condition, or is suffering from recent overindulgence in alcohol. Meticulous attention should be paid to all details of a dive, with an accurate record kept of time of dive, length of dive, depth of dive, and details of decompression. No diver should exceed the optimum exposure times given, and the U. S. Navy Air Decompression Tables should be rigidly adhered to, with a slightly longer time at all stops being allowed, if possible, as a safety factor.

In addition to the above mentioned divers' diseases, there are various accidents which can occur. Probably the most common cause of fatal accidents, using selfcontained breathing devices, is air embolism.

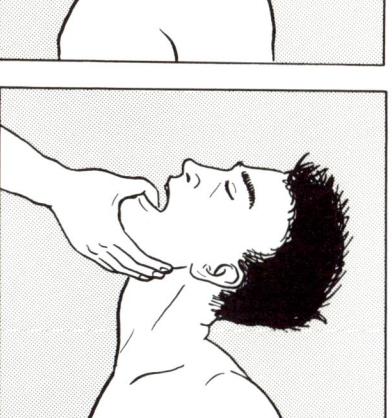

Fig. 48a. Don't waste time. Start "mouth-to-mouth" artificial respiration immediately.

Fig. 48b. Tilt the victim's head all the way back to open the throat air passage.

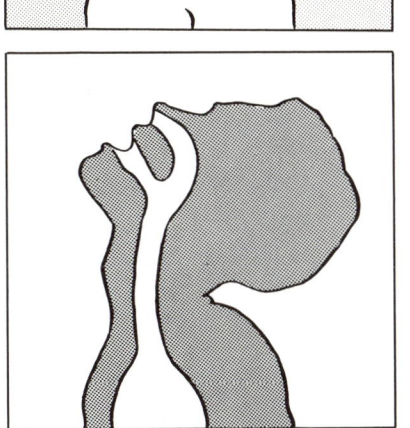

Fig. 48c. Hold his jaw forward with your thumb so tongue won't block the air passage.

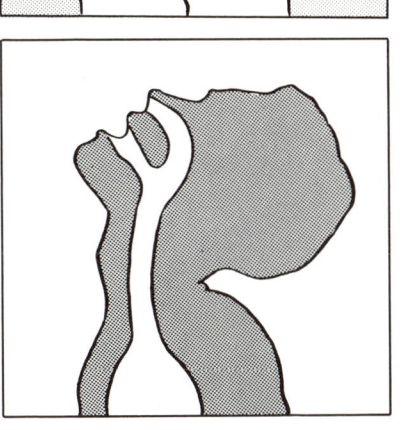

Fig. 48d. Or push his jaw forward with your fingers.

Fig. 48e. Open your mouth wide and place it over the victim's mouth.

Fig. 48f. Press your cheek against his nostrils to prevent air leak.

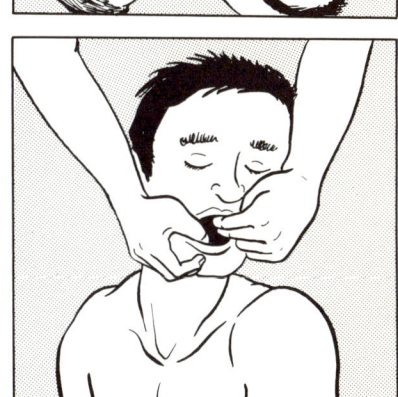
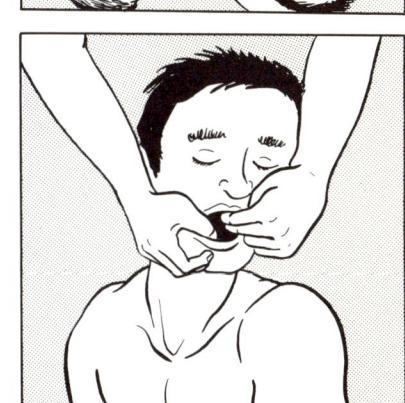

Fig. 48g. If blowing effort fails, clear victim's mouth and throat of obstructions.

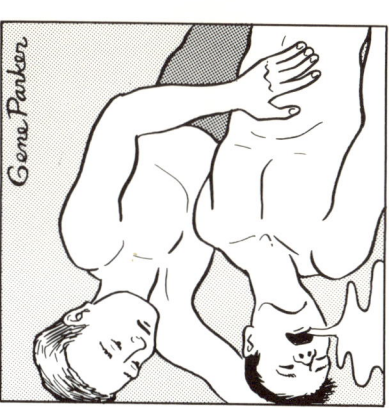

Fig. 48h. If water or air in stomach prevents blowing, press his belly to force it out.

Symptoms include bleeding from the nose and mouth, rigidity of the arms and legs, unsteadiness, mushy speech, and loss of consciousness. Treatment requires prompt medical attention and generally the use of a recompression chamber or underwater recompression using treatment tables. Death has been known to occur from an ascent of only a few feet without exhaling.

Because of the seriousness of this accident, the importance of proper knowledge and training before using SCUBA cannot be overestimated. No ascent should be made at a rate faster than sixty feet per minute, and the breath should never be held while ascending. Ordinarily, if a diver attempts to hold his breath, the discomfort and sensation of pressure in the lungs will force him to exhale almost continuously. However, fright, which may occur as a result of equipment having to be jettisoned underwater due to emergency, may cause a spasm of the throat muscles which prevents air from escaping freely. For this reason a thorough and gradual training period with SCUBA is essential, and no breathing equipment should be jettisoned underwater unless absolutely necessary. Even then if panic is avoided, the diver can usually ascend safely. E. R. Cross, owner of a diving school and author of a diving manual, mentions having made a successful ascent from a depth of 140 feet, after abandoning faulty breathing equipment. The important thing in an ascent of this kind is to exhale continuously, regulating the rate of exhalation according to the depth.

Spontaneous pneumothorax is another accident caused by overexpansion of the lungs, and may accompany air embolism. It is the result of air being trapped in the chest cavity, outside the lung, and as the diver ascends, the increasing pressure of the trapped air may collapse the lung and cause displacement of the heart toward the other side of the chest, sometimes resulting in death. Symptoms include extreme shortness of breath, sharp pain in the chest, distention of neck veins, irregular pulse, and bluish discoloration of the skin. Since the treatment includes the insertion of a needle to allow the trapped air to escape, prompt medical attention is necessary.

Overexpansion of the stomach and intestinal organs can also occur through the expansion of air swallowed or intestinal gases formed while under pressure. This may cause serious discomfort, and even impair the function of the bowel due to stretching. This disorder is not as common among divers, who are exposed to pressures for relatively short periods of time, as it is among aviators. However, it is unwise to eat gas-producing foods or beverages just before diving.

Probably the most common cause of fatalities among skin divers is drowning. The absence of swimming skill and lack of knowledge of the ocean are the greatest factors in diving accidents. For this reason it would be wise for all skin diving clubs to insist that members acquire sufficient swimming skill and endurance before going on diving excursions, particularly in deep water or in areas where there are currents and strong surf. No diving should be done without a float or small boat handy and secured against drifting, and no one should dive when fatigued or immediately after eating. If the water is cold, the body should be immersed gradually in order to allow a gradual adjustment to the temperature.

Since more drownings have been caused by weight belts than any other single factor, it is essential that all weight belts have quick-release buckles, for rapid removal in case of emergency. One drowning occurred when a young diver who had built his own diving helmet wore weighted shoes instead of a safety-release weight belt, and when the helmet accidentally came off his head he was unable to reach the surface in time because of his heavy shoes.

An unbreakable rule is that no one should ever dive alone, or even stray too far from his group while diving. All divers should have some knowledge of life-saving rescue techniques and know how to administer artificial respiration. The best method of artificial respiration is the "mouth to mouth" (or "mouth to nose").

In a case of drowning, don't waste time getting him to shore (Fig. 48a). You can breathe for him while standing or kneeling in the water. You can administer "mouth-to-mouth" on an inner tube, over the side of a boat, or while buoyed up by life vests. Fig. 48b: Tilt his head back as far as possible to open his throat air passage. Fig. 48c: Hold his jaw forward by hooking your thumb in his mouth or (Fig. 48d) pushing his jaw forward with your fingers. Fig. 48e: Open your mouth wide and place it over the victim's. Seal your lips over his. Pinch his nostrils or (Fig. 48f) press your cheek against his nose to prevent air leak. Blow air into the victim until you see his chest rise. Then remove your mouth to let him breathe out. Continue inflations at least 10 times a minute for an adult, up to 20 times a minute for a child. While you are giving artificial respiration, you can be bringing the victim to shore.

If the first blowing effort fails, make sure that his tongue or some foreign object is not blocking the air flow to his lungs. Fig. 48g: Clear his mouth and throat with your finger. If the obstruction persists, roll the victim over and strike him *hard* between the shoulder blades until the obstruction is coughed up. Then proceed as before. Press his belly

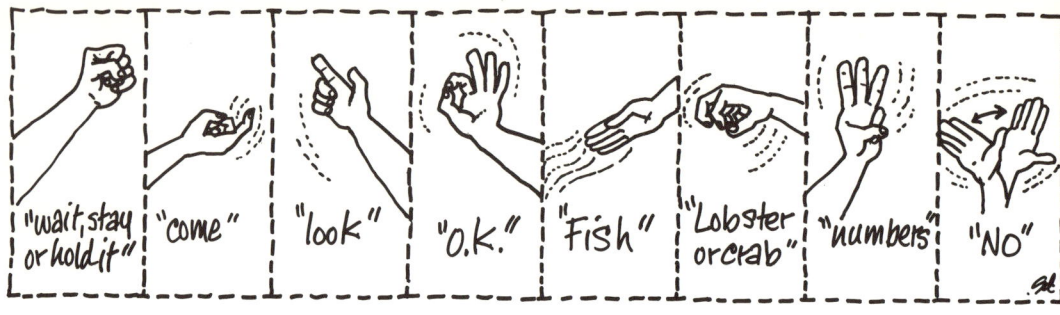

Fig. 49a. Visual hand signals.

Fig. 49b. Additional visual signals, as seen mainly from underwater.

if air causes it to bulge. Fig. 48h: Press his belly to force excess water out. It may take hours to revive a victim. Continue "mouth-to-mouth" until the victim is breathing on his own, until a physician pronounces him dead, or the person appears dead beyond *any* doubt.

Since other accidents or minor injuries caused by sharp rocks, corals, spears or other equipment are frequent in diving, a waterproof first aid kit should be an additional item of equipment on any spearfishing or skin diving excursion. This kit should include a first aid pamphlet, a good pair of surgical tweezers for removing sea urchin or other fish spines, a scalpel for small incisions to remove fishhooks or barbed spines, a good antiseptic for application to wounds and for sterilizing instruments, a tourniquet (to be used according to directions in the first aid book), an ammonia inhalant, and a good supply of bandages.

Additional items which may be helpful are rubber finger cots which can be worn over bandages to permit going into the water again, sunburn oil or salve, a wire splint, and a bottle of potassium permanganate crystals to relieve the pain of wounds caused by poisonous fish.

In spite of all the above described possible diving accidents, skin diving is a relatively safe sport, with far fewer fatalities proportionately to driving an automobile on the highway today. If proper precautions are taken and with adequate understanding of the principles of diving and the use of equipment, skin diving can be a safe and fascinating and thoroughly rewarding sport.

Fig. 50. Demonstration of the "buddy breathing" system. Some regulators have attachments for an "octopus rig" whereby two divers can breathe from the same regulator without exchanging mouthpieces. Where only one mouthpiece is available one diver passes it to the other diver for alternate breaths. *Courtesy, Poseidon Systems, USA*

IV Equipment and Its Uses

Man in his first attempts at developing diving equipment might profitably have observed the natural world around him. Certain aquatic insects have highly developed systems for breathing under water.

The larva of the Dipterous fly, which lives buried in mud and decaying vegetable matter and in polluted water, has a telescopic tail which can be extended to the surface to take in air. Another of the so-called "rat-tailed maggots," *Eristalis tenax*, can extend its tail in a similar manner to a length of as much as six inches. Inside are air tubes which coil up in the same way as a diver's hose, when the tail is retracted.

The gnat larva has an arrangement similar to the air tube and float used by early divers (Fig. 51). It opens the tip of its respiratory siphon to form a miniature basin which adheres to the surface film of the water, taking in air and holding the insect suspended while it feeds. When it wishes to descend, it simply closes its siphon valves, making the surface tension no longer effective.

The aquatic beetle Dryopidae forms a plastron by which it stores air and which functions as a sort of self-contained breathing apparatus. This plastron is an air store, or gaseous layer, held in position on the body by tiny hairs. The surface film of the plastron, in contact with the water, functions as a diffusion membrane; dissolved oxygen diffuses into it from surrounding water and carbon dioxide is given off into the water. This plastron must be replaced from time to time, but with one the insect is able to live underwater from seven to forty days without coming up for more air. If there are enough oxygen bubbles given off by green plants in the water, the insect could probably stay submerged indefinitely.

The water spider constructs a form of diving bell spun from his own silk and anchored to the bottom by silk threads, with the open end down. He gradually replaces the water in it with air, by trapping air bubbles under hairs on his back and diving to release them at the mouth of his container. He is then able to breathe and keep dry under water. (It is interesting to note here the similarity between this insect's underwater activities and Halley's diving bell described in the first chapter, in which the air was replenished by air carried down to it in barrels.) There is some indication that the spider's diving bell also functions as a self-contained breathing apparatus, taking oxygen from the water and giving off carbon dioxide, so that the spider is able to stay submerged for weeks at a time.

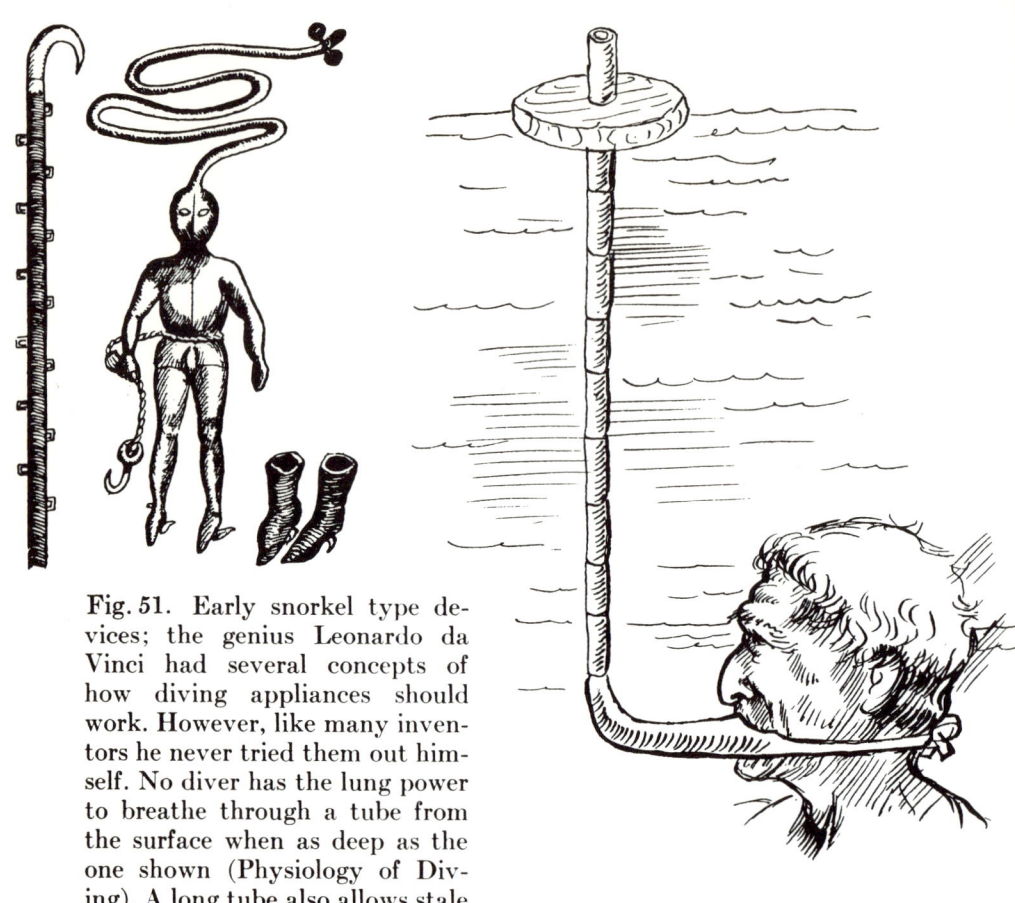

Fig. 51. Early snorkel type devices; the genius Leonardo da Vinci had several concepts of how diving appliances should work. However, like many inventors he never tried them out himself. No diver has the lung power to breathe through a tube from the surface when as deep as the one shown (Physiology of Diving). A long tube also allows stale air to collect, since it cannot be flushed out thoroughly with each breath.

Many people have speculated about the possibility of man's developing some similar equipment which would allow him to stay underwater indefinitely with no outside source of air necessary.

The mask for sight, fins for extra power, and snorkel for breathing are the basic equipment of the skin diver. From a casual glance one might think that the items shown are all fairly new developments. However, by studying their history it will be found that certain of these appliances are quite ancient in origin. For instance, the plastic tubes used by skin divers today to breathe while swimming slightly under the water surface are just another variation on an old principle which had its antecedents in the siphons of various fly larvae, in the hollow reeds used by heroes of story and legend, and later the leather air tube and cork float of early divers. The mask and flippers also are not new ideas, as will be explained later in this chapter.

Quite a few people who are interested in skin diving but have not yet tried it, seem to think that they must have an artificial breathing device in order to participate in the sport. Nothing could be further from reality. Every month the *Skin Diver* magazine carries articles about famous divers, most of whom dive wearing only basic equipment: mask, flippers, etc. Free divers (natural divers using no breathing equipment) have accomplished some remarkable feats, including dives up to 170 feet, the spearing of fish weighing hundreds of pounds, and many other achievements which demonstrate the possibilities of free diving. Most skin diving clubs have

Fig. 52a. Wide-angle-view types of masks. a. U. S. Divers "Aqua-Lung" Pro Mask with purge. b. Swimaster (Voit) Wide View Mask. c. Seamless Maxvue. d. Seamless Oporto. e. Sportsways "Water-Lung" mask. f. Healthways Pinocchio "Clear-Ease."

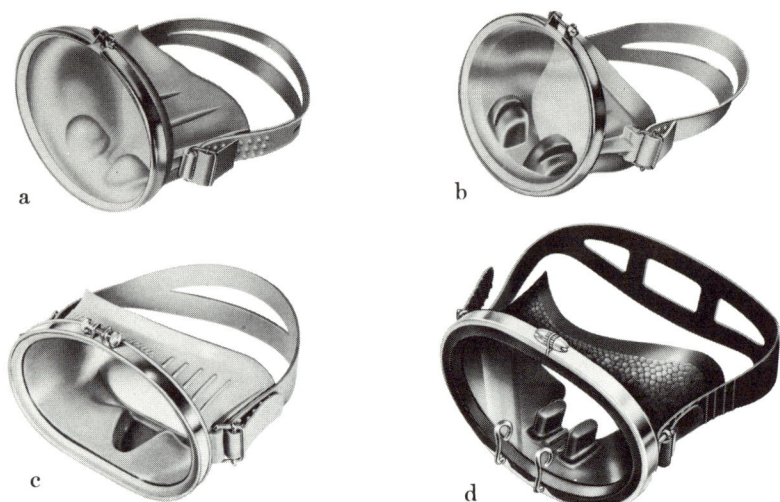

Fig. 52b. "Nose squeeze" masks permit divers to squeeze the nose to aid in equalizing air pressure in the inner ear. (See Fig. 75.) a. U. S. Divers Champion "Equi-Pressure." b. U. S. Divers Deluxe "Equi-Rama." c. Adolph Kiefer Pro Pinocchio "Riva." d. Voit "50 Fathom." (Squeeze levers in front of lens.)

Fig. 53. Snorkeling skin diver. *Courtesy, Seamless; photo by Burton McNeely.*

rules prohibiting the spearing of fish while wearing SCUBA. Of course for activities requiring prolonged periods underwater, such as undersea exploration, scientific research, underwater photography, or salvage, some form of breathing apparatus becomes necessary.

Of all the various items of equipment which are available to skin divers today, the mask can be singled out as the most important, for without it man cannot see underwater, since light is refracted differently through water, focusing the image behind the retina and creating a blurred image. Basically, the mask is the diver's window to the underwater world. Forms of goggles and masks have been used for years by native divers in the Pacific.

The earliest type was the binocular or goggle, originally constructed with wooden frames. However the depth to which divers could go wearing these was limited, because of the effects of squeeze on the eyes. Later the problem was solved by the addition of small leather air sacs with tubes leading to the inside of the goggle frame. Later, the development of the monocular mask—one large eyepiece—with nasal protection eliminated the squeeze problem since the diver could snort into the mask to equalize the pressure on the eyes.

All of the masks available today are merely developments of these basic ideas, the binocular or goggle, or the monocular or single lens (Fig. 52a). Face-plates for diving masks are made of ordinary plate glass, safety glass, or plastic. It is unwise to purchase a mask containing plate glass or to use it to replace the face-plate in a mask, since plate glass may shatter if it receives a sharp blow from coral, rocks, or a spear-gun while underwater (due to the combined forces of the shock and water pressure), possibly resulting in serious injury to the eyes and face. If the safety glass in a mask gets a crack in it, a replacement can be obtained from a local sporting goods store or by writing to the manufacturer.

The rim, buckles and bolts of a good mask should be made of a noncorrosive metal like stainless steel or chrome-plated brass.

The flexible parts of masks today, such as the body and straps, are usually made of rubber. Occasionally, neoprene or flexible plastic is used. Most accomplished divers prefer a mask that does not have a snorkel built into it. The body should be stiff and the skirt (Fig. 54) should be soft so as to form a watertight seal around the face. Rubber straps must be soft and live (soft, flexible, and springy), and all buckles should be designed to hold tight when the strap is adjusted and under tension. A mask should always be tested first in shallow water to make sure

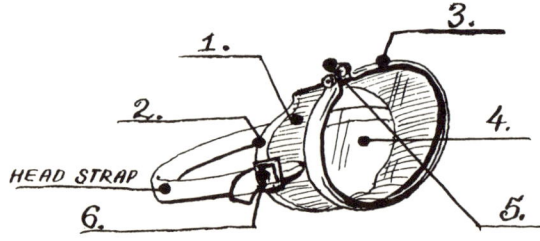

Fig. 54. Parts of the mask: *1.* Body, *2.* Skirt, *3.* Rim, *4.* Face plate, *5.* Adjusting screw, *6.* Buckle. The best way to be-

Photo by George Knoblach

come accustomed to new equipment is to test it in a pool (or sheltered waters) with an experienced diver to give instructions. When a pool is used, wash the equipment thoroughly after each use, since usually there are chemicals in pools that will dry out rubber goods.

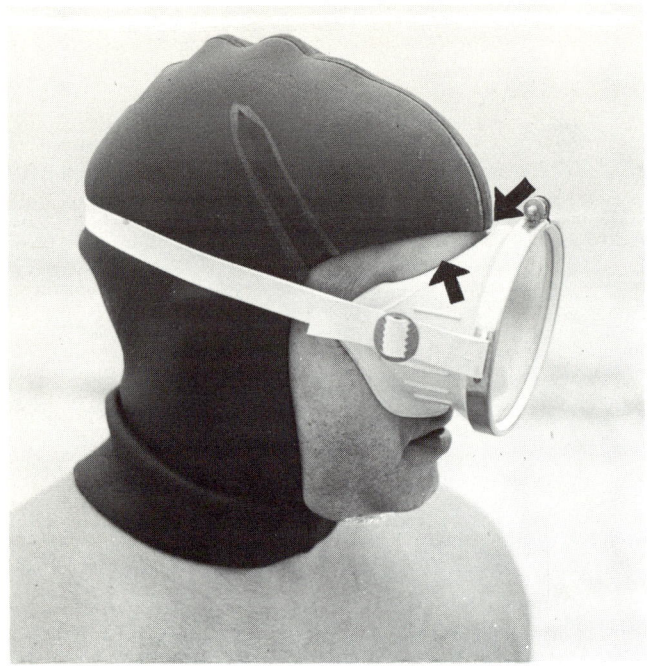

Fig. 55a. The skirt of the mask should seat snugly against the face with no turned-over edges.

Fig. 55b. Water pressure will hold the mask on even though the strap is missing. c. If the mask should fill with water, the diver needn't surface to clear it. d. Press the top of the mask to the forehead and snort hard but gradually. The bubbles will rise to the top, form an air pocket and drive the water out of the bottom.

e Shows the method for clearing the mask when using SCUBA. Roll over on the back and blow air out the nose. Bubbles will collect under the face plate and force the water out around the edges of the mask.

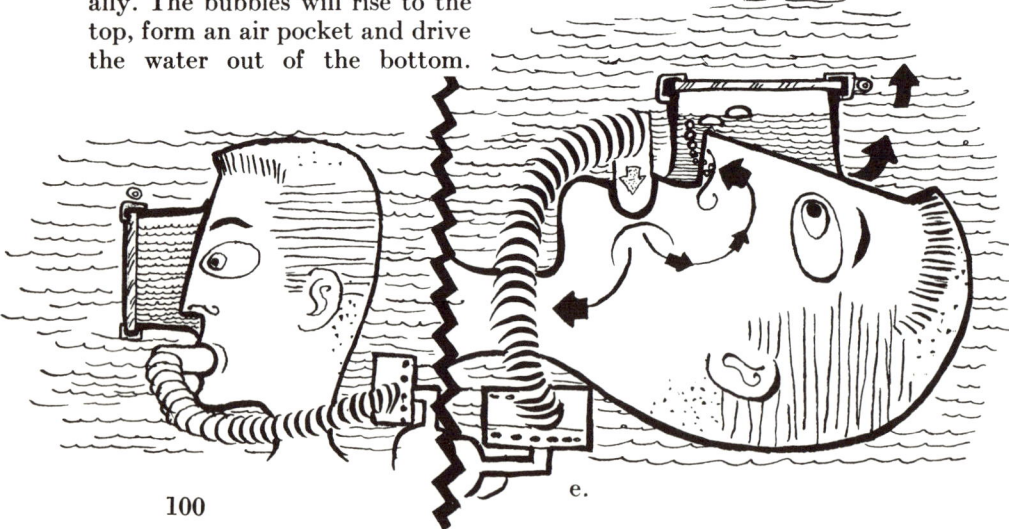

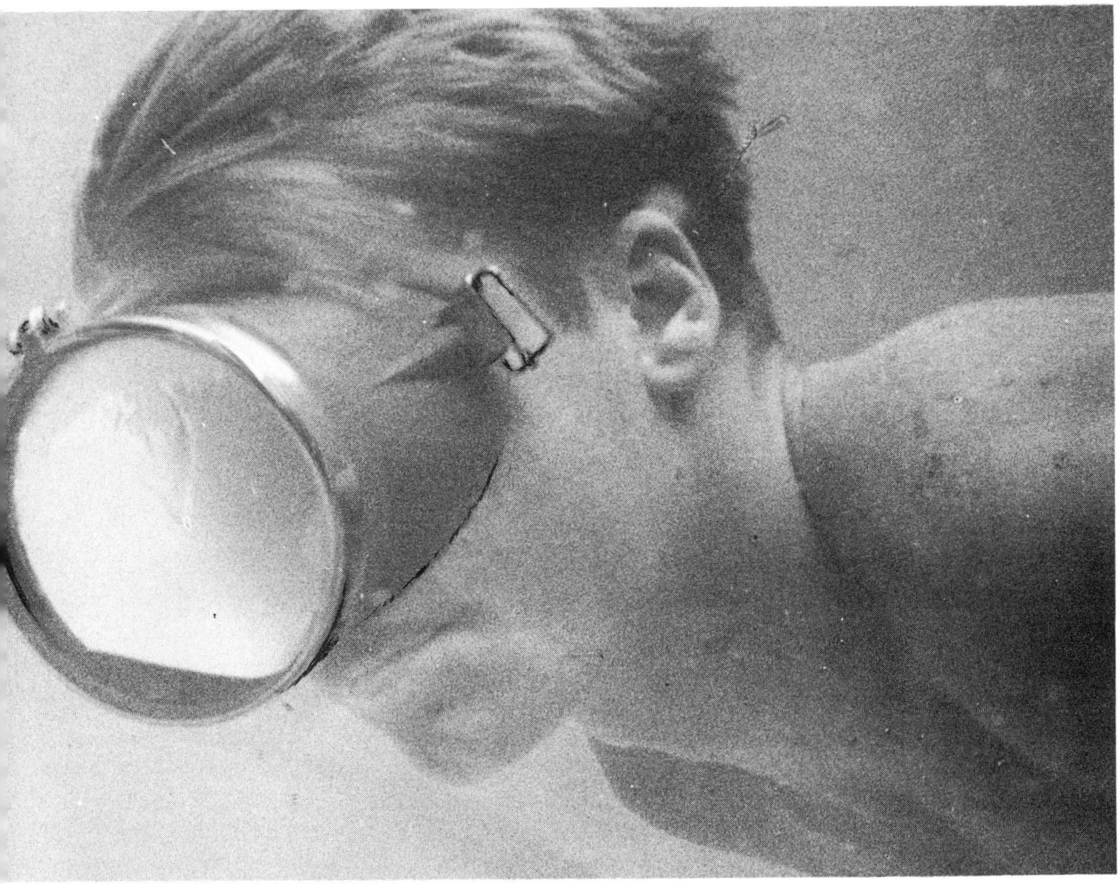

b.

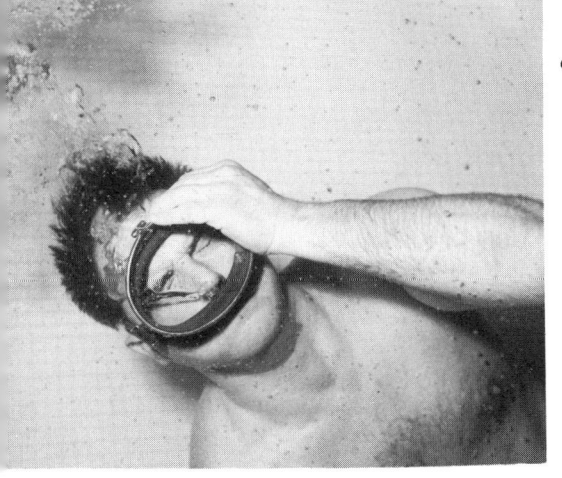

c.

d.

it is adjusted to be completely watertight. A good way to test a mask for good fit before purchasing it is to put it on the face without fastening the strap, and inhale slightly. The mask should stay on. This same procedure will hold the mask on the face underwater in the event that the strap should break while diving. (Figures 55b and 55c illustrate the technique for purging a water-filled mask.)

In order to eliminate fogging of the mask while underwater, the face-plate should first be rubbed with saliva or with a bit of tobacco from a cigarette until it squeaks, and then rinsed with sea water before putting it on. The novice diver on his first submersion will notice that underwater objects appear larger and closer than they really are, and that he must readjust his perception of depth in order to grasp an object underwater. This illusion is caused by the physics of light refraction through water, which makes all objects appear one fourth larger and one fourth closer than they actually are. Thus a fish eight feet away could seem to be only six feet from the spearfisherman and the lobster, which at first sight looked like the *pièce de résistance* for a beach party, the hungry diver may decide to keep all for himself when he sees its actual size out of the water.

There are some possible dangers connected with the phenomenon of visual distortion underwater. One example might be an exhausted diver, completely out of air and making his final effort, who lunges for the boarding ladder (Fig. 56) and misses because he misjudges its distance. This is an extreme example but it serves to illustrate the fact that visual perceptions must be reinterpreted underwater for safe and successful diving. One mask has special lenses built in to compensate for underwater distortion but it is very expensive.

A good, well-fitting diving mask is almost accident-proof when used properly. However there are certain precautions which must be observed. One should never dive or jump into the water while wearing a mask, since injury to the face or eyes may result, or the mask may flood, causing a delay and perhaps an accident. If it should be absolutely necessary at any time to jump into the water (see Fig. 58), the mask should be held firmly in place with one hand. The diver should enter the water carefully, adjusting the mask as he submerges.

The growing popularity of diving equipment has extended even to young children, who should not, however, be permitted to use masks or snorkels except under supervision, and for very small chil-

Fig. 56. Fatigue is a diving hazard. A boarding ladder is a welcome piece of equipment for getting in and out of the water. The spare tanks (fully charged) on the boat locker are a must when diving beyond the 35 or 40 foot level. Better yet, have them available every time SCUBA is used. If a diver should foul or need more air while decompressing, extra air flasks will be needed at once. Above, picture is from one of the first movies based on SCUBA diving for treasure, as can be noted by the "do-it-yourself" aspect of the diving rigs. *Courtesy, RKO Pictures*

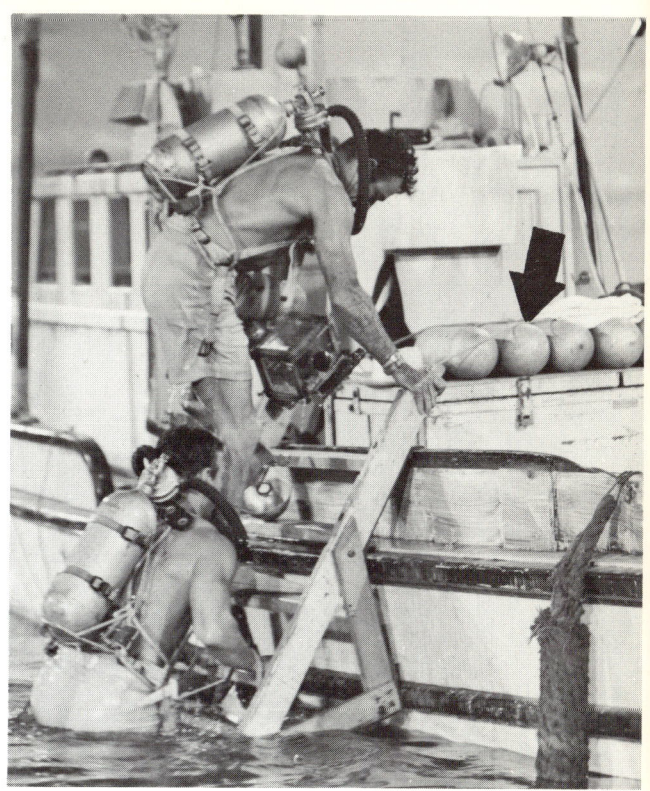

Fig. 57. Snorkeling, with the aid of a good wet suit, can be enjoyed practically all year round. For cold water and weather a head covering such as that illustrated on page 132 is recommended. *Courtesy, Parkway Fabricators*

Fig. 58. Foolish divers enter the water in this fashion. Nearly all diving accidents happen when common sense is not used. Divers wearing equipment should enter the water feet first, backing down the ladder or descending line.

dren "froggles" or goggles, rather than masks, are preferable. A mask for a child, as for an adult, should fit snugly and be watertight. Goggles and masks have helped many children overcome a fear of the water, since they are less frightened when they can see what is under the water and also are fascinated by the new experience.

Diving masks are also being used more and more by swimming instructors in their training programs as an aid for people who have sinus trouble, and also to eliminate the possibility of nose and eye infection.

Since excessive bulk around the head creates water resistance and makes diving more difficult, the emphasis, in a diving mask, should be on simplicity of design. A good mask is one which is light and compact, which affords the greatest possible angle of sight, is easy to put on and take off quickly, is well made and of the best materials, and which will accommodate a snorkel with no difficulty. All of these points should be checked when purchasing a mask.

Skin divers who wear glasses have a special problem. Corrective lens holders are available at most sporting goods stores for the Champion and Squale masks, and the Squale goggles can be adapted with prescription-ground lenses. However, as mentioned earlier, goggles restrict the depth of dives. Another method is to have prescription lenses attached to the face-plate of the mask with balsam cement, but this requires that the lenses be specially ground with a flat optical plane and compensation allowed for the added distance from the eye. The drawbacks to the above methods are that the changing focal length caused by imperceptible variations of pressure or shifting of the mask is fatiguing to the eye and may distract the diver's attention at a crucial moment; furthermore, since these lenses are part of the diving mask, they cannot conveniently be worn when out of the water.

Another solution is to get army surplus spectacle frames, intended for use with gas masks, and mount prescription lenses in them. These frames are built with flat temples and thus will allow the skirt of the diving mask to "seat" snugly against the face. In addition they are extremely rugged, and can also be worn when out of the water, and so would be excellent glasses to take on a skin diving trip where ruggedness and practicality count more than looks.

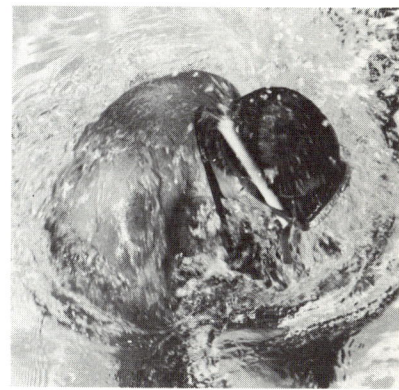

Fig. 59. Take it easy when first using new equipment. The diver here is wisely learning to use the snorkel in a pool. Long, easy breaths should be taken; then if a wave swamps the tube, the throat can be closed before the water gets into the mouth. If the diver breathes heavily, he stands a good chance of getting a lungful of water. *Photo by John Brooks*

Fig. 60. Longer immersion times can be achieved if the diver first takes several long breaths, ventilating the carbon dioxide from the lungs. A slight dizziness may be felt. The procedure then is to exhale about half a lungful, hold the breath and dive. Then slowly let the air out while rising, keeping enough air in the lungs to clear the snorkel with a short hard blast when the head breaks the surface. *Photo by John Brooks*

Approximately two decades ago Drs. Curtis F. Nagel and James B. Monical from the University of California at Berkeley, devised a set of contact lenses for underwater wear. The front of the lens is optically flat, making them somewhat conspicuous out of water, but they eliminate the need for a diving mask underwater, and also the fogging which creates a problem with glasses mounted inside a mask. The only possible drawback to these seems to be that they may slip when the diver swims rapidly, causing an effect of double vision.

In order to keep a diving mask in top condition and prolong its life, it should be rinsed off with fresh water after each use in salt water, dried thoroughly, and sprinkled with talcum powder or hydrous silicate of magnesia. These few minutes of care for masks or any other rubber goods used in salt water will really pay, since it will prevent drying out and cracking.

The items of next greatest importance to the skin diver after the mask are the swim fins and the snorkel. The snorkel (Fig. 59) permits the diver to breathe while swimming face down in the water, or slightly under the surface, thus eliminating constant raising of the head for a breath of air, and allowing uninterrupted vision. Figures 61a and 61b show several of the various models available.

The breathing tube is usually made of plastic with the mouthpiece of rubber; however, snorkels are now on the market which are made entirely of flexible rubber. A good snorkel should have a smooth, comfortable mouthpiece which adjusts to any mouth or position and which does not wobble when the snorkel moves through the water, since this will cause irritation of the gums. Most divers thrust the snorkel through the strap of the diving mask to keep it in position (Fig. 54), but some snorkels have attachments which clip onto the outside of the strap.

Many snorkels come with a ball attachment at the top of the tube to shut out the water when the diver submerges or when a wave hits. However most divers find that this arrangement causes additional vibration and water resistance, and the water flow can be shut out just as easily simply by holding the breath when submerging and then blowing the water out of the tube with one strong expiration upon surfacing. The water will come only part way down the tube, since the air already in the tube prevents its flooding completely, and a good snorkel should have a tube small enough to permit the water to be cleared with one hard blow. The top curve and ball arrangement can simply be removed from any snorkels that are constructed this way, once the diver is used to the technique of using a snorkel. Long easy breaths should be taken when breathing through a snorkel, and it should never be "blown out" while underwater since then it will have to be removed from the mouth in order to clear the pipe of water.

Probably the earliest pictorial indication of swim fins or flippers being used is the drawing of a diver shown in the first chapter of this book (Fig. 7a). Some authorities feel that these are foot weights, but the construction certainly resembles a swim fin. Leonardo da Vinci, in his notes and drawings, conceived the idea of hand fins as an aid to swimming. However, it was only recently that

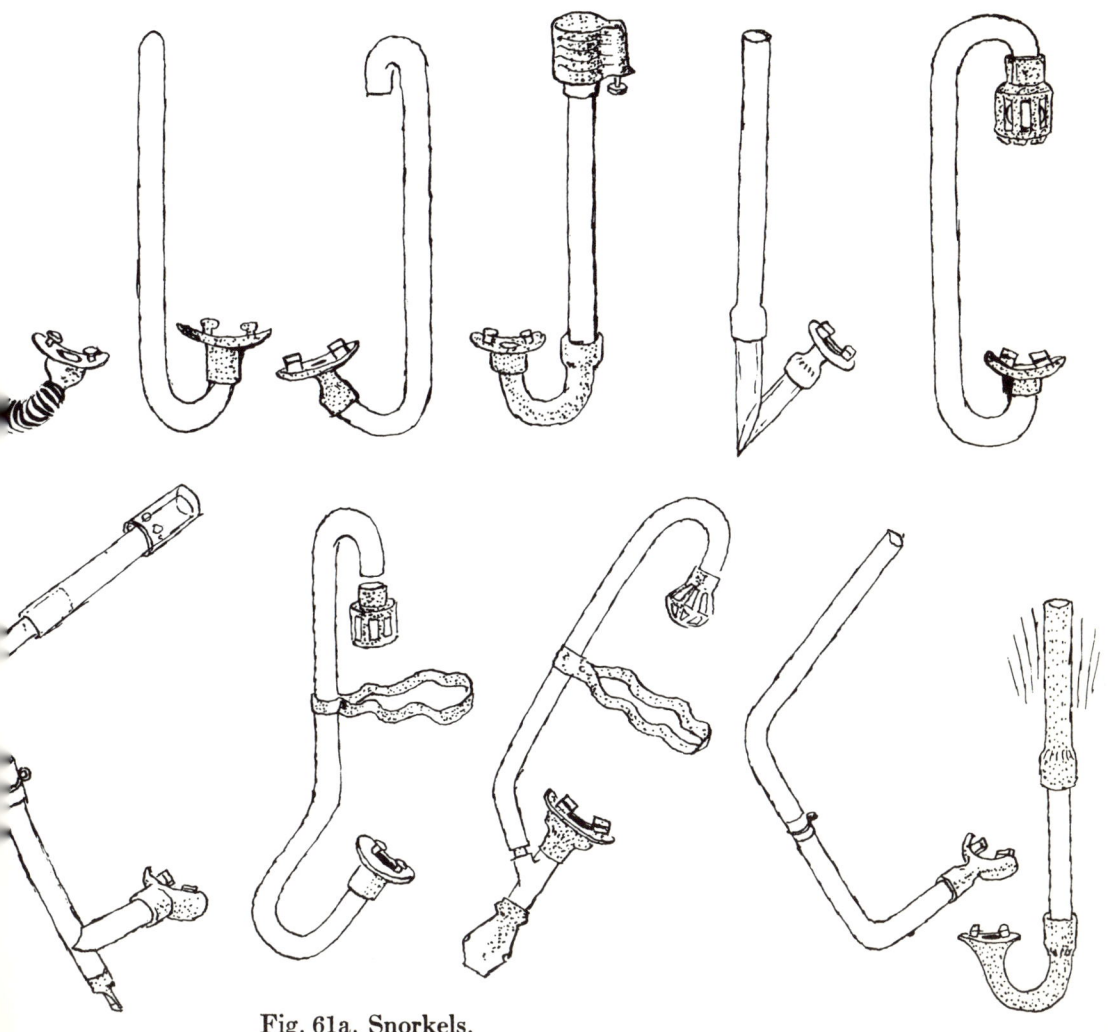

Fig. 61a. Snorkels.

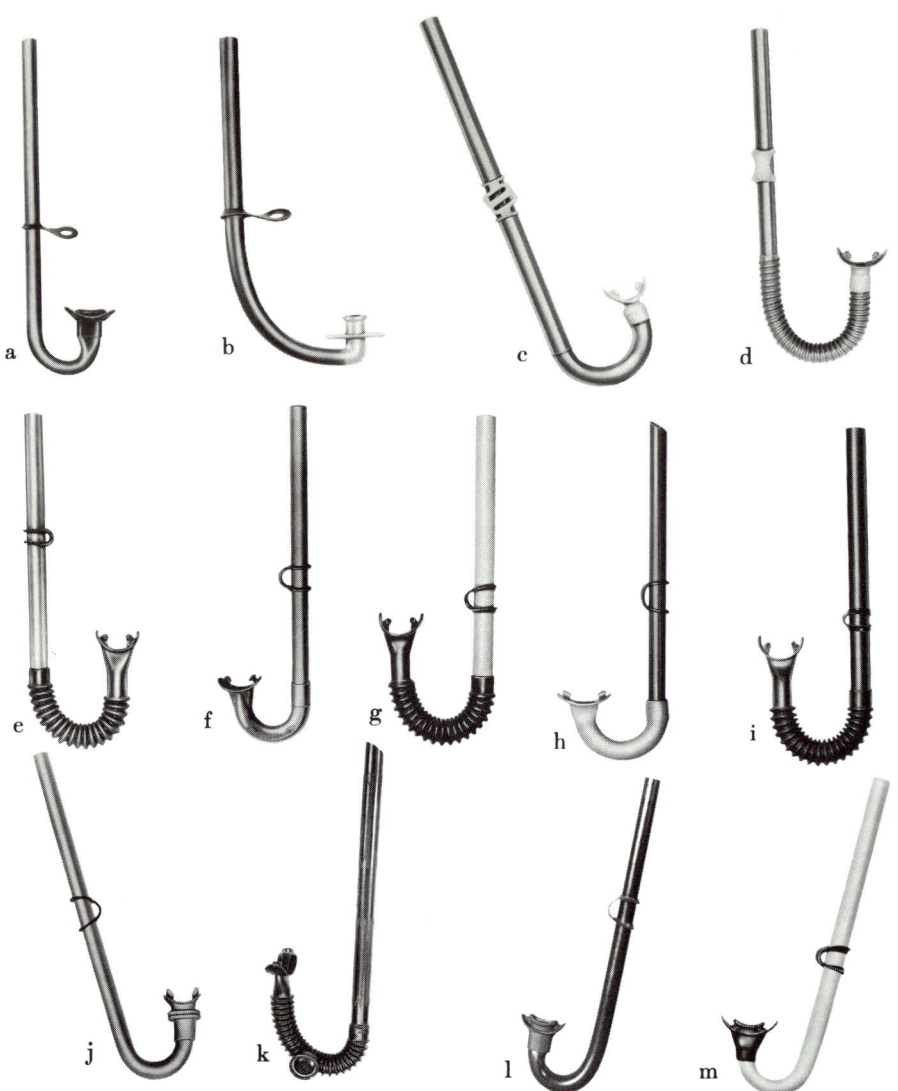

Fig. 61b. Snorkels. a. Swimaster (Voit) Bel-Aqua. b. Voit. c. Voit "Skindiver. d. Voit Deluxe. e. Sportsways "Waterlung." f. U. S. Divers "Aquatic." g. "Eel-S" by Adolph Kiefer. h. Adolph Kiefer "Eel-C." i. Voit 2 S 10. j. Healthways "Haiti Professional." k. Seamless Deluxe, with purging valve. l. Dacor ST. m. U. S. Divers "Aqua-Master."

There are two basic types of snorkels shown on this page. They are the "J" type which is permanently curved at the bottom of the tube, and the corrugated, flexible type. Each has its advantages. The mouthpiece on the permanently curved snorkel is easy to locate when switching from SCUBA to snorkel. The flexible type hangs limply when not in use and is not likely to become entangled in the SCUBA hose.

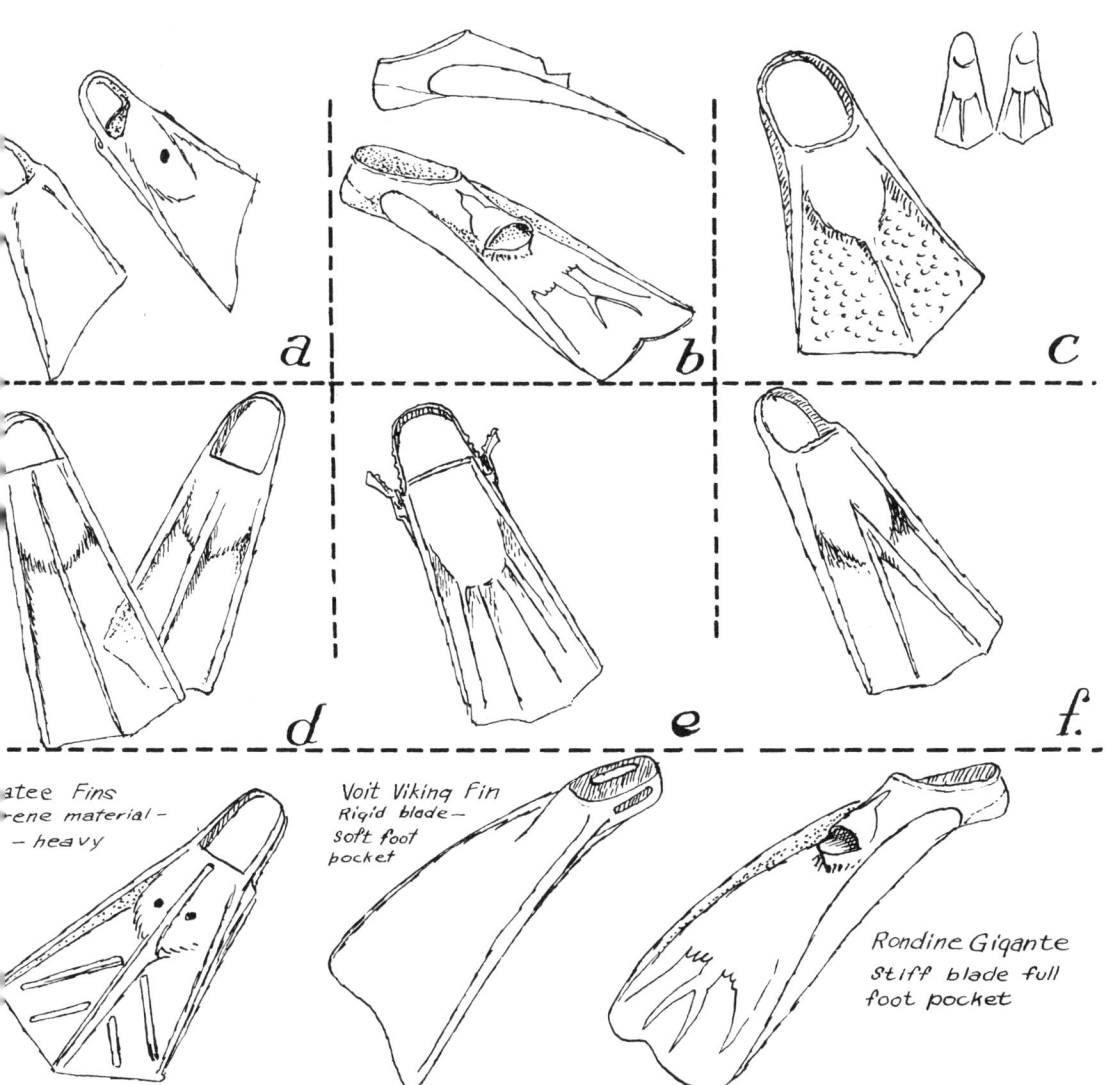

Fig. 62. Most brands of fins are available in sizes to fit most feet. Therefore the diver should choose the type most suited to his capabilities. The following styles are recommended by the majority of skin divers: a. Voit fins are marked "top right foot," "top left foot," and the hole must be under foot. Wet fins and feet first; hold back straps with thumbs and insert foot into foot pocket and slide back strap up over heel. Pure gum green or amber rubber; they float. b. Rondine fin forms a straight line from knee to tip of fin while foot is in a natural position; the fin completely covers the bottom of the foot; comes in colors, is lightweight, nonfloating. Fins are interchangeable. c. Hass fin—designed by the famous explorer and photographer—green; very rigid in the larger sizes, softer in the smaller; nonfloating, nonadjustable. d. Giant duck feet; for experienced divers only, they give a tremendous push; natural rubber, sizes from nine up. e. Frogman, which is adjustable, for all-purpose use, fairly rigid—a practical fin; sizes 8 to 13; smaller sizes use standard web feet. f. Senior web feet—a pure rubber fin soft at the foot with rigid side supports; non-adjustable; floats.

Fig. 63. Swim fins. Two basic types are shown. They are open-heel and the full-foot types. The open heel permits the diver to carry them looped on his arm. They are often considered easier to put on and take off, in or out of the water. Many people feel that the full-foot type is more comfortable and gives better protection to the bottom of the heel.

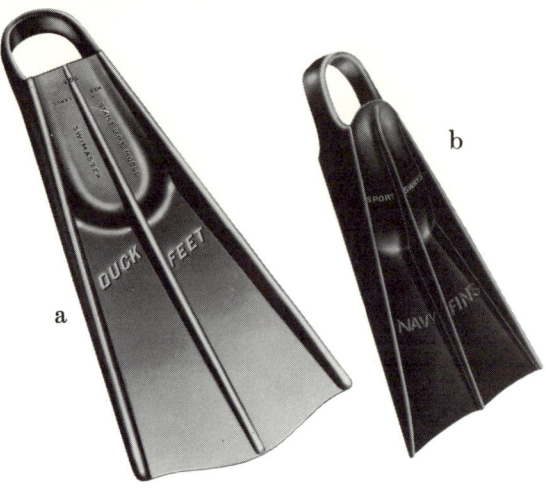

a. Swimaster Duck Feet fins. The regulation model duck feet range in size from small (shoe size 5–7) to large (shoe size 10–11). The Giant UDT duck feet shown here in size med.-lge. (shoe size 8–9) can be obtained in the super extra lge., (shoe size 13–14). Divers with small feet but powerful legs use one or two pairs of foam neoprene bootees to fill in the extra foot space. b. Sportsways "Navy" fins.

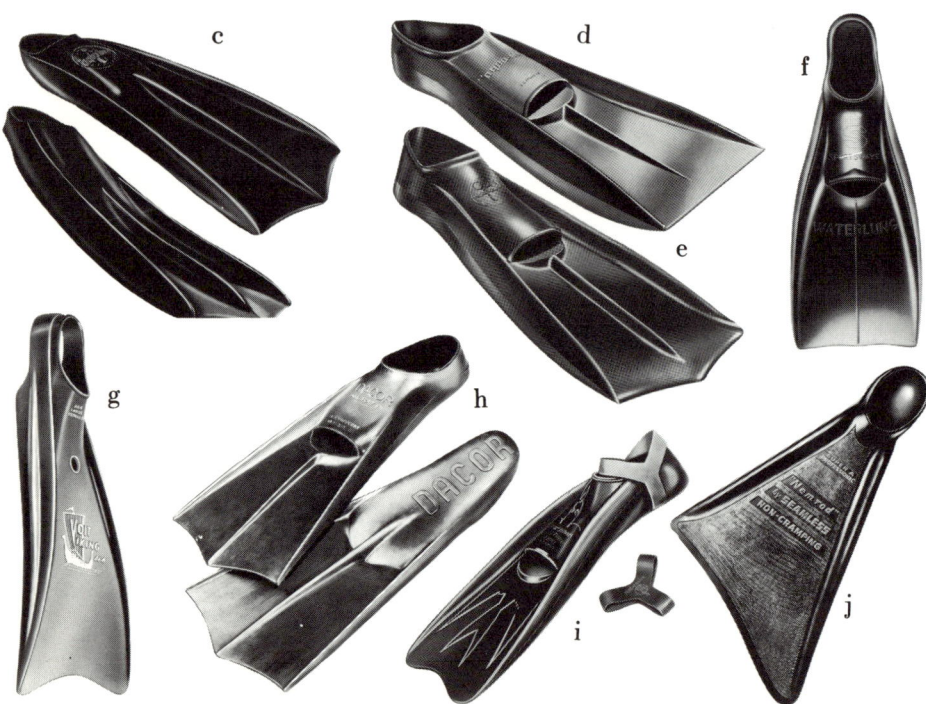

c. U. S. Divers "Aqua-Lung" fin. d. U. S. Divers "Aqua Fin." e. U. S. Divers "Aqua Master." f. Sportsways "Waterlung" fin. g. Voit "Viking." h. Dacor "Streamline" Power Fin. i. Healthways Cressi Rondine Competition Professional fin. j. Seamless Super A "Professional."

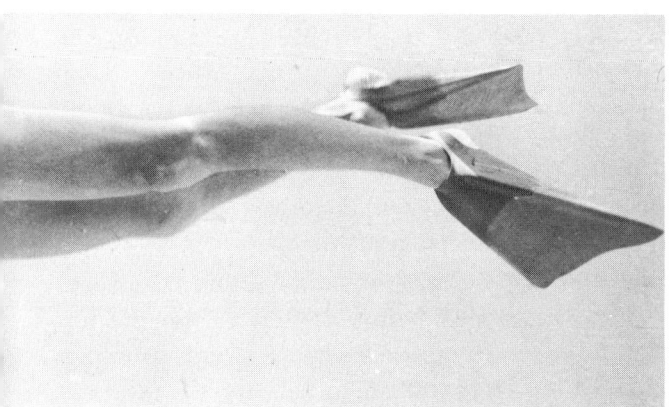

Fig. 64. Fins add about fifty percent more swimming speed. Comfort is the most important factor. Sanding will eliminate any high spots on the straps or slippers. *Photo by George Knoblach*

the foot flipper, developed by Commander Le Corlieu, became a standard item of diving equipment.

Fins enable a swimmer to move about fifty percent faster than he could ordinarily. However conserved strength and endurance, rather than increased speed, are the main advantages gained by the use of fins. With them many swimmers have been able to swim safely to shore through currents and rough surf which might otherwise have caused a fatal accident. Recently a forty-seven-year-old man succeeded in swimming the twenty-three miles from Catalina Island to the mainland of California wearing swim fins, without which he said he could never have made it. Often they provide the extra thrust which enables a diver to reach the surface before his air runs out. In swimming with fins, a slow, steady flutter kick (Fig. 64) is best, since rapid kicking while wearing fins puts too much strain on the legs and quickly exhausts the diver.

In purchasing fins, comfort is the most important consideration, since fins which press on any part of the foot will cause chafing, and when used for long periods of time may create sores which will not heal when the foot is frequently immersed in salt water. A fin should feel comfortable on the foot, with no pressure on any particular area. It should be smooth inside and free from irregularities, and should not wobble when the foot is moved up and down, since this too may cause chafing and sores. (If a blister should occur on a skin diving trip, it should be covered with a bandage and then socks or foam neoprene boots worn over it before trying to use the fins again.) Fins should be snug enough on the foot to prevent wobbling, but not too tight to be completely comfortable; and if they are intended to be worn over socks or rubber suits, they should be tried on over socks.

Figure 62 shows some of the many different types of fins on the market today. All are excellent for their purpose, and divers vary a great deal in their preferences in fins. It is wise to try several styles before buying in order to determine which are best for the individual foot and for the purpose for which they are intended. Beginners should not buy very large or rigid fins, since these will tire the legs too quickly.

When purchasing any rubber equipment it is important to make sure that the rubber is live. Sometimes merchants put rubber goods in display windows where it dries out over the summer, so it is wise to be cautious when buying end-of-season-sale merchandise.

Once the diver has acquired some degree of skill with these basic items of equipment, and is ready for more ambitious diving, certain additional equipment may become necessary.

Most divers find that they need extra weight in order to descend quickly and with a minimum of effort to any depth or to swim comfortably underwater, particularly when wearing SCUBA, without constantly having to fight against their own buoyancy (see Chapter III on the physiological problems of diving). The safest method of adding this extra weight is in the form of a weight belt with a safety-release buckle in case it must be removed quickly.

Since several skin diving fatalities have been caused by weight belts which could not be jettisoned quickly enough in an emergency, the type of safety-release buckle used is extremely important. War surplus military buckles, with the exception of the pilot's quick-release buckle, are not safe to use with weight belts, since they require two hands to operate.

Safety release buckles should be used on all straps which attach equipment to the body. Figure 67b shows safe and unsafe types of closures. For a simplified version of the safety-release buckle, see Chapter V for how to build it yourself. Weights should never be attached to the body by a rope or cord. A recent drowning was ascribed to the diver's having had fourteen pounds of lead tied around his waist with a cord. Weight belts should also provide for interchangeable weights to regulate buoyancy as needed, both for the individual diver and for use with different equipment.

A diver should carry a sharp knife at all times, since he may have to cut his way free of kelp or of snagged equipment. A good underwater knife should have a strong blade (for prying). This blade should be of high-tempered steel, preferably of chrome steel to prevent rusting. Stainless steel will not rust, but also does not keep a good edge. If a knife is not rustproof, it should be oiled after each exposure to salt water. The knife should be worn in a sheath and attached to the harness in such a manner that it can be drawn quickly in an emergency without danger of injuring the diver (Fig. 65).

If a diver finds himself trapped under seaweed or kelp, which may happen when he is engrossed in following a fish, he should look up to get his bearings, surface to take a breath where the growth seems thinnest, pushing it aside with his hands as he rises, then drop straight down, fins first. He can then work his way gradually away from it, swimming to a new position and repeating this procedure. It is never wise to attempt to swim over it; and if a diver

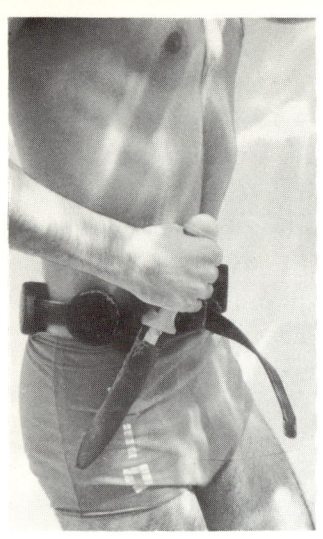

Fig. 65. Quick accessibility is the keynote in locating the knife on the diving belt. If the diver becomes fouled he should try to remain calm while cutting himself loose with the knife, to eliminate the risk of serious wounds.

becomes entangled under water he should remain calm and cut himself free with the knife.

One of the best safety precautions is to carry a carbon dioxide self-inflating float. Many skin diving clubs have rules providing that every diver should wear one whenever he enters the water. They are required equipment in most skin-diving contests. The life preservers illustrated are activated by squeezing a trigger mechanism which perforates the neck of a CO_2 capsule. The carbon dioxide inflates the float. The full vest type will support an unconscious 250-pound man so that he will float with his face out of the water. These floats should never be inflated under water while wearing SCUBA. The added buoyancy may pull the diver to the surface too quickly, causing an air embolism. Experiments have shown that a CO_2 inflatable life vest normally will not fully inflate itself when triggered in deep water. At a depth of a hundred feet it would have very little lifting power. Near the surface it would expand, causing the diver to ascend at a potentially dangerous rate of speed.

Nose clips were used when diving with goggles or a mask by divers who had trouble equalizing pressure in their ears. Fig. 75: Some recent makes of masks have provisions for squeezing the nose to aid in equalizing.

Many other items of equipment (Fig. 76) are helpful but are not absolutely necessary except in certain cases.

Ear plugs may be found in most sporting goods stores, but they can be hazardous to use in diving, as explained in Chapter V. Many skin divers find they help to lessen the discomfort of pressure on the ears in shallow depths, but when they attempt to go deeper wearing them, they run into trouble. It is better to learn to equalize

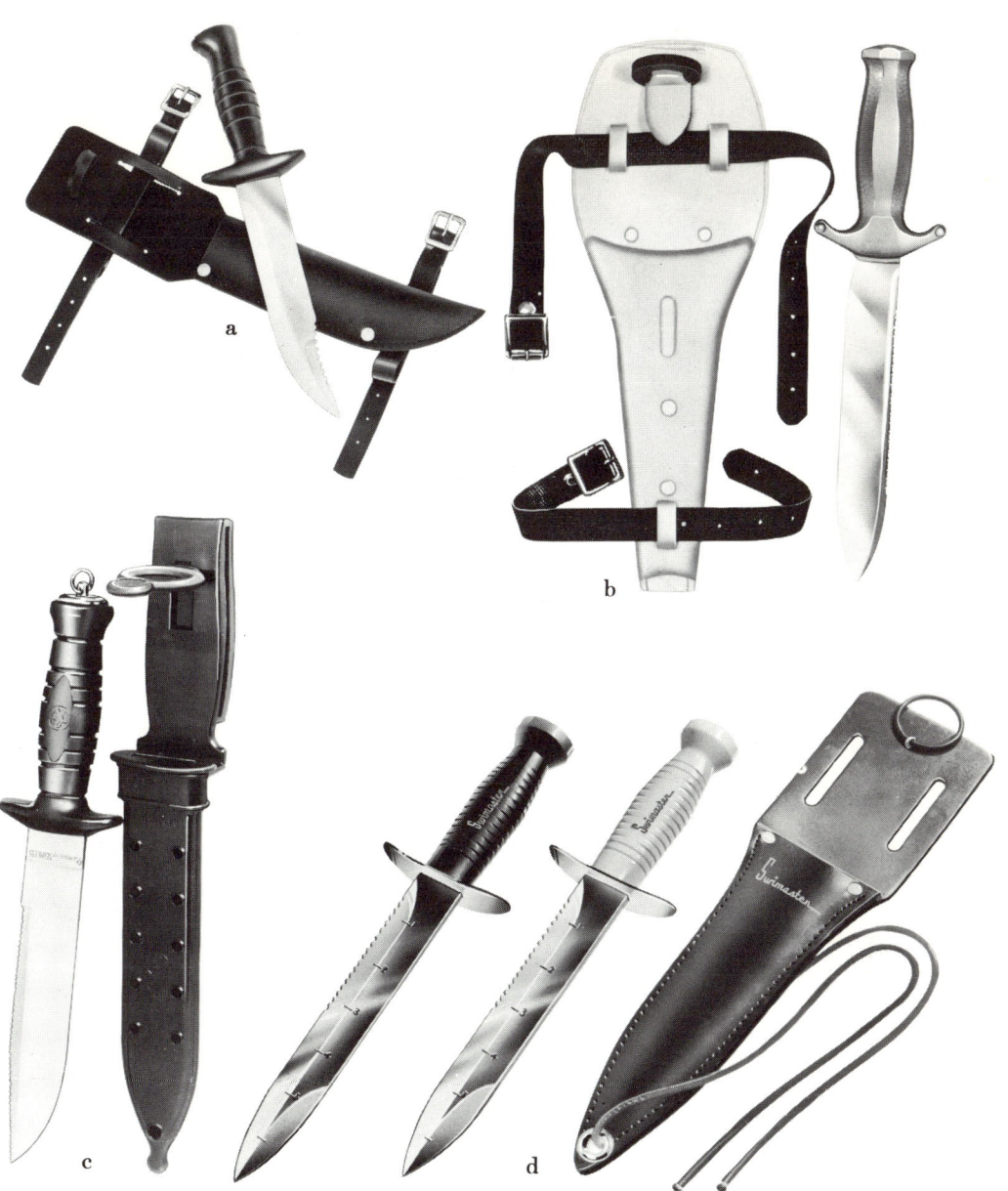

Fig. 66. There are some fine, rugged diving knives of which the above are good examples. A thin or narrow blade is useful for cleaning fish but is an inadequate prying or gouging tool. A diver's knife is not primarily intended as a weapon. Most divers need a knife to cut fishlines, wire, rope, and to chip and pry at rusted or encrusted objects. a. Voit "Deluxe Skin Diver" knife. b. Healthways "Espadon." c. Seamless. d. Swimaster knives marked in inches can be used to pry abalones off rocks.

Fig. 67a. Weight belts. a. Voit, three 5-pound, white vinyl-coated weights. Airplane type, quick-release buckle, nylon belt. b. Voit, six 2-pound, cast-iron weights, white vinyl-coated. "D" ring buckle on cotton belt. c. U. S. Divers 15-pound weight belt with Safe EZ buckle, 8-pound weight belt with hook-type release. d. Swimaster Slip-On Weight belt. e. Healthways "Big Jim" belt breathes with the diver. Weights can be easily removed. f. Lu Jo's Klampon weights can be easily fastened or removed. g. Seacraft Nylon tape friction fastener.

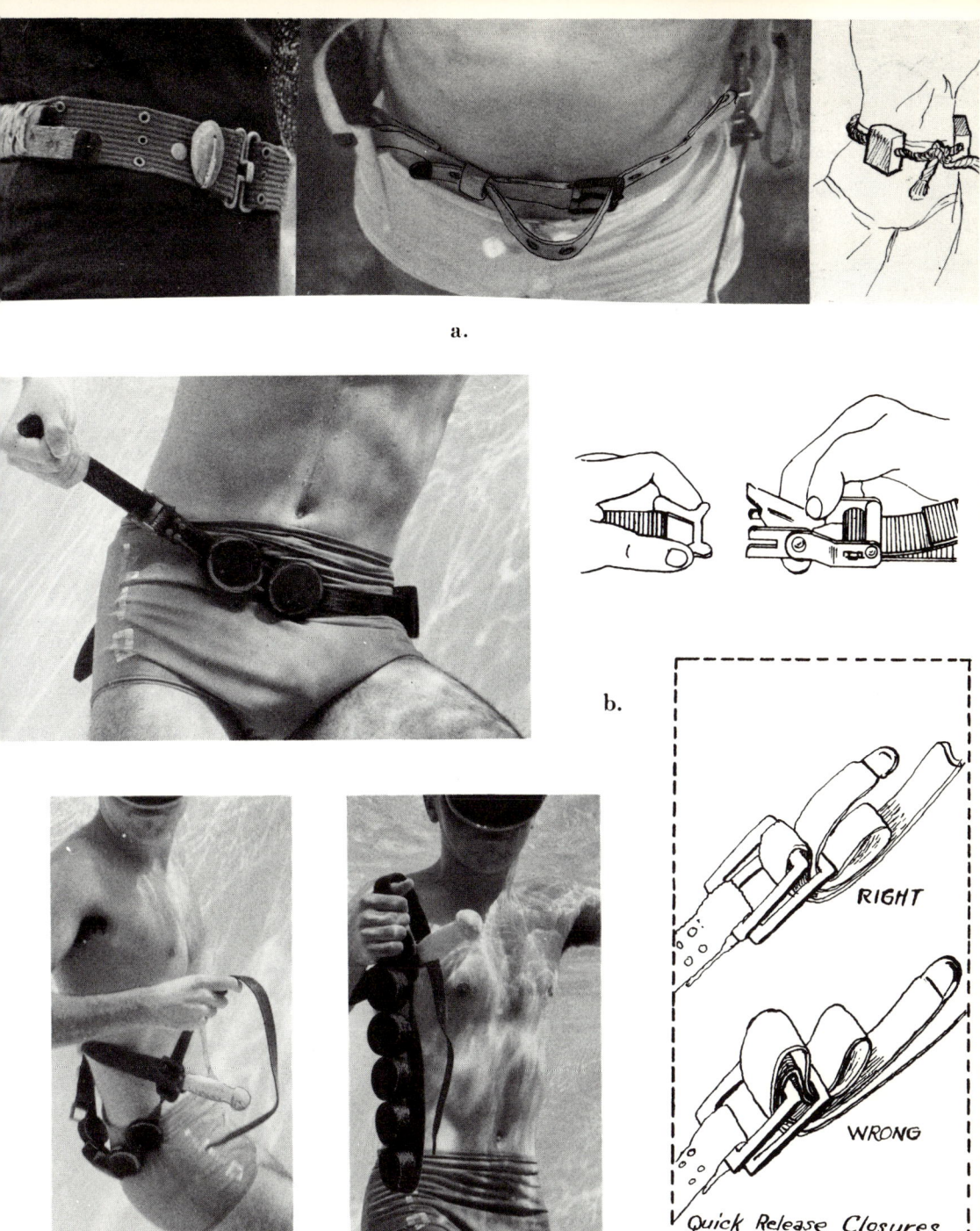

Fig.67b. Weight belts are expendable. a. Dangerous types—NEVER use these closure methods on a weight belt. b. The types that must be used are styled so that they may be removed using one hand and in a single motion.

pressure by other methods—swallowing, yawning, snorting into the mask with the mask pressed against the face.

A depth gauge and a watertight wrist watch should both be used when diving with SCUBA in order to determine if decompression is necessary (see Decompression Tables, Chapter III), and if so, to time the stops, and also to check on the amount of air left in the tank. The depth gauge (Fig. 76) works on the principle of Boyle's Law, and gives accurate readings at depths from 1 foot to 140 feet. The underwater compass is another helpful item of equipment. Facing page shows deep water depth gauges and compass-depth gauges.

An item of importance to the skin diver is the float (Fig. 72). A float is necessary as a place to rest while diving, especially when wearing a weight belt, as a means of carrying equipment to and from the scene of operations, and for spearfishermen to carry the day's catch. It can also be a help in carrying the diver himself through the surf and over underwater obstructions, especially if he is wearing heavy equipment.

In order to keep the float from upsetting and spilling all the equipment when going out to sea through surf, equipment should be lashed down and the float trailed behind the diver. When going back to shore through surf, the diver can push the float along in front of him, making sure to hold it securely and with all spears attached horizontally across it.

Often divers have problems with floats blowing away or being carried away by currents. If there is no way of mooring the float to pilings, kelp, or other underwater objects, a sea anchor is the best solution. The construction of this is described in Chapter V, as well as the method of making a float from an inner tube and gill netting.

Since the temperature of most of the ocean is below 60° F., and never above 85° F. in the warmest surface waters of the tropics, some form of protective clothing becomes necessary when diving in cooler climates, for deep diving, or even for long periods spent in waters of moderate temperature. The normal body temperature is 98.6°, and whenever the body surface is in contact with water of a lower temperature, there is a transfer of heat from the body surface to the surrounding water. This means that calories are consumed in order to help maintain a normal temperature equilibrium over the surface of the body, and the colder the water, the more body energy has to be expended. If this is carried on at too great a rate over a period of time, exhaustion follows and finally unconsciousness and death. The following table on cold water survival, compiled by the

Fig. 68. Depth gages are mandatory for the deep diver who must keep track of his depth to obviate the possibility of decompression sickness. They are also helpful in convincing the amateur that he is deeper than he may think. a. U. S. Divers 100-ft. Bathometer. b. U. S. Divers 100-ft. "Nemo." c. Voit 140-foot "Professional." d. U. S. Divers 150-ft. "Navy." e. U. S. Divers 200-ft. "Calypso." f. Dacor 200-ft. "Thin Line." g. Voit 140-ft. Combination Compass & Depth Gage. h. Taylor 140-ft. Combination Compass & Depth Gage. i. Voit 300-ft. Combination Compass & Depth Gage.

Fig. 69. A diving watch is necessary in deep diving to keep track of "bottom time" and to time decompression stops. The rest of the time the watch becomes a handsome wrist watch that identifies you as a diver. a. Lady Dacor. b. Dacor hand-wound. c. Automatic self-winding with calendar indicator. d. U. S. Divers "Date-O-Matic." e. U.S.D. "Chronomatic" automatic with stopwatch feature. f. Voit Automatic. All of the above watches have a lapsed-time movable bezel and are waterproof to at least 500 feet deep. A special Rolex watch (not shown) spent 20 minutes on the Pacific Ocean floor, 35,797 feet down, and came up ticking!

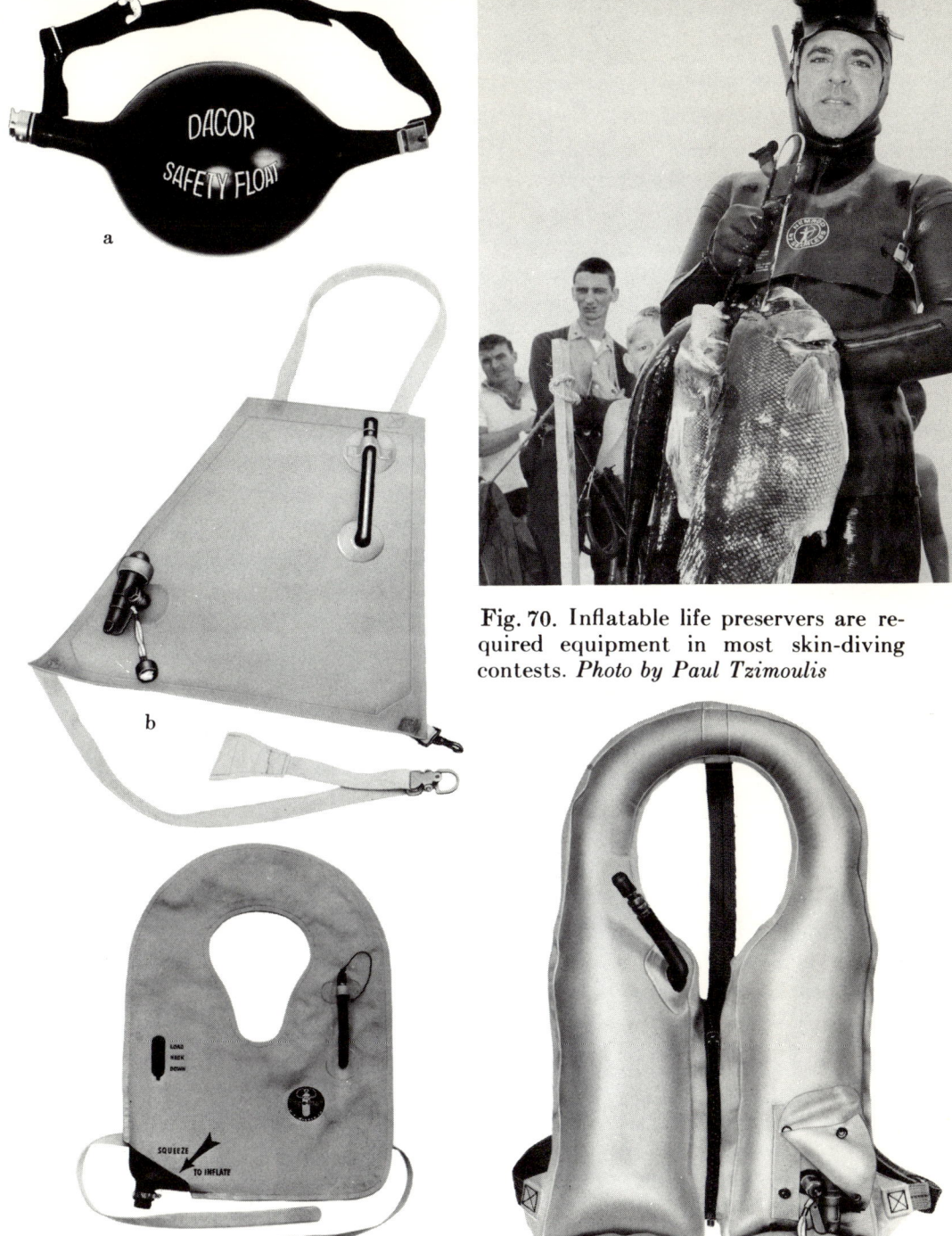

Fig. 70. Inflatable life preservers are required equipment in most skin-diving contests. *Photo by Paul Tzimoulis*

Fig. 71. a. Dacor CO_2 inflatable life preserver can be fastened around the waist. b. Voit c. U. S. Divers d. Sportsways CO_2 inflatable life vest can also be mouth-inflated.

a.

Fig. 72. Innertubes or floats are used not only as a safety precaution against fatigue, but also to serve as a storing place for guns, spears, cameras, weight belts, fish, etc. The divers in picture a are swimming too close behind each other. A large wave rolling in could mix these divers into a melee of tangled lines, bodies and spears. b illustrates the safe method of entering the surf. c. When using a boat or raft, head into the surf. (Make certain equipment items are well secured and all sharp points covered.) When broaching large waves, e, and the boat is loaded like d, the swamping, f, will scatter the gear so thoroughly that many hours or weeks will be spent diving and searching for lost gear. Many pieces may never be found. Try to anticipate this type of accident. *Photos by Hal Reiff, George Knoblach, RKO Pictures*

b.

c.

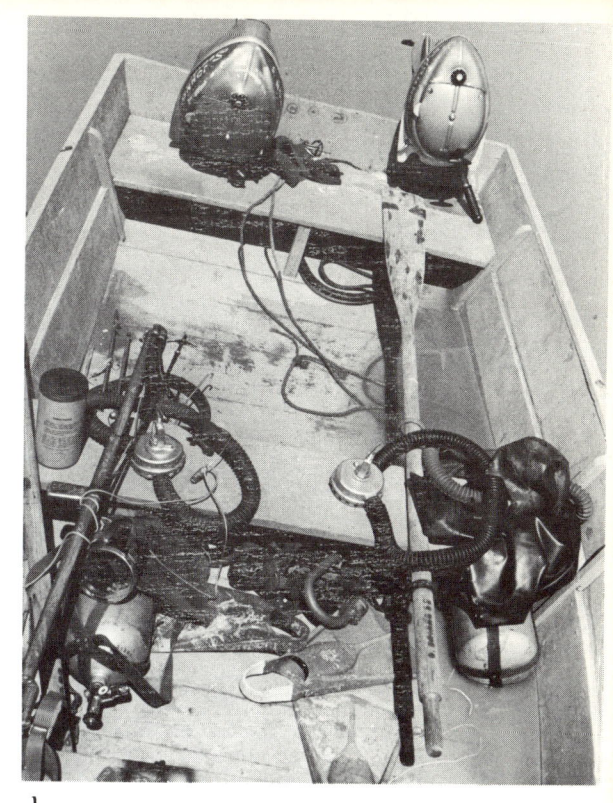

d.

e.

f.

United States Naval Institute, graphically illustrates this, and may be something of a shock to divers who question the necessity of a rubber suit (reprinted from *Skin Diver* magazine):

Water Temperature (in degrees F.)	Approximate Time to Exhaustion or Unconsciousness (in hours)	Death (in hours)
32	¼	¼–1½
50	½–1	1–2
60	2–4	6–8
70	3–7	?
80	12	relatively safe

This chart is not intended to be used as an indication of how long a diver may stay in the water, since the specific period after which symptoms of fatigue may be felt depends on the individual.

Captain Phillipe Tailliez, in his book *To Hidden Depths*, tells of an experience he had while swimming one New Year's Day near Toulon. Wearing only a jersey and woolen trousers, he became paralyzed from the cold a hundred yards offshore. He managed to reach shore finally but was unable to dress himself. Fortunately his dog covered him with his warm body and saved his life.

Rubber suits have been designed to protect the diver from the effects of cold water. There are two basic types of rubber suit—the "wet suit" and the "dry suit" (Fig. 73).

The principle of one type of wet suit is that the water is permitted to enter the suit, usually through an entry valve on the chest or back and then prevented from circulating by seals at the arms, neck and legs. The trapped water is then warmed by the body heat of the diver and serves as an insulating barrier against the temperature of the surrounding water.

Another type of wet suit is the foam neoprene suit, which is more resistant to snagging and tearing than thin rubber suits. Although water enters the suit, the construction and close fit keep it from circulating, and the isothermic quality of the material makes it an excellent insulating layer between the body and the cold water. The pull-over style also makes these suits easier to put on and take off.

Kits can be obtained for making foam neoprene and sheet-rubber suits yourself, and also for coating fabric with liquid latex to

Fig. 73. Types of wet suits—full length and short. Divers are equipped with single hose regulators and are jumping into the water while holding their face masks in place. The girl already in the water is holding an underwater camera housing which also doubles as a ladder. *Courtesy, Parkway Fabricators*

Fig. 74. The couple leaving the water are wearing full-length wet suits made of Sharkskin Two, a material permitting increased flexibility. Consequently, there is less effort expended by the diver when he moves underwater. Note: The divers are carrying their gear in their hands once they have a firm footing—a procedure recommended in the surf. *Courtesy, Parkway Fabricators*

make wet suits. Since ready-to-wear rubber suits are quite expensive, it would seem well worth the time and trouble for people who are good at making things to construct their own.

Since air is much better insulation than water, dry rubber suits with a dead air space would be the warmest type of suit possible. However suits constructed on this principle, such as the Cousteau Constant Volume Suit, are usable only with artificial breathing equipment, and in any case are too expensive and complicated in operation for the average sport diver.

Probably the next best thing is the use of a sealed sheet-rubber dry suit worn with one or more suits of long underwear or wool sweaters underneath. These help to create an air layer over the body and thus insulate against the cold water. The main problems with these suits are leakage, tearing on coral, rocks or other projections, and loss of maneuverability due to the constricting bulk of the suit and undergarments. Weight belts will be needed with all rubber suits to counteract excess buoyancy, and a carbon dioxide inflatable float should be carried in case the suit should fill with water.

For ice diving, northern divers formerly wore several layers of long underwear, or heavy clothing, under a dry suit. Today, many of these divers prefer the one-quarter-inch-thick wet suit. Some wear a size larger dry suit over their wet suit. If the dry suit rips, the diver does not become immediately chilled. Talcum powder is a help in putting on a rubber suit. Soap lather can be an emergency substitute in a wet suit.

Some rubber suits come with a helmet attached, and some without. The main difficulty with an attached helmet on a dry-type rubber suit is that it creates a dead air space between the hood and the outer ear, which may cause pain or even rupture of the eardrum outward when breathing air under pressure. The best solution seems to be a wet-type hood with a neck seal suit, or a mask and hood combination which is worn under the hood of the dry suit. Separate hoods are also often worn alone in warmer water, making them the most generally used form of rubber cold-water protection. Often a helmet worn with a T-shirt and trunks will be adequate protection for short periods of time, even in fairly chilly water, since most helmets cover the back of the neck, an area which is particularly vulnerable to cold.

Every diver, except in the warmest tropical waters, should carry some sort of cold-water garment to have available when needed since otherwise unexpectedly cold water may completely ruin a skin diving trip. A diver can become quite chilled after spending long periods of

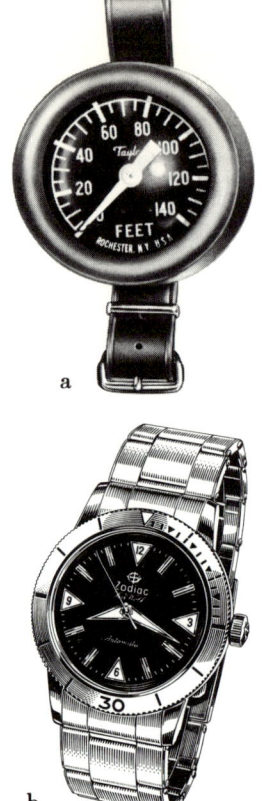

Fig. 75. This diver is wearing a special mask that permits him to squeeze his nose. As he blows gently against this constriction, air is backed up into his inner ear. This will equalize the air pressure in his ears with the water pressure surrounding the diver.

Fig. 76. Depth gauge, waterproof watch, compass, and Navy flashlight used in SCUBA diving.

time under water, even in water which at first seems quite warm. If a diver should become chilled, the reflected heat of a fire is much more effective than wrapping in blankets or administering a shot of whiskey, even though the diver may prefer the latter method.

Nothing could be more frustrating for a diver than to buy an expensive rubber suit, wear it one season and then store it, only to find when it is dug out of the closet the following spring that it has dried out, stuck together in spots, and is for all practical purposes ruined. This unfortunate experience can be prevented if certain precautionary measures are followed. The rubber suit should be rinsed with fresh water after each submersion in the sea. All rips or tears should either be vulcanized or patched with a tire repair kit or special patch kit for rubber suits. Before hanging it (rubber suits should never be stored folded) in a cool dry closet, it should be dusted liberally with talcum powder or with hydrous silicate of magnesia.

Different brands and styles of rubber suits are appropriate for different purposes, and the diver should investigate the types available before buying, letting his choice be determined by the amount of money he wants to spend, the purpose for which the suit is intended, the fit, comfort, freedom of movement and ease of donning the suit, as well as the quality of the material and workmanship.

Some years ago, *Skin Diver* magazine featured a controversy between the proponents of wet suits and the users of dry suits for diving under the ice. The dry suit can be put on over ordinary warm clothing. After diving the diver could peel off the dry suit while out of doors.

More recently the wet suit has gained favor for all kinds of diving including diving under the ice. One drawback still remains. In winter a wet suit poses the problem of dressing and undressing in frigid temperatures. Normally however, this Spartan regimen is not necessary. A warm camp or automobile is usually available.

Most early wet suits were only 1/8-inch thick. A diver did not remain comfortable for very long in ice water. More recent wet suits are available in 3/16- and 1/4-inch thicknesses. It is possible to remain comfortable for an hour among floating ice cakes when dressed in a full length 1/4-inch wet suit.

Wet suits have other advantages over the dry suit. A small hole in the wet suit may only be a minor nuisance. In a dry suit it can be a near catastrophe. When a dry suit punctures or rips, the water soaks the clothing worn underneath. The diver becomes cold and loses

Fig. 77a. Diver, resting in hole in ice, is holding a safety line and watching another diver beneath the surface. *Photo by Gene Parker*

Fig. 77b. Fish-eye-view of diver and line tender. Note the safety line attached to the diver. *Photo by Gene Parker*

Fig. 77c. Ice divers using Unisuits, an underwater sealed suit equipped with valve control enabling diver to ascend or descend by pushing a control button which supplies or removes air from within the suit. *Courtesy, Poseidon Systems USA*

buoyancy. A self-inflatable safety device becomes an absolute necessity.

Wet suits have become more popular than the dry suits for several reasons. For one thing, a dry suit can cause "suit squeeze." At greater depths the water pressure squeezes the rubber, actually pinching folds of skin caught in the wrinkles. In severe cases the diver's skin becomes covered with welts. Another problem of the dry suit is that it makes it impossible for the water to reach the outer surface of the eardrum. Air pressure from the SCUBA presses against the eardrum from within. Since there is no compensating water pressure on the eardrum from without, the eardrum may be ruptured outward.

The dry suit is usually a one-piece suit. The diver is sealed into the suit. It is not easy to get into or out of. He cannot wear only the jacket portion of the suit as he can with a wet suit. In moderately cool water, where he may want only a wet suit jacket, the diver with a one-piece dry suit has to wear the entire suit. When on the beach, a diver can easily take off a wet jacket and quickly shrug it on when he is ready to re-enter the water. Not so the dry suit.

Fig. 78b. There is virtually no age limit for skin diving as long as one can swim and feel at home in the water.

Fig. 78a. As more women are attracted to skin and SCUBA diving, style and color are receiving more attention in the underwater world. Much SCUBA diving is being performed in lakes and rivers, where such colorful attire is both attractive and easily identifiable to other members of the diving group. A theory exists that bright colors, worn in the ocean, may tend to attract sharks. But this seems to be lacking in proof. The famous Ama pearl divers in Japan wear white to *drive away* sharks, with apparent success. *Courtesy, Parkway Fabricators*

Fig. 78c. Some headcovering is almost always necessary for deep diving in cold water, especially for those lacking long and thick hair. *Photo by Rick Carrier*

Sooner or later, most divers want to try spearing a fish, and then their interest turns to the various types of underwater weapons available.

The simplest form of underwater hunting device is the lightweight hand spear. This can be merely a long pole sharpened on one end, or it can be a finely balanced, flexible shaft tapered at both ends and with a sharp steel spearhead attached. Some hand spears used have been as long as fifteen feet. It takes an extremely skilled spearfisherman to catch fish using this primitive device, and many experts consider the use of the hand spear the true test of the sportsman (see Chapter VI).

Ben Holderness of the Aqua-Gun Company has developed a fiberglass spear which is light and flexible, yet tough. Various types of spearhead can be attached to a hand spear, provided the end of the spear is threaded to accommodate the threads on the spearhead.

Fig. 79. Diver using Hawaiian sling equipped with Shark Dart against an oncoming shark. *Courtesy, Farallon Industries*

Fig. 80. The spearheads vary in metals. Some are made of soft steel while others are very hard molybdenum steel. Some have interchangeable heads. The type of spearhead used will depend largely on the type of fish sought. However, the types with the detachable head seem to be preferred for most game fish.

Somewhat more powerful weapons are the rubber-powered spearing devices, notably the Hawaiian sling and the Arbalete. The principle of all of these is the same: a rubber sling is drawn back under tension, and released, propelling the spear toward the prey. The Hawaiian sling is the simplest device of this kind (Fig. 81).

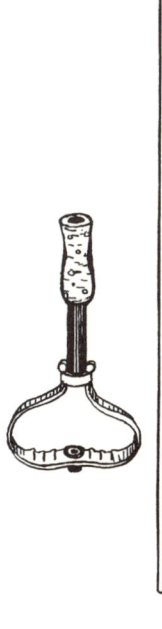

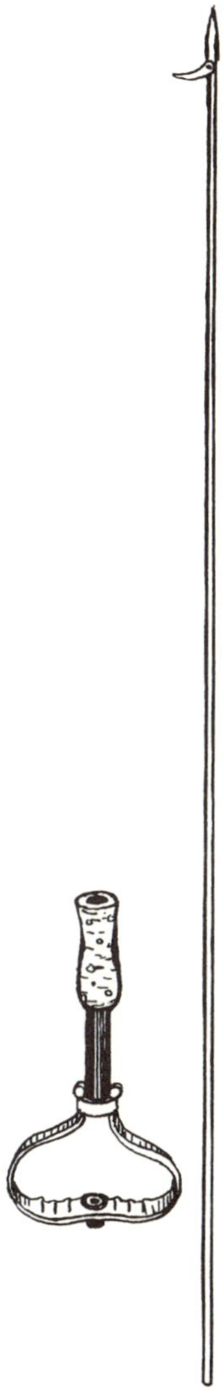

Fig. 81. Hawaiian sling.

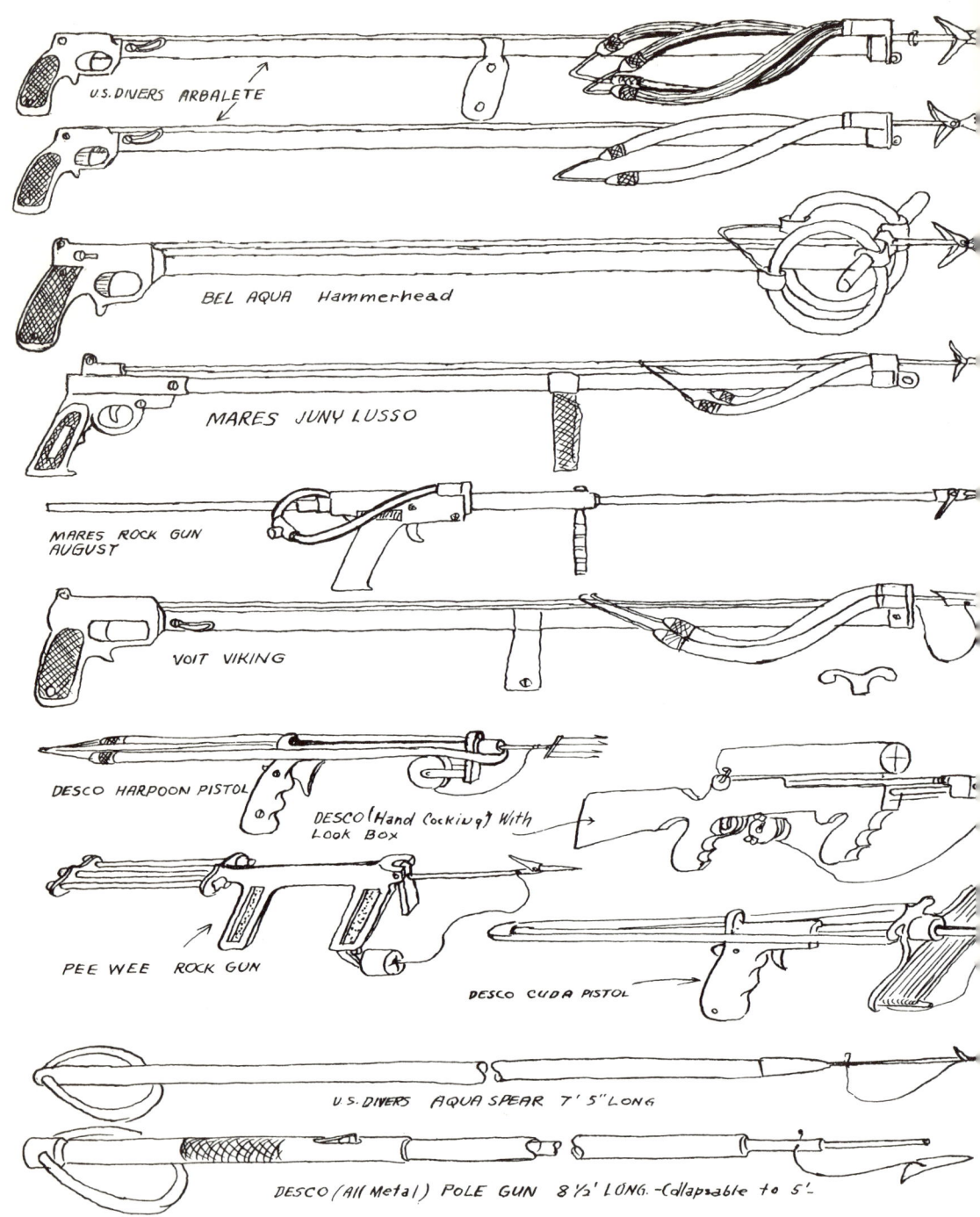

Fig. 82. Rubber-powered spear guns.

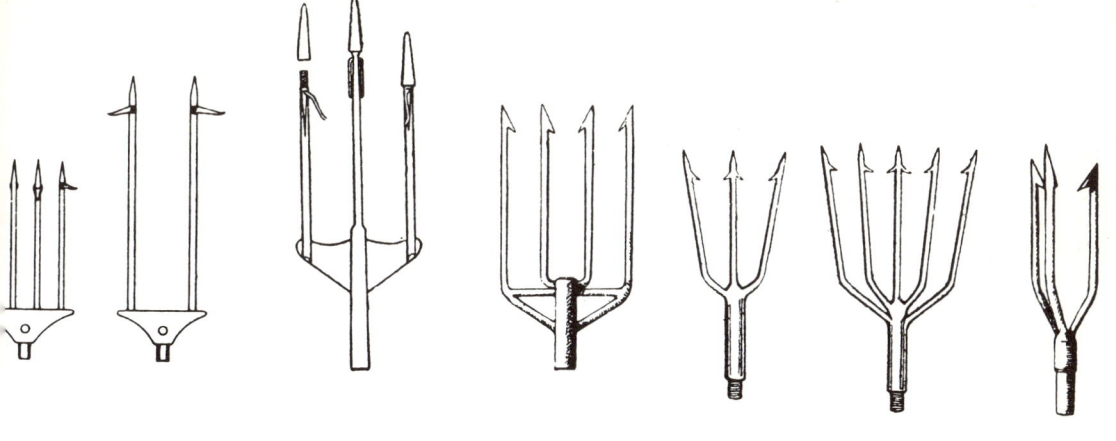

Fig. 83. Most of the tridents or harpoons are made with tines of soft steel, so that they may be straightened and sharpened when bent or blunted. Others made of tempered steel are soft at the tip and hard at the base. These harpoons are usually used on bottom fish.

More powerful is the two-strand Arbalete rubber-powered spear gun, and the four-strand is more powerful still. These guns are constructed so that the spear rides above the tube frame, whereas in certain other brands of rubber-powered guns the spear is inside the barrel and is propelled by the slings being drawn back and attached to a impeller inside the barrel. For a schematic diagram of a four-strand Arbalete, see Fig. 82.

The Arbalete is fairly easy to load if a specific procedure is followed. The spear is first passed through the muzzle and under the wishbones (see page 143), seating the end of the shaft in the trigger mechanism (a loading bar can be used here). Then the wishbone is held firmly and drawn back, seating the loop in the notch at the end of the spear. The same procedure is followed with the other wishbone. Then the nylon line should be folded carefully and slipped under the spring clip on the right side of the gun.

Instead of the spring clip, a small rubber ball with a half-inch hole in it may be used to stuff the line into. This will keep the line out of the way while hunting, and when the gun is fired it will play out freely.

The rubber-powered guns are the least expensive of all the underwater guns, yet are powerful enough, particularly the four-strand Arbalete, for most spearfishing purposes. Record catches have been landed using these guns.

The styles of rubber-powered guns range from small rock-hunting

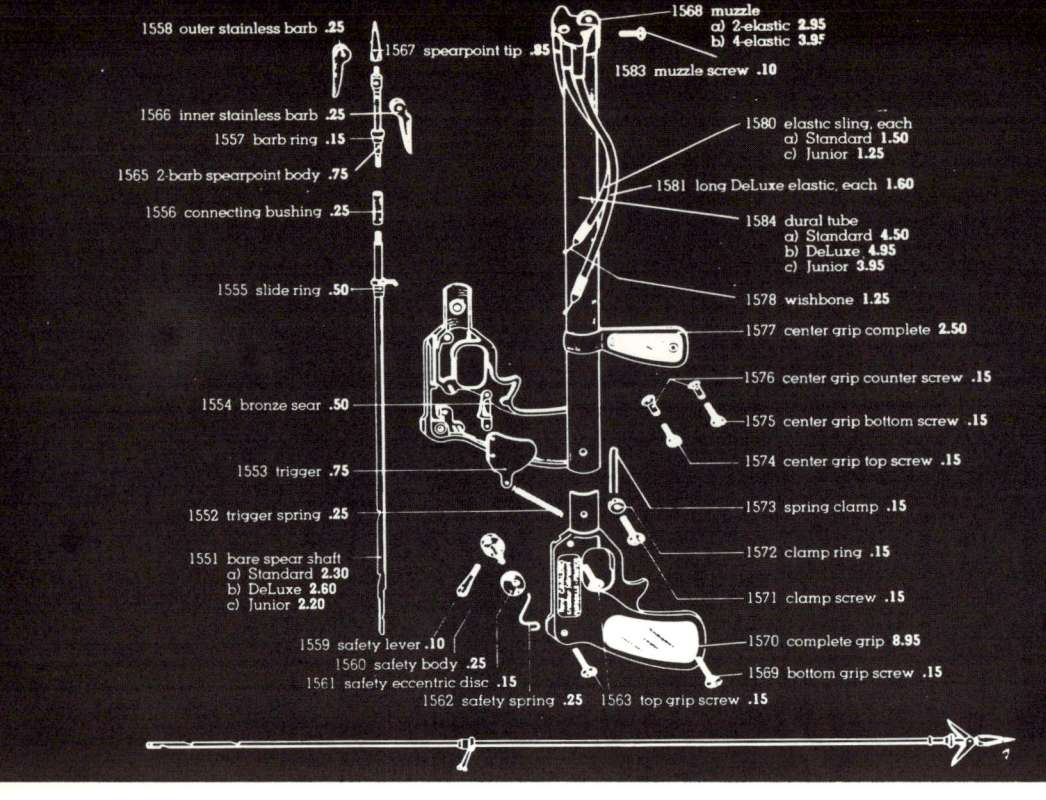

Fig. 84. Schematic diagram of Arbalete. *Courtesy U. S. Divers Corp.*

types to larger big-game pieces (Fig. 82). As with all spears and spear guns, certain safety precautions must be observed. The most common accident when using these guns is head injury caused by the rubber tubing breaking, while the gun is being cocked, or pulling free owing to a crack in the muzzle. These weapons should be carefully examined periodically to check on any possible danger spots and thus prevent accidents.

Spear shafts can be purchased commercially, or the diver can fashion them himself (see Chapter V). Since spears are frequently lost or bent out of shape by big fish, it is advisable to take several extras on any spearfishing trip.

Various higher powered underwater guns, spring guns, and the even more powerful gas guns and powder guns, are available, but must be handled with extreme care (Fig. 85). As we all know, laws exist regulating the use and possession of firearms in order to protect the lives of innocent people. Underwater weapons can be equally lethal if misused, and laws restricting their use have already been passed in certain sections.

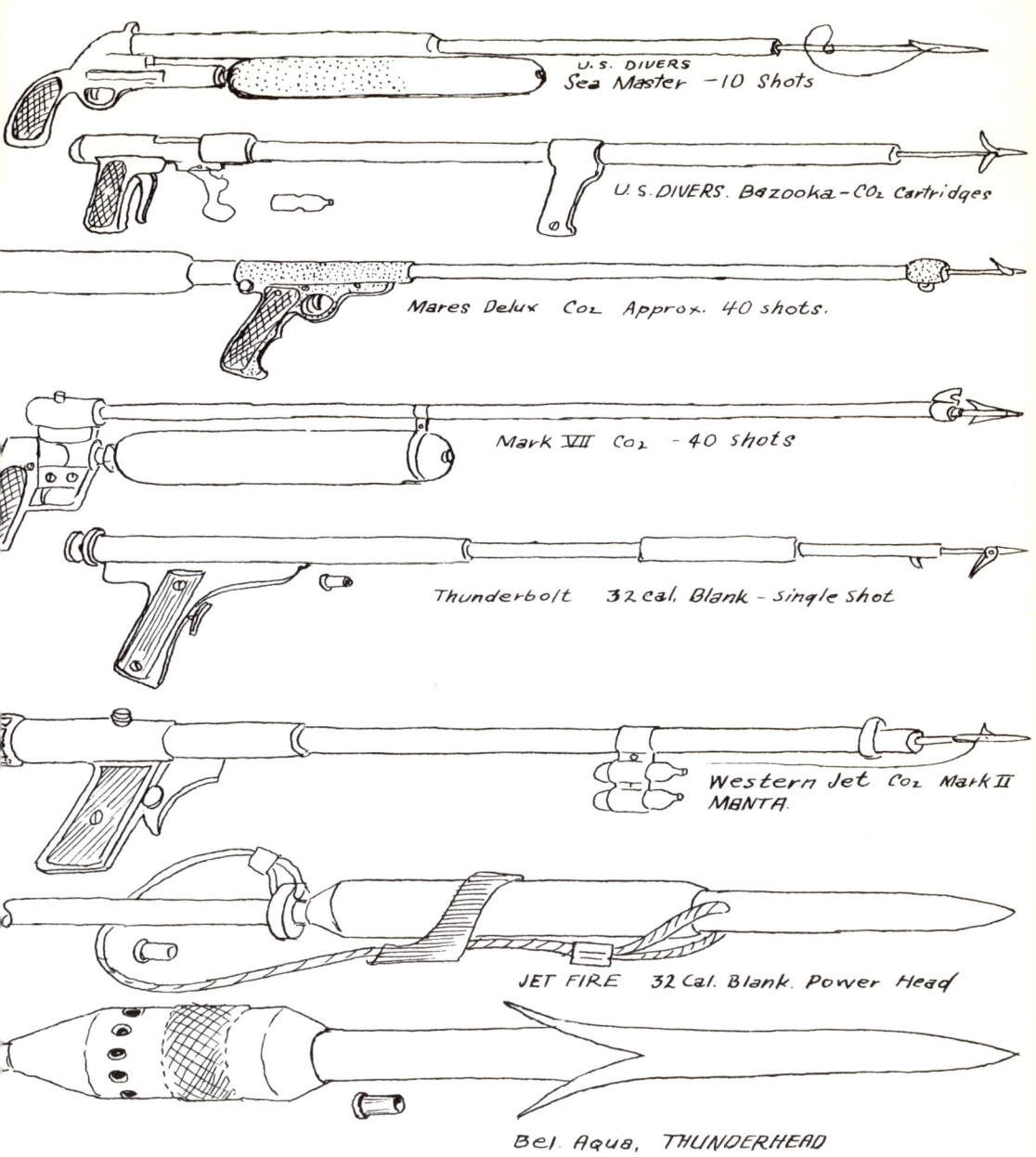

Fig. 85. Power guns should be handled carefully. A recent report in the *Skin Diver* magazine tells of a carbon dioxide gun that was left on a beach uncovered. The heat from the sun caused the gas to expand beyond the rated pressure of the cylinder and the valve blew up, temporarily blinding a man nearby.

An example of the potential power of a carbon dioxide gun will serve to illustrate the dangers of carrying or using loaded guns on public beaches. A carbon dioxide gun when fully charged will propel a spear approximately thirty feet underwater. However, in air, which offers much less resistance, the same spear might travel one hundred yards with lethal force, and if a powerhead is attached, the striking force is enormously increased. It can easily be seen why groups like the Bottom Scratchers diving club of California have been instrumental in the passing of restrictive legislation governing the handling of spears and spearguns on public beaches.

The following rules should be observed by all spearfishermen. No spear gun should be loaded on the beach, or while entering or leaving the water (this includes rubber-powered guns). All self-contained guns such as carbon dioxide, pneumatic, and powder guns should have the spears removed, and all spearheads should either be detached or covered while on a public beach. No spear or spear gun of any type should ever be tested on a public beach, and equipment should not be left where anyone can accidently injure himself on it.

Photo by George Knoblach

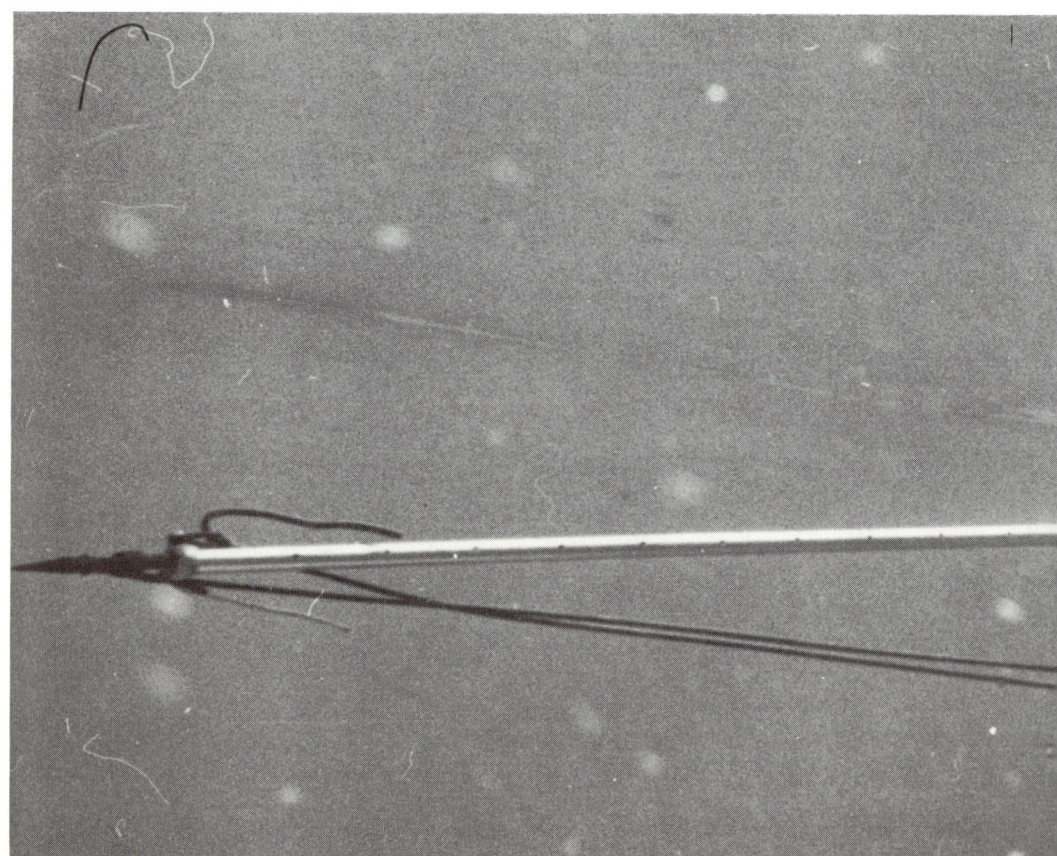

There are two main types of spring guns, the compression and the extension models (Fig. 87a). The compression type is preferable in that the possibility of spring breakage is eliminated. A compression spring will lose power over a long period of use, but this can be corrected by removing the spring and pulling it back into shape or by replacing it.

All spring guns will lose their efficiency if allowed to become rusty or if sand gets into the moving parts. Oiling all metal parts before and after each use and dismantling the gun and cleaning it thoroughly if it should accidentally fall into the sand will keep the gun in top working order.

The spring gun is loaded simply by sliding the spear down the barrel until a slight resistance is felt; then the loading bar is placed over the spear and shoved down until it clicks. An advantage of this type of gun is that the pistol grip is in the center (Fig. 86), giving it excellent balance and maneuverability and enabling the spearfisherman to manipulate it using only one hand. Also the nylon line need only be doubled once to fit into the spring clip at the breech of

Fig. 86. The spring gun in ready position.

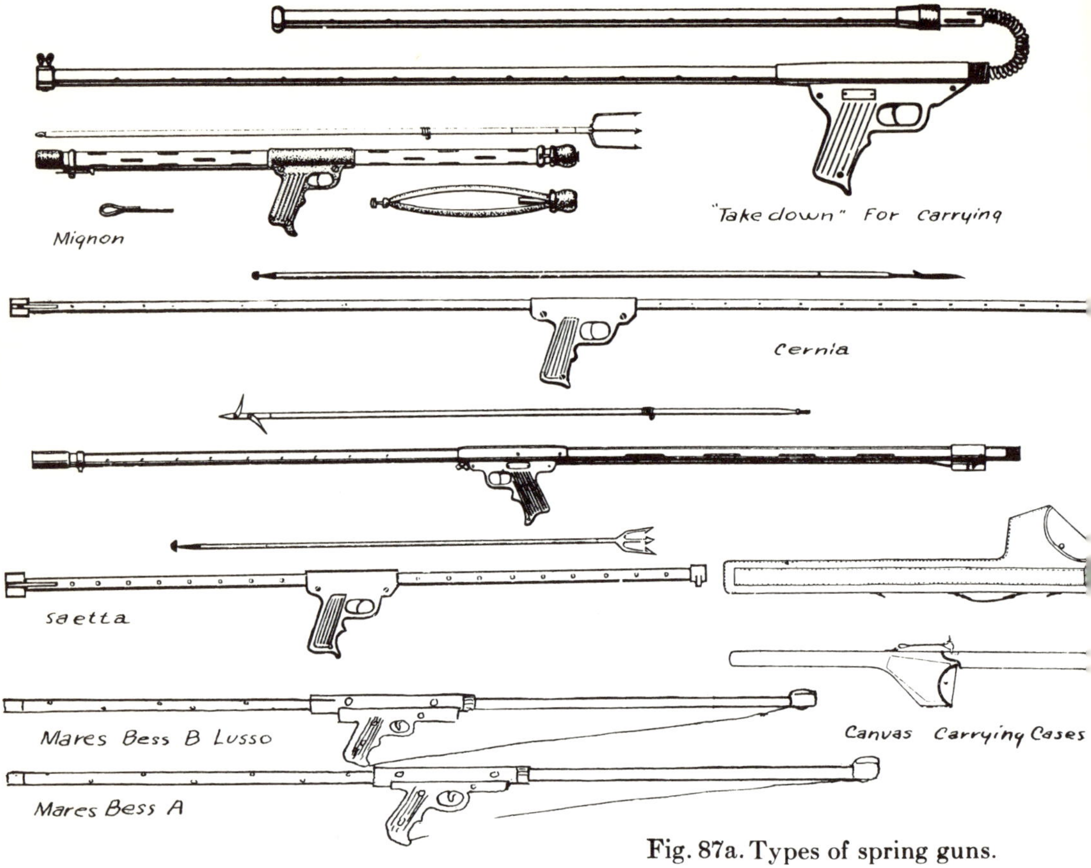

Fig. 87a. Types of spring guns.

Fig. 87b. Diver with Hawaiian sling looking for "the big ones that live down deep!" *Photo by Paul Tzimoulis*

Fig. 88. Loading the gun underwater is safer and saves time. a. The Arbalete. b. The spring gun. c. Be calm when loading the spring gun even though the fish may get away. It can easily be imagined what will happen if the diver fires the gun with the line wrapped around his neck.

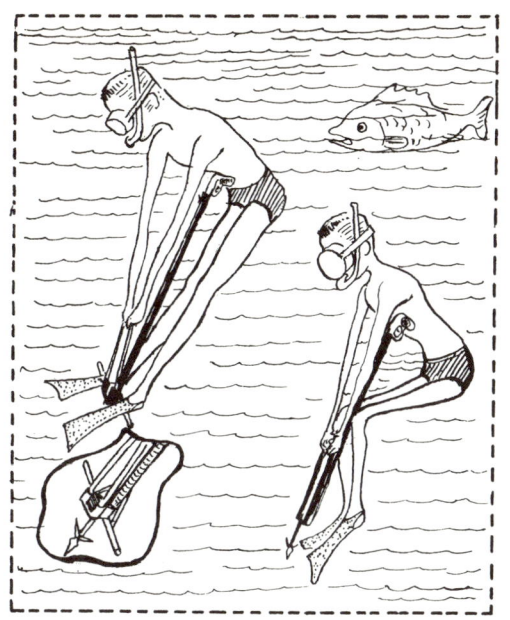

Photo by George Knoblach

the gun. Some guns come with fishing reels attached to accommodate the nylon line or they can be added by the diver.

The gas and powder guns are designed for hunting large fish and should never be used unless the diver be really expert. Their operation is fairly simple since no cocking is necessary. The spear is simply placed in the barrel until it touches the breech; then the gun is ready to fire.

The carbon dioxide guns have two types of power supply, one is a large reservoir of gas and the other is a small single shot carbon dioxide cartridge like those used for making carbonated water at home. The pressure in the cylinder remains constant as long as there is a drop of liquid CO_2 remaining in the tank. This gives a constant breech pressure for every shot. See Figure 85.

Underwater powder guns are a fairly recent development. In these guns the spear is propelled by a .32 caliber blank cartridge covered with wax or lacquer for waterproofing. With this type gun it is essential to keep the barrel free from obstruction, since otherwise the barrel could explode when the gun is fired. Some divers have converted rifles to make underwater powder guns, but this is dangerous unless the builder is an expert on guns. The use of explosive-powered weapons to catch fish is illegal in some areas, so this should be checked before buying or building a powder gun. As with all power spear guns, it is not simply how much power a gun has that counts most in spearing fish, but rather the diver's skill in stalking the prey and how the fish is handled after it is speared (see Chapter VI).

Power heads for spears are also used to take fish which are very large or have extremely tough hides. The Bel-Aqua "Thunderhead" is powered by a blank cartridge and is made to fit on various types of spear guns and even on a hand spear. When carried in "safe" position, this spearhead is an ordinary detachable spearhead, but when set in the "fire" position, it will penetrate any sea monster encountered. Therefore it can be used for spearing ordinary fish as well as larger varieties. Extreme care must be taken to follow the safety precautions set up by the manufacturer, since these spearheads can be dangerous if misused.

A useful item on any spearfishing trip is a canvas or heavy plastic pouch to carry extra speartips, and other miscellaneous items such as pliers, screwdriver, triangular file, small hammer, scissors, oil, a container of grease, an extra bar loader, and five yards of wire and nylon leaders (see Chapter V).

Sooner or later most skin divers, particularly those who are more interested in exploring the underwater world than in spearfishing, or who have some specific project such as underwater photography, research or salvage, become interested in self-contained underwater breathing apparatus.

Fig. 89. The equipped SCUBA diver, John Pritzlaff, wearing a wet suit, CO_2 inflatable life vest, SCUBA, mask, snorkel, fins, weight belt, compass, and depth gage. A knife (not shown) is fastened to his leg. The divers flag is mandatory in many waters. The diver is holding an underwater camera. Two more cameras are in the raft. An equipped diver as a companion is necessary to insure safe diving. *Photo by Gene Parker*

There are many widespread misconceptions regarding SCUBA. Most people know that the description "self-contained" means that the diver can swim freely using this equipment without being dependent on air hoses leading to a surface air supply. However in popular terminology, as well as in magazines, movies, etc., the term "oxygen" is often used to denote the breathing medium used in all equipment of this type. This is a dangerous misstatement.

Oxygen is used as a breathing medium only in the recirculating type breathing apparatus and cannot safely be substituted for the compressed air used in the "demand type" (i.e., the air flows automatically and only when needed and exhaled air is given off into the water) units such as the Aqua-Lung.

The principle of the oxygen recirculating unit is that it operates on a closed circuit; oxygen is breathed in from a cylinder and the air exhaled is purified by the use of a carbon dioxide absorbent so that it can be rebreathed. There are several possible dangers in the use of this equipment. For one thing, oxygen becomes toxic to the human body when inhaled under pressures of depths greater than about thirty-five feet or for long periods of time (see Chapter III). Also if the carbon dioxide absorbent becomes ineffective through overlong use or through becoming water-soaked, carbon dioxide poisoning can result. In addition, the self-valving of oxygen necessary in some of the equipment of this type takes time to become accustomed to, and requires the diver's constant attention. For these reasons, as well as the fact that the oxygen must be exhausted from the breathing bag whenever the diver returns to the surface, in order to avoid a dangerous build-up of pressure, thus using up the oxygen supply too rapidly if frequent trips to the surface are made, this equipment is not suitable for the sport diver and therefore will not be considered here. Oxygen recirculating equipment is economical and convenient for certain shallow water work by professional divers, and has been used by the frogmen because it produces no betraying bubbles. However most skin divers are not expert enough or careful enough of their exact depth, to make this equipment safe for general use.

The principle of the Aqua-Lung and other "demand type" apparatus such as the Sportsways or Healthways unit, is that compressed air is inhaled from a cylinder carried on the back, valved automatically by a demand regulator to compensate for varying external water pressures and then is exhaled into the water in the form of bubbles.

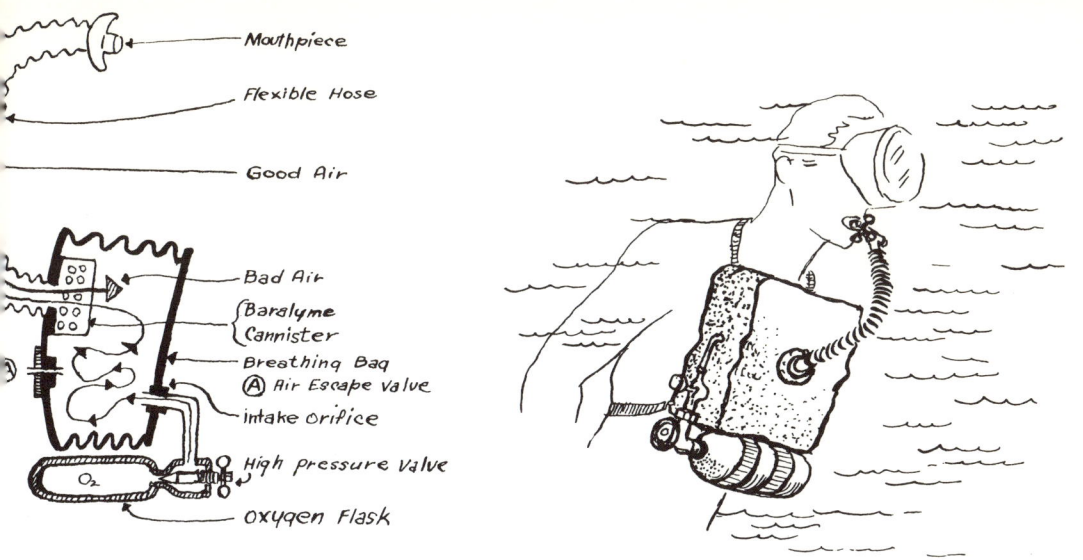

Fig. 90. Closed circuit lungs. The re-breathers should be left for the experts as there are too many dangers in using this type of equipment.

Fig. 91. a, Detail of the two-stage regulator.

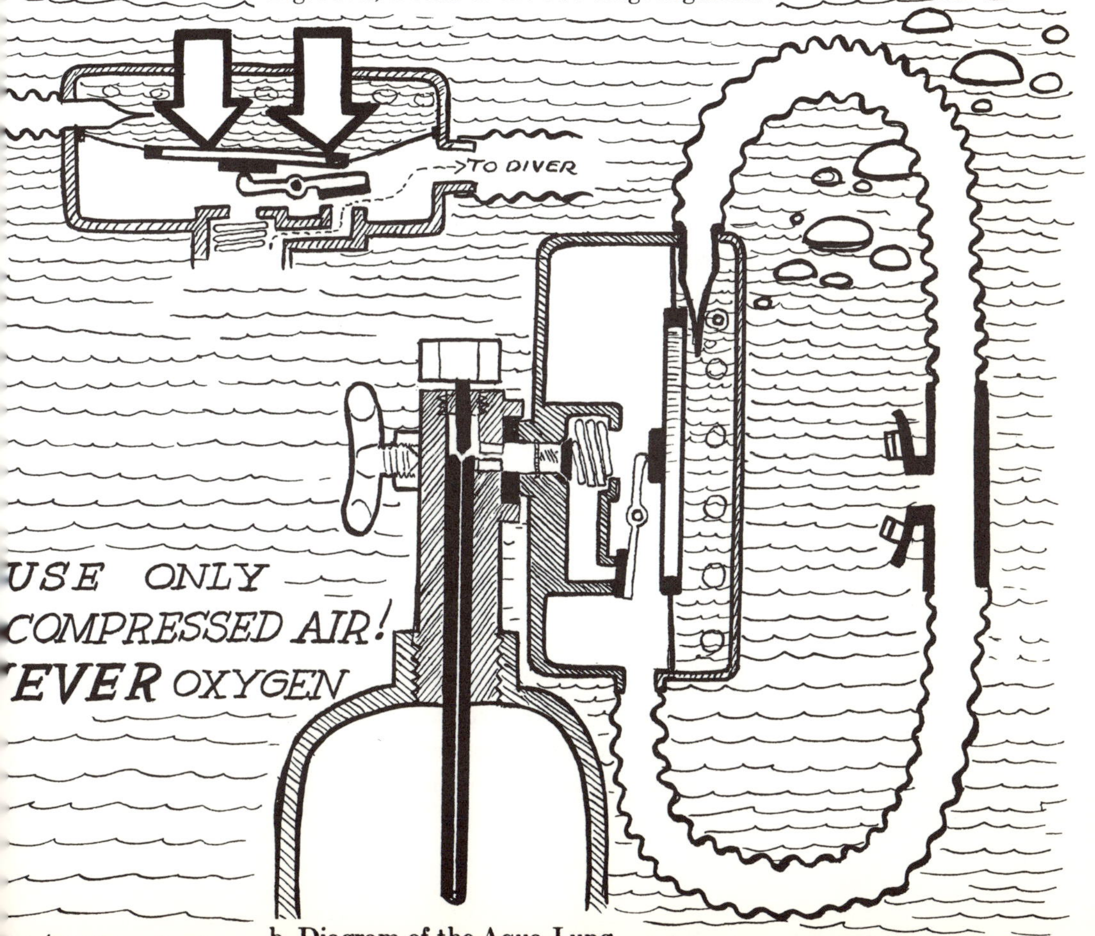

b, Diagram of the Aqua-Lung.

Figure 91b shows the two-hose regulator. This unit consists of a rubber mouthpiece attached to two corrugated flexible rubber hoses, one for inhaling and the other for exhaling, which are connected to the regulator which in turn attaches to the outlet valve on the top of the steel cylinder (see Fig. 93 for how to attach it). The regulator (Fig. 91a) is a two-stage, pressure-reducing, demand regulator. The pressure in the 70-cubic-foot cylinder, when filled to capacity, is about 2,365 pounds per square inch. Since this pressure cannot be breathed directly into the lungs, the two-pressure-stage regulator was designed to reduce this high pressure to breathing pressure and to allow the diver a continuous even flow of air at a pressure equivalent to the outside water pressure, even though the pressure in the cylinder decreases. The air from the cylinder is filtered and valved into the first pressure reducing stage where it is maintained at constant pressure of about 100 pounds per square inch. From there it is valved into a larger area (the second pressure reducing stage) from which it passes into the inhale tube leading to the mouthpiece. As the diver inhales air from this reservoir, the vacuum created depresses the diaphragm, thus opening the valve to admit more air as in the diagram. The water outside also exerts pressure on this diaphragm, thus opening the valve to admit air to compensate for outside water pressure. When the diver exhales, the exhaled air passes through the exhale tube and out the flutter valve at the back of the regulator. It is necessary for this exhaust valve to be placed close to the diaphragm, since the diaphragm is sensitive to very small pressure variations, and if the exhaust were more than two inches above the diaphragm the difference in water pressure, the rapid expansion of the exhaled air (Boyle's Law) would create a pull on the inside of the diaphragm, thus opening the valve and exhausting the air from the tank. If the exhale valve were set much lower than the diaphragm, the diver would have to force the exhaled air out the tube.

It is also because of the variation in water pressure at different levels that the regulator is mounted on the top of the tanks, approximately on a level with the diver's lungs. If it were set higher, the reduced pressure on the diaphragm would not allow enough air to enter the diver's lungs to compensate for the water pressure outside the chest, and if it were lower than the lungs, the air would enter the diver's lungs at too high a pressure. As it is, the diver can swim in any position and still maintain a free flow of air.

Figures 93a, b, and c show the proper methods of installing the regulator on the tank and mounting the Aqua-Lung on the diver. The harness should have safety-release buckles and should be adjusted so that the regulator fits squarely between the shoulder blades and close to the back. It should fit comfortably and not wobble or float when submerged.

Fig. 92. Unlike the earlier versions, the latest SCUBA equipment is light enough for anyone to carry, place, and fasten into position with minimum effort. The girl is carrying a cryogenic SCUBA filled with liquid air which a condensor turns back into a gaseous state. This will enable the diver to expand his normal air supply and stay underwater nine or ten times longer than if the tank were filled with normal expanded air. *Courtesy, Parkway Fabricators*

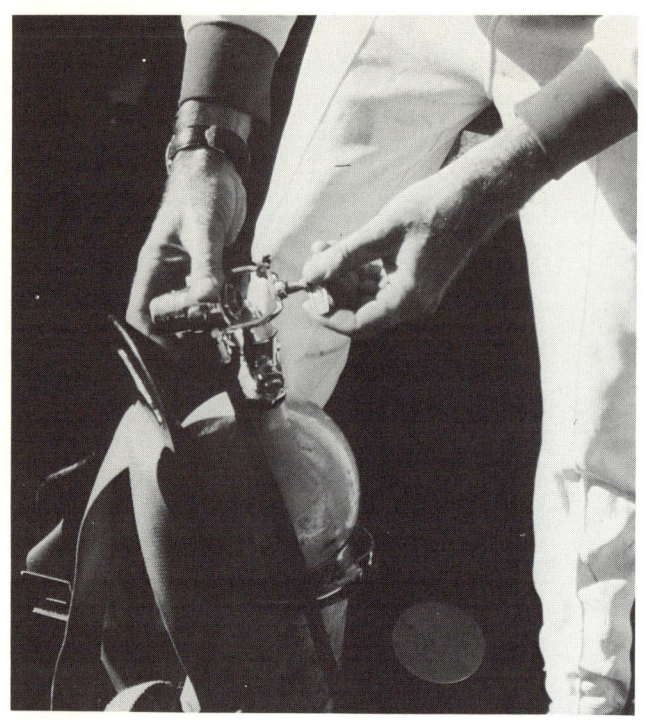

How to attach the regulator to the tank.

Fig. 93a. Step 1: Make sure that the thumbscrew on regulator yoke is fully open and then slip yoke over the tank valve. Align valve seat on regulator with valve seal on tank. *Courtesy, Aqualung School of New York*

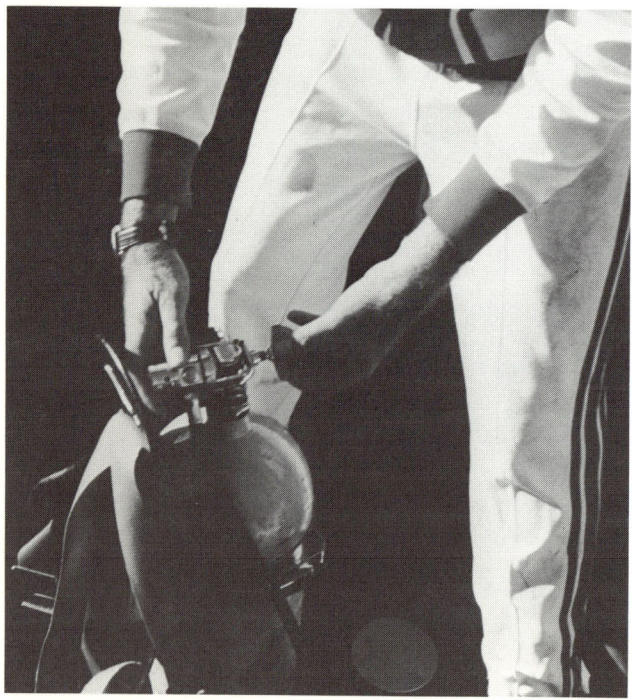

Fig. 93b. Step 2: Tighten regulator yoke thumbscrew until secure. *Courtesy, Aqualung School of New York*

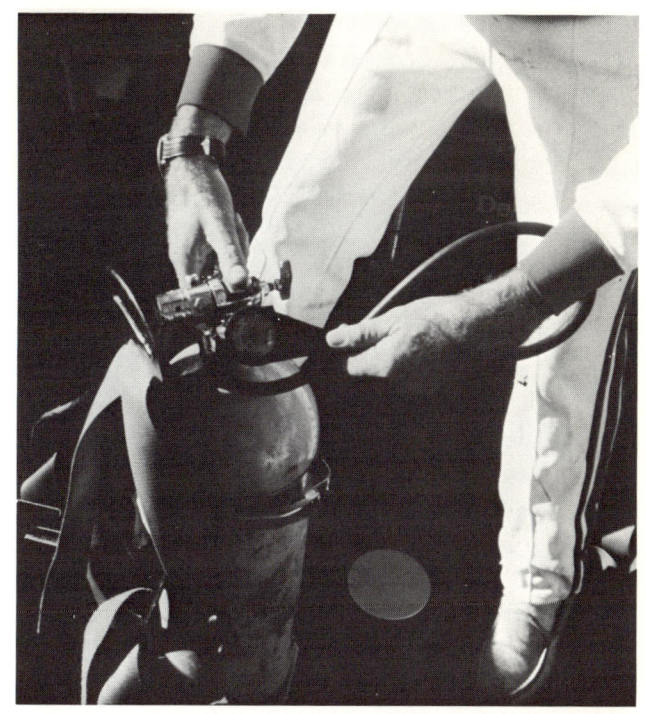

Fig. 93c. Step 3: Turn tank valve handle slowly until air enters regulator. The gauge in this photograph indicates tank pressure and will monitor pressure during the dive. The regulator should not be fastened to the tank until just before the actual dive. It should be removed immediately after diving, as it is a delicate piece of machinery which can easily be damaged during transportation if left on the heavy cylinder. Make certain the air reserve bar is up. *Courtesy, Aqualung School of New York*

Fig. 94. Monitor gauge as seen underwater, attached to regulator by long hose to afford easy viewing. *Courtesy, Aqualung School of New York*

SCUBA cylinders are made of special steel alloy and can be filled with compressed air at pressures ranging from 1,800 to 2,600 pounds per square inch. These should never be filled beyond the rated pressure stamped on each cylinder. In the early days of diving it was frequently necessary to contact an oxygen supply house for compressed air. Now almost every diving area has a diving shop nearby, where air for SCUBA can be obtained. Figure 94 shows a portable compressor that divers can use to fill their own tanks. These cylinders should be handled with great care, since, if the nipple should be broken off accidentally when the cylinder is full, the cylinder could take off like a rocket, leaving a wake of destruction in its path.

Some SCUBA feature a safety reserve in the cylinder valve. In the Aqua-Lung this is called a "J" valve. When the pressure in the tank becomes very low (300 pounds per square inch), this valve shuts off the flow. The diver can then manually trip a lever, releasing a flow of air which is sufficient for approximately five minutes.

This reserve feature has been incorporated into some of the new single hose regulators. Instead of buying two or three "J" tanks a diver may purchase the lower cost "K" tanks which do not have a reserve mechanism. (Some divers own several tanks so that they do not have to interrupt a day's diving to get air-fills for a one-and-only tank.) Since the reserve is located on the regulator it is not necessary to have another reserve on the tank.

Regulator mouthpieces are made of soft rubber and have two bits which are clenched between the teeth. Modern two-hose regulators have non-return valves in the mouthpiece so that the entire hose does not fill with water if the mouthpiece is accidentally dropped out of the diver's mouth. The very small amount of water that has collected in the mouthpiece can be blown out very easily. No water can get into the hose of the single hose regulator. The mouthpiece on most of the single hose regulators can be cleared of water by pressing a button located in front of the mouthpiece. Although the mouthpiece which must be gripped in the teeth might seem less convenient than the air flow from a full face mask, it has its advantages; where in case of breakage of a full face mask the flow of air is interrupted, this risk is eliminated with the separate mask and SCUBA mouthpiece.

The Desco "Dolphin" lung also has a full face mask, and has a "free-flow button" which makes purging the mask of water simple. The cylinder or cylinders (50 or 70 cubic feet) are attached to a comfortable plastic backboard with valves downward to eliminate

TABLE 1

	1 Cylinder	2 Cylinders
At the surface	100 minutes	200 minutes
At a depth of 33 ft.	50 "	100 "
At a depth of 100 ft.	25 "	50 "

TABLE 2

Gauge Reading on Cylinder	Number of Cubic Feet of Air Remaining in Cylinder	Gauge Reading on Cylinder	Number of Cubic Feet of Air Remaining in Cylinder
2200	71.7	1200	39.12
2150	68.5	1100	35.8
2000	65.2	1000	32.5
1900	61.8	900	29.3
1800	58.6	800	26.0
1700	55.5	700	22.8
1600	52.2	600	19.6
1500	49.0	500	16.3
1400	45.5	400	13.0
1300	42.3	300	9.8

For finding the approximate cubic feet of air in the cylinder in between the numbers given, simply take the gauge reading and multiply by .032. (When connecting the gauge to the cylinder, make certain the gauge is seated on the washer of the valve. Open the cylinder valve long enough to get a reading, close it, and remove gauge. The reading tells how much air is in the tank.)

Fig. 95. With practice in conserving air, the diver may increase the immersion times as given in Table 1.

Fig. 96. The Cornelius Air Compressor is perfect for the sport diver who wants to charge his own tanks with air. This compressor is portable and is available with a gasoline or electric motor. It weighs 47 pounds and will fill a 70 cubic foot tank in 100 minutes to a pressure of 2350 pounds per square inch.

bumping the back of the diver's head. The cylinders can be refilled without removing them from the backboard. The waist strap has a quick-release buckle in case of emergency. This unit is in the same price bracket as the Aqua-Lung. The Desco full face mask can be purchased separately to convert a mouthpiece type unit to the full mask type.

All of the above SCUBA units are safe, functional, and pleasant to use. With them the diver can explore and feel himself a part of the underwater world, swimming with the freedom of a fish. By weighting himself properly (usually about 2 to 9 pounds in salt water, or more when wearing rubber suits, the diver can start out slightly overweighted since he will become more buoyant as the air in the cylinder decreases) he can achieve a delightful sensation of weightlessness in a dreamlike world.

However publicity about self-contained diving equipment has led the public to believe that it is completely free from danger and that preliminary training is unnecessary. It would be just as ridiculous to say that anyone can fly an airplane, steer a battleship, or play a good game of golf without special training. Situations may occur unexpectedly underwater which demand a high degree of skill and training in order to prevent a serious accident. The trained diver can usually cope with a situation which might panic the inexperienced—for instance, a flooded air hose at a considerable depth. Before trying any SCUBA unit, the diver should fully understand the physiological principles of diving, the way the equipment functions, the possible dangers, and how to cope with emergencies. Preferably he should first be skilled in the use of the basic equipment, mask, fins, and snorkel, and should try the SCUBA first in shallow water, supervised by someone experienced in its use. Many diving clubs provide this training.

The following pages display several makes of SCUBA. Prices have not been listed since cost is not necessarily the criterion of the best SCUBA for your particular purpose. If you do not contemplate diving deeper than about forty feet, for a short period, it is possible to purchase SCUBA for about fifty dollars. On the other hand, if you intend to do salvage work at greater depths it may be worthwhile to buy a more expensive rig for about two hundred dollars.

Generally, a 30 cu. ft. tank holds about a half-hour air supply at depths to 33 feet. A 70 cu. ft. tank is considered good for about an hour at 40 feet. The double "70" may provide enough air for two hours. (See pages 145 to 174 for SCUBA information.)

Many divers still prefer the two-hose regulator. It may "blow air" if the mouthpiece is held higher than the regulator mechanism. A camera lanyard draped around the diver's neck tends to pull down on the SCUBA hoses. There is more water resistance when the diver is being towed. However, one can hardly lose the mouthpiece since it is within easy reach. No neck strap is needed to hold it in place. Modern 2-hose regulators include non-return valves in the mouthpiece to inhibit water accumulation in the hoses.

The single hose regulator is a recent innovation. It is more compact. The mouthpiece can be cleared by pressing a button which causes a rush of air to force out the water.

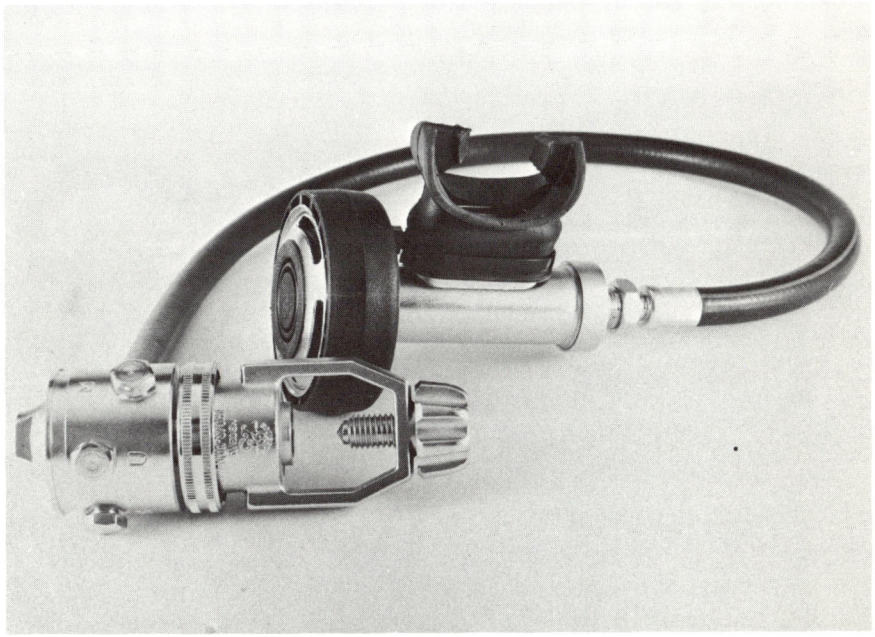

Fig. 97. A Poseidon Cyklon 300 Regulator, developed for easy breathing. Extra attachments on regulator are for connection with Unisuit, air gauge, and "octopus (multi breathing) rigs." This regulator can be used on present American tanks (capacity 2250 lbs. per square inch) or new European ones (capacity 4500 lbs.). In the future, most tanks will have the latter capacity, making it possible for divers to stay underwater much longer without changing tanks. *Courtesy, Poseidon Systems, USA*

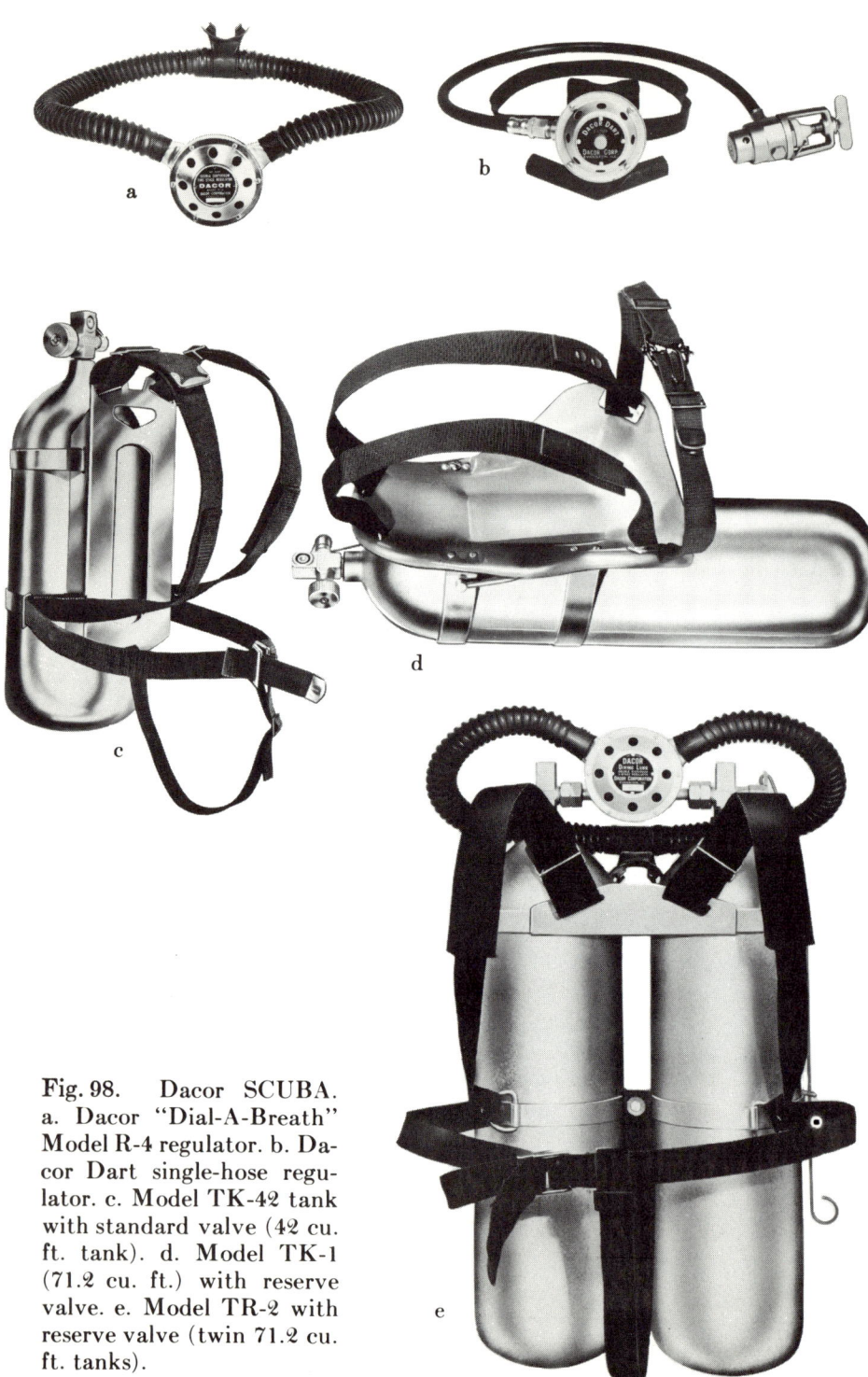

Fig. 98. Dacor SCUBA. a. Dacor "Dial-A-Breath" Model R-4 regulator. b. Dacor Dart single-hose regulator. c. Model TK-42 tank with standard valve (42 cu. ft. tank). d. Model TK-1 (71.2 cu. ft.) with reserve valve. e. Model TR-2 with reserve valve (twin 71.2 cu. ft. tanks).

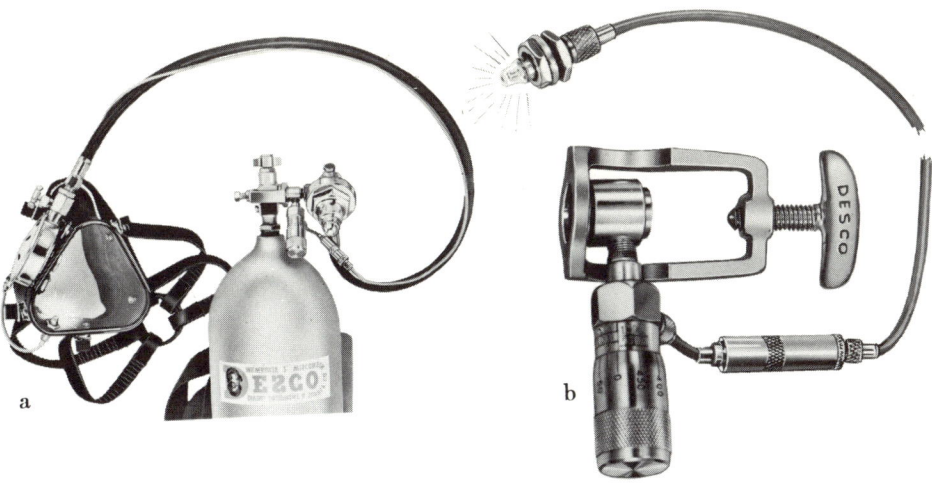

Fig. 99. Desco (Diving Equipment & Supply Co.) SCUBA. a. Saf-t-eye Mask with reserve selector and cylinder pressure indicator. b. Close-up view of Saf-t-eye reserve selector and cylinder pressure indicator. The light flashes on automatically when the air reserve is low.

Fig. 100. SCUBA diver swims by coral head and sea ferns. Nassau, Bahamas. *Photo by Paul Tzimoulis*

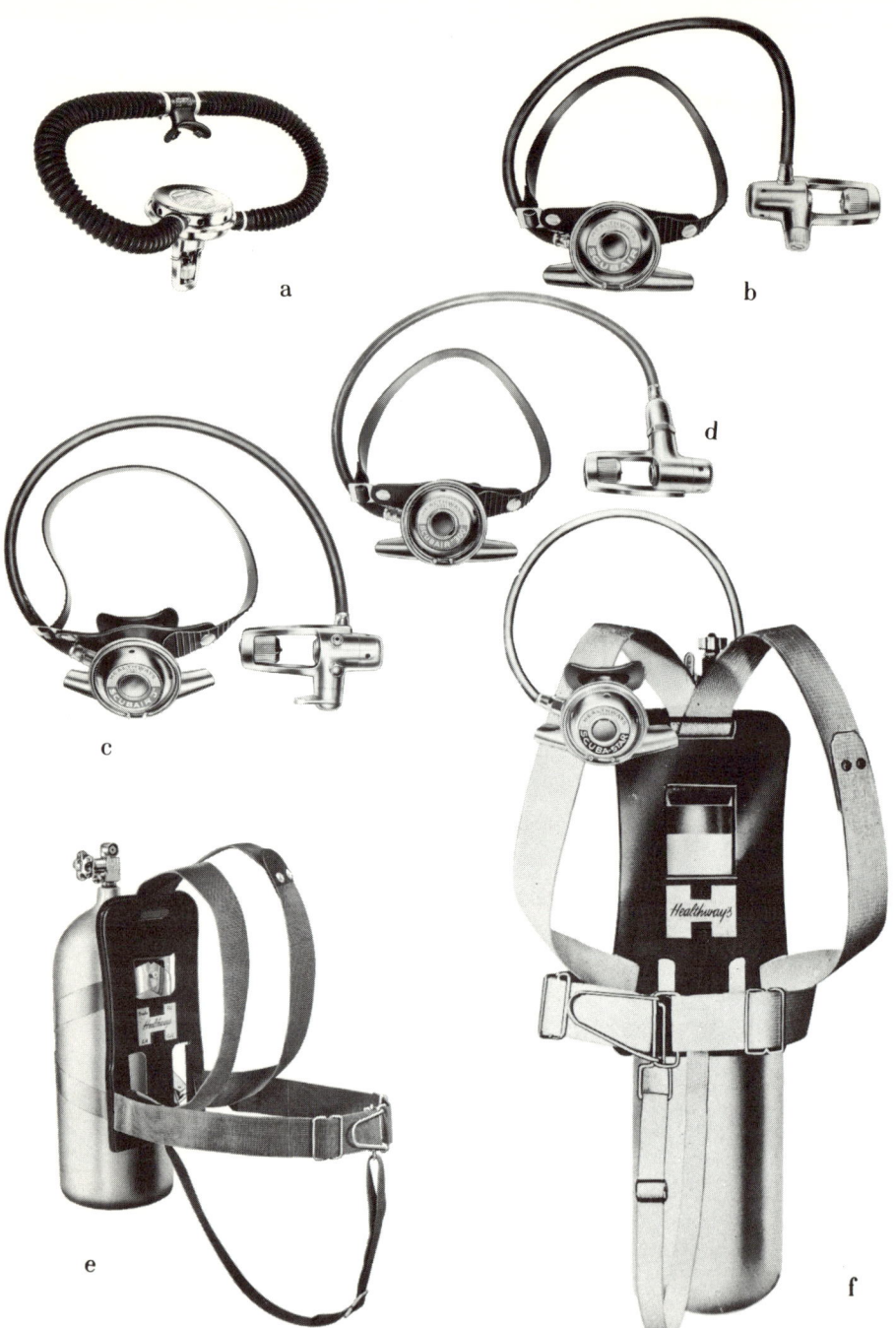

Fig. 101. Healthways SCUBA. a. Deluxe "Model 1962." b. Scubair single-hose, 2-stage. c. Scubair "J" has reserve feature on regulator. d. Scubair "300" contains an alarm which sounds when the tank pressure has been depleted to 300 p.s.i. e. 42 cu. ft. tank. f. 71.2 cu. ft. tank with SCUBA-Star regulator.

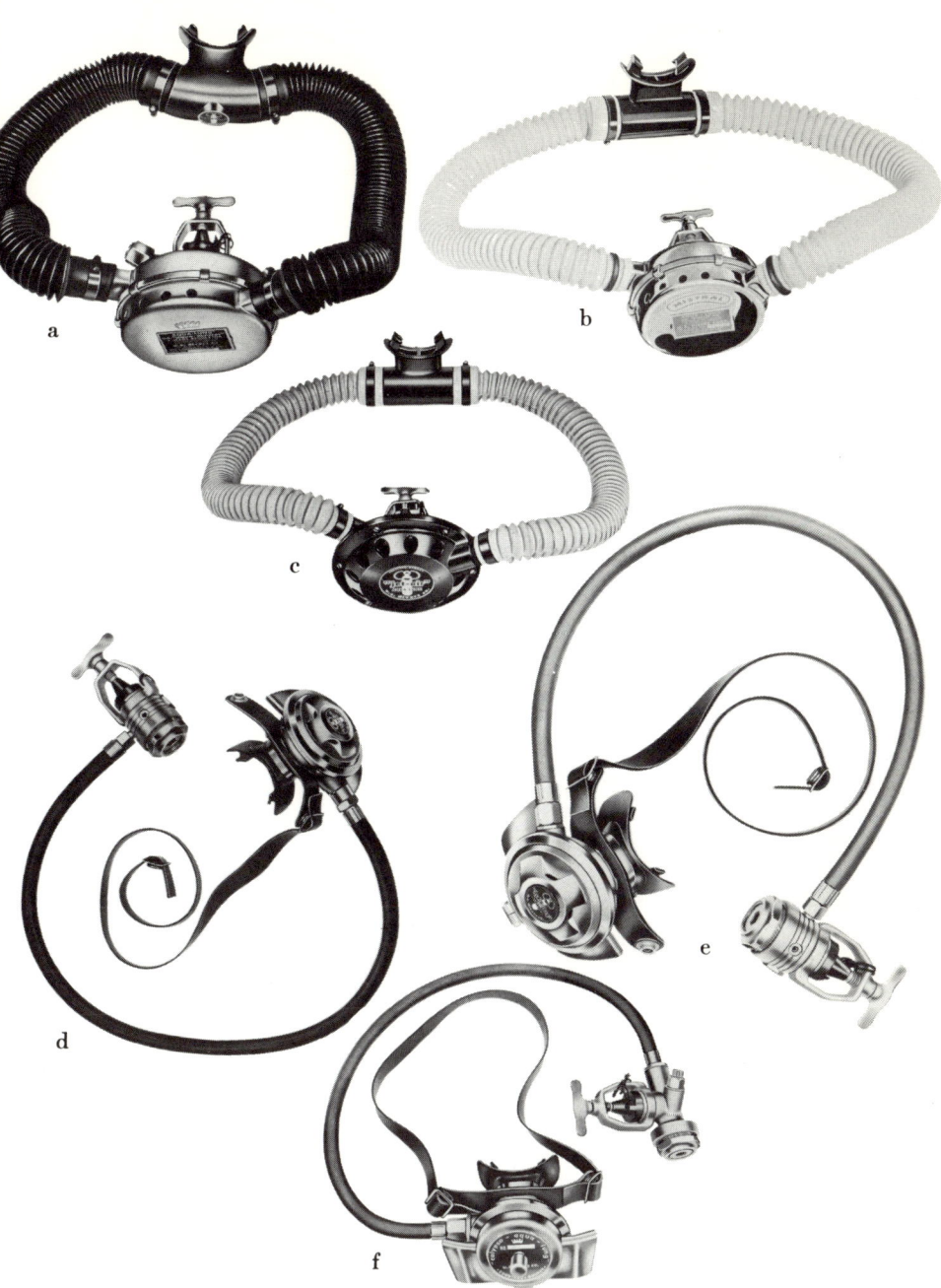

Fig. 102. U. S. Divers regulators. a. "Aqua Master" 2-hose Aqua Lung regulator. b. "Mistral" single stage, 2-hose. c. "Jet-Air" has a high impact Cycolac plastic housing. d. "Aqua-Div" Deluxe single-hose. e. "Hydro Lung Supreme." f. The "Calypso" which was selected by Hans Keller for his world record dive to 728 feet.

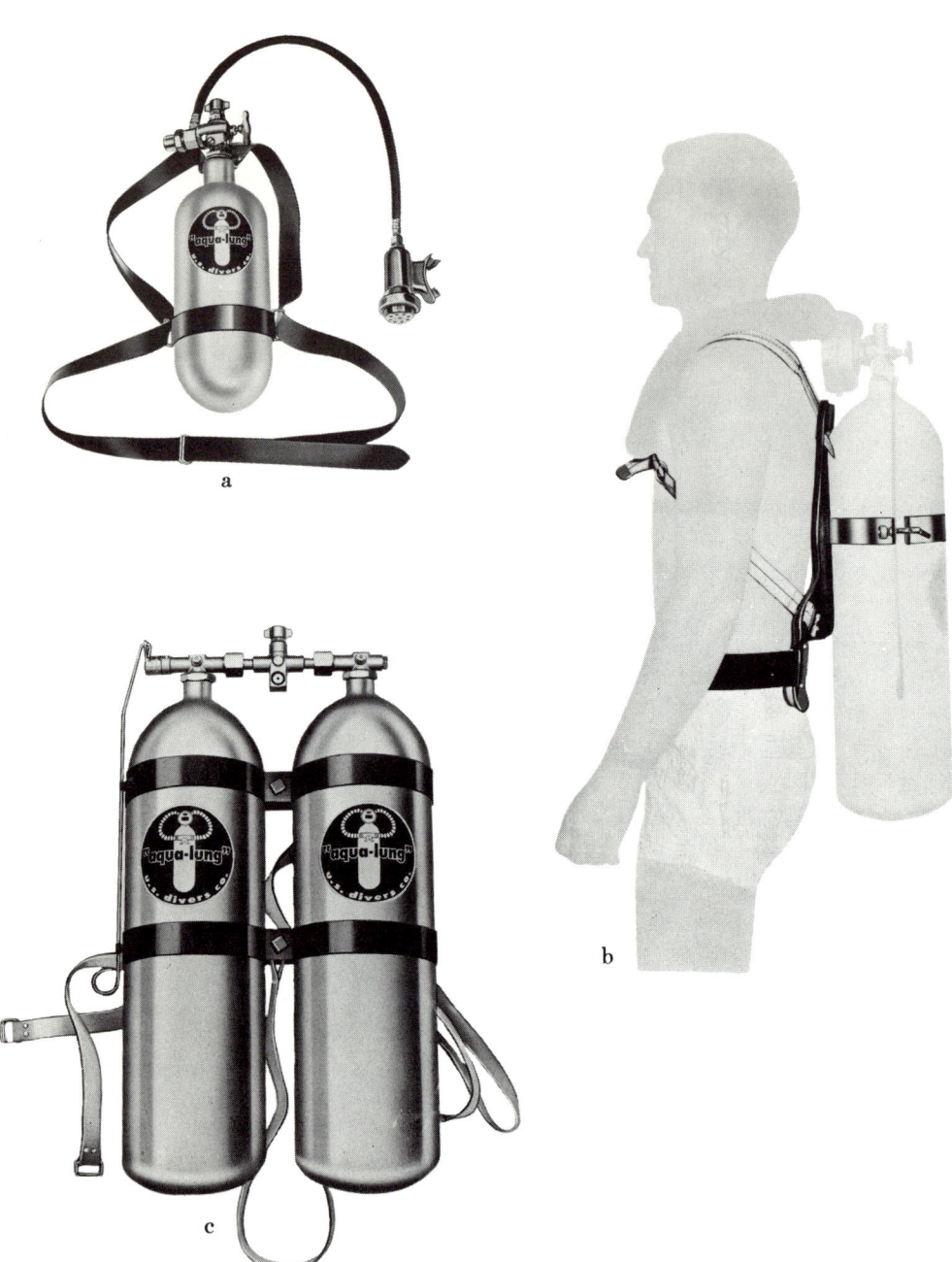

Fig. 103. U. S. Divers SCUBA. a. The tiny Vigo "Aqua-Lung" 18 cu. ft. tank with special Aqua-Div regulator. This is a good unit for quick, shallow dives such as for inspecting the bottom of a boat. b. "Aqua-Lung" Pac is a comfortable harness that permits of quick changes of tanks. c. Twin tank block for rugged underwater work.

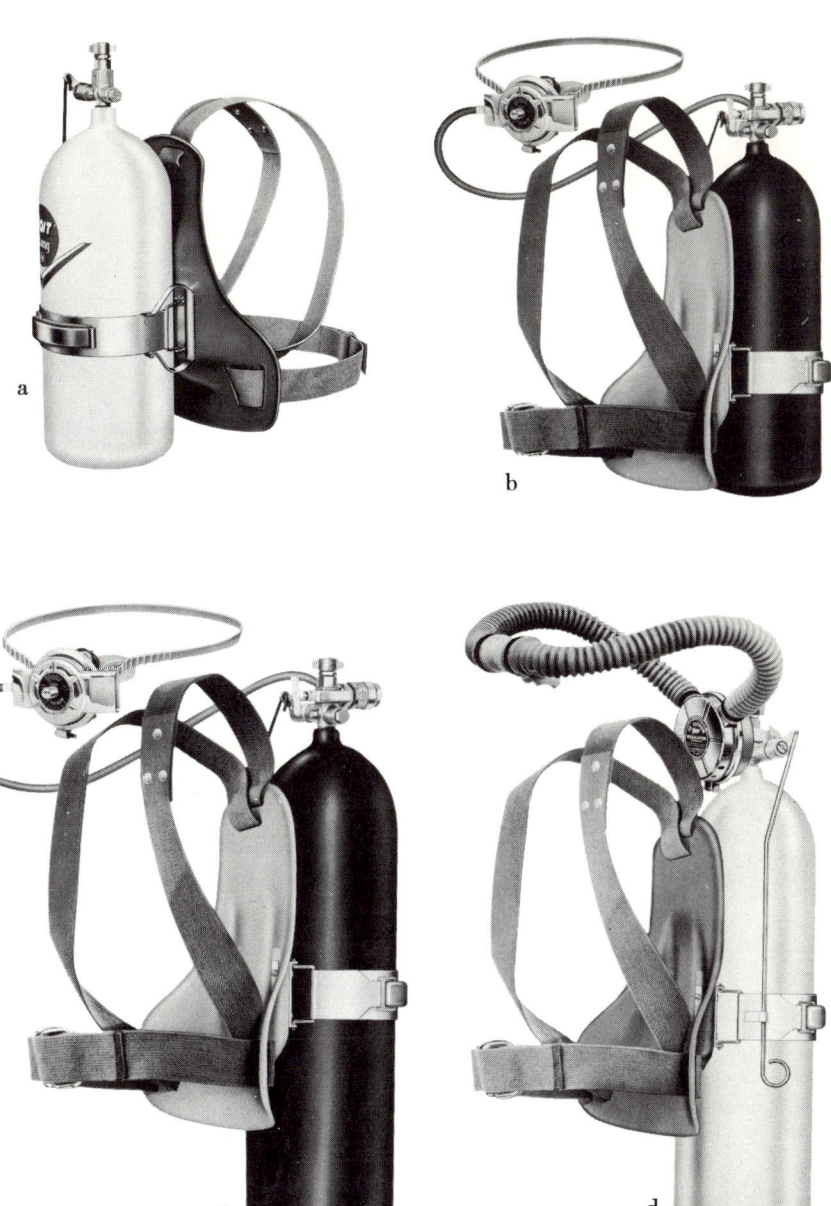

Fig. 104. Voit SCUBA. a. 50 cu. ft. tank in Snugpack. White vinyl coating on tank. b. 50 cu. ft. tank in Snugpack. Black vinyl-coated tank. c. 71.2 cu. ft. tank in Snugpack, single-hose regulator. d. 71.2 cu. ft. tank with 50-fathom, 2-hose regulator. Voit tanks are also available in double tank blocks.

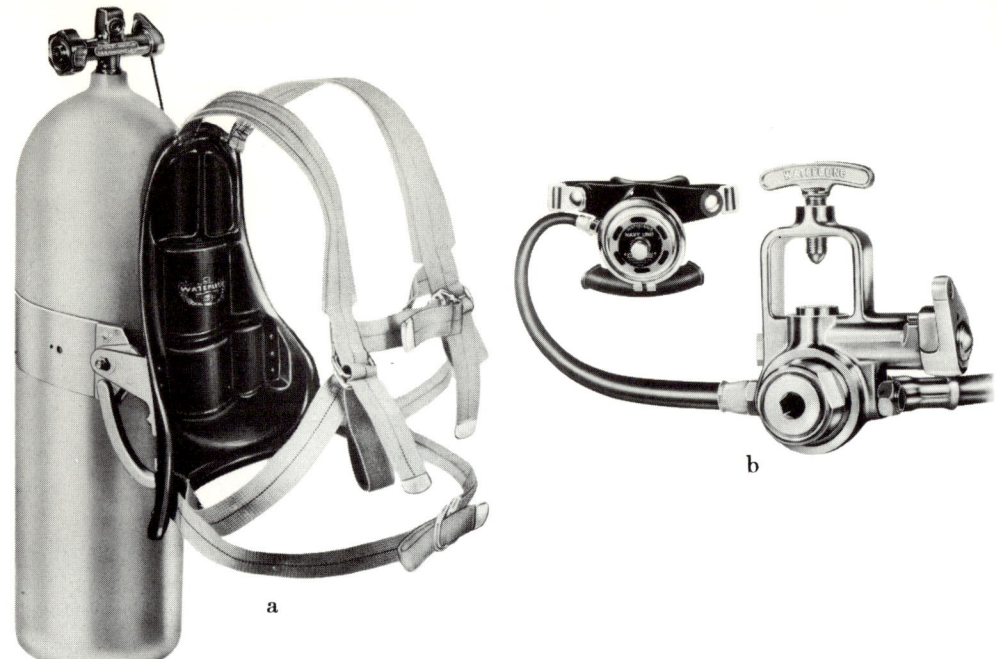

Fig. 105. Sportsways waterlung. Sportsways makes several excellent regulators including a 2-hose. They pioneered the easy-to-reach, shut-off valve at the top of the tank. a. 71.2 cu. ft. tank with Cam Pac harness. The diver needs only one harness to accommodate quick change of tanks. The tanks are galvanized steel, coated with plastic. b. Waterlung Navy Unit with reserve. A "Sea Vue" gage can be attached for determining air pressure remaining in the tank. c. Waterlung divers relax in the Florida sun. *Photo by Ambrose Gaines III, Florida Cypress Gardens*

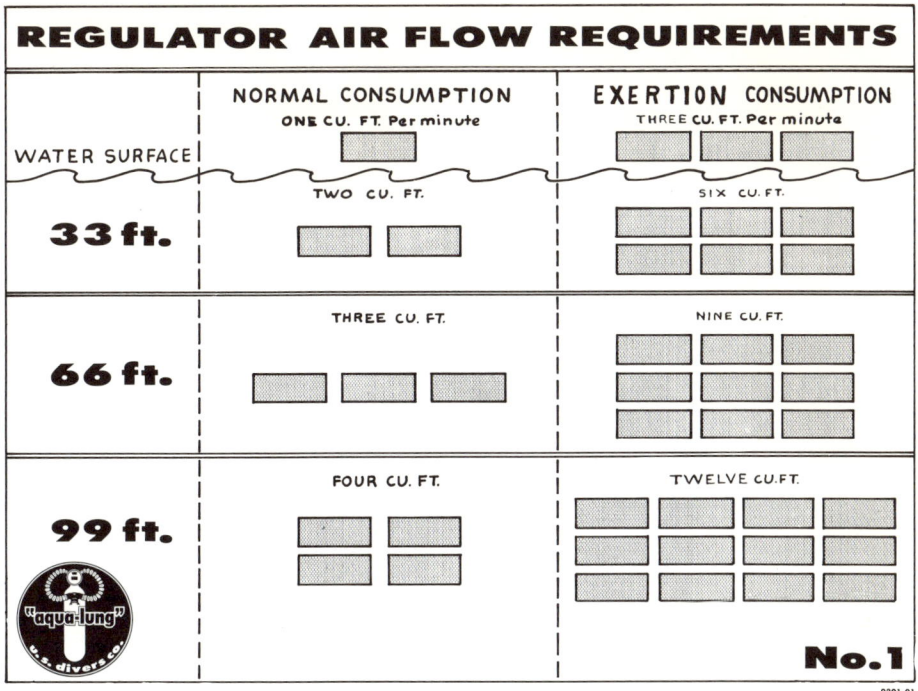

Fig. 106. Increase in Air Flows
The extremely large volumes of air flow demanded from a regulator are illustrated in the drawing above. The figure of 1 cu. ft. per minute normal consumption is not accurate as air consumption varies between individuals. But 1 cu. ft. per minute is close enough to illustrate the huge increase in volume of flow required during exertion. The estimate of three times normal consumption during exertion is conservative. But it is obvious that a tremendous volume of flow is required below 50 feet. At 100 feet, a diver under working conditions consumes 12 cubic feet per minute. This is an enormous air flow. Any restriction to breathing in a regulator will give the same effect as trying to run around the block while breathing through a straw. The large air flows must be obtained with *no increase in suction effort.*

The result of restriction to breathing has been experienced by every "old time" diver who has attempted to work underwater at any appreciable depth. With insufficient volume of air flow he becomes starved for air. Increased suction effort accelerates his exhaustion and causes a demand for ever greater volumes of air flow. At this point even-stopping to rest while still under pressure will not ease the demand for great volumes of flow and the diver is gasping for breath until he returns to more shallow water or the surface. *Courtesy U. S. Divers Co.*

Fig. 107. Many husband-and-wife teams spend exciting hours exploring the fascinating underwater world. The girl is wearing a single-hose Dacor regulator on a single tank. The man is using a "two-hose" Dacor regulator and double tanks. Regulators are interchangeable on several makes of tanks. *Photos taken by Sam Davison Jr. at Weeki Wachee Springs, Florida.*

Fig. 108. Recovery of SCUBA diver from sea by hook which is lifting him into the aircraft. The line attached to his belt will be used to haul up an inflated boat once he is aboard. To enter the water from a helicopter, the frogman simply dives from a reasonable height as the aircraft hovers or, if it is very high, uses a parachute. SCUBA divers were of paramount importance in astronaut recoveries, fastening a flotation collar around the space capsule, opening the door, and assisting the astronauts to the helicopter sling. *Courtesy, Établissement Cinématographique des Armées*

Fig. 109. Early type of French Navy underwater sea scooter, used for recovery work, location of wrecks, underwater exploration, and often for underwater archaeology. The diver steers with his fins the self-propelled vehicle, which operates like a torpedo. Italian divers in World War II were remarkably successful in riding earlier versions of self-propelled torpedoes up to the hulls of British battleships, attaching time charges, and frequently sinking the vessels. *Courtesy, Établissement Cinématographique des Armées*

Fig. 110. Diver is wearing a Unisuit with valved air control. If he wants to carry a heavy object he pushes a button on the suit which sends air inside the suit enabling him to carry or ascend with minimum effort. However, if he should drop it, he would experience an "express ride" to the surface. *Courtesy, Poseidon Systems, USA*

Fig. 111. Divers at work at Perry Oceanographic Hydrolab Habitat. The "Jules Verne effect" of walking on the bottom of the sea is attained by use of the exhaust button on the Unisuit, giving maximum negative buoyancy. *Courtesy, Poseidon Systems, USA*

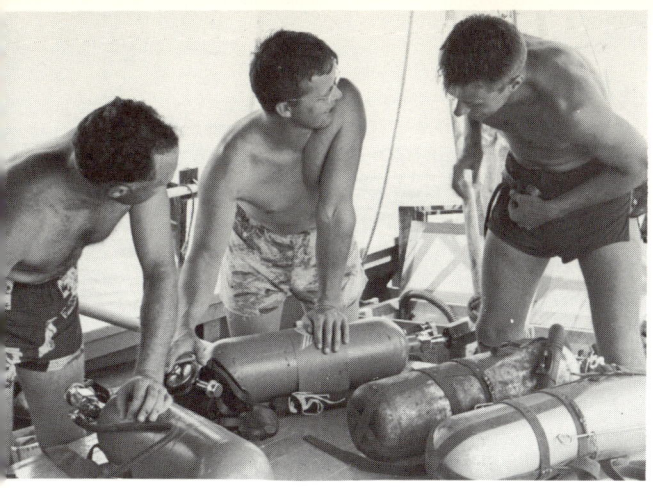

Fig. 112. Safety precautions. a. For maximum comfort, the equipment should be adjusted and in top working order before entering the water.

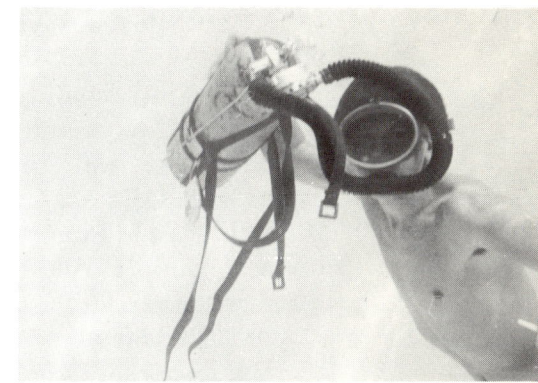

b. Never dive alone. c. Learn to switch tanks underwater. *Photo by George Knoblach*

d. Since impure air can cause a serious and chronic type of pneumonia, cylinders should be filled only at reputable and regularly checked sources of supply. *Courtesy, RKO Radio Pictures*

Basic rules for diving with SCUBA. Reprinted courtesy U. S. Divers Corporation. (*The author's additions are italicized.*)

1. No breathing unit can eliminate the inherent risks of swimming and diving. There is no substitute for the diver's alertness, common sense, and self-discipline. Respect the ocean—avoid panic.

2. Before attempting ocean diving, one should first seek an opportunity to train in a swimming pool.

3. The weight belt should be the last piece of equipment secured to the diver. This will allow it to be quickly released if necessary. The amount of weight to use to offset buoyancy can be determined by preliminary test, considering that when half of your air is used, your buoyancy must be neutral.

4. Never hold your breath. Keep on breathing while returning to the surface and slow up your rate of ascent when near the surface. Take at least 90 seconds to ascend the last 35 feet. Breaking this most important rule may result in air embolism.

5. Shoulder straps, belt, and weight belt must be fastened with "a quick release."

6. If the "Aqua Lung" features a constant air reserve valve, make sure the air supply is closed before submerging (lever up). To release the reserve or to refill the tank, pull the lever down.

7. Avoid undue exertion under water. Do not get out of breath.

8. Use a snorkel to go back and forth from your base (shore or boat) to save your precious supply of air. Blow once into the mouthpiece to clear it of the small amount of water which accumulates between the two non-return valves.

9. Head and regulator should both be either above or below the surface, as air loss (hissing) will otherwise occur.

10. Beginners and users of the shallow water unit without an air reserve device should stay within a depth of 25 feet.

11. Observe the safety curve rules and decompression tables if more than 1 cylinder of air is used below 50 feet during any 6-hour period.

12. Although record dives have been made to 300 feet, amateur divers should not exceed 130 feet.

13. If far away from your base when out of air, swim on your back as this will prevent the weight of the tank from tiring you.

14. Some find it difficult to climb back into the boat with a 2 or 3 tank-block on. It is current practice to slip off the harness while still in the water, get in the boat, and then pull in the equipment. (*Better yet, use a boarding ladder.*)

15. Swimming fins are a "must." Locomotion should depend on the flutter kick only, leaving the arms free for other purposes.

16. Screw the regulator on hand tight before opening the cylinder valve (for a better seal, moisten the washer). If you have a leaky connection:
- A. Turn off the valve.
- B. Breathe out the air from within the regulator.
- C. Tighten up the screw again.

It is impossible to tighten the screw while the full pressure is in the regulator. For the same reason, breathe the air out before taking off regulator.

17. The regulator should never be left on the cylinder when not in use. Never carry the cylinder using the regulator as a hand-hold.

18. Whenever possible, dive two at a time (buddy system) and stay together.

19. Extreme cold may cause fatal accidents. Use a rubber suit when the surface water is below 70 degrees F.

20. NEVER use ear plugs while diving with the "AquaLung."

21. IMPORTANT: The 71.2 cu. ft. tank holds the maximum air capacity to be used in any six-hour period without possible need for decompression.

22. Double and Triple "AquaLung" tank-blocks make it possible for the diver to stay long enough and deep enough to necessitate following the decompression rules during ascent. **Be on the alert!**

23. There is no time limit for diving within 40 ft. with an "Aqua-Lung."

24. Those who suffer from the following should refrain from diving:
- A. Chronic bronchitis, bronchial asthma, emphysema, sinus trouble or a cold. (*In some cases, diving has helped sinus conditions, but check with a doctor first.*)
- B. Perforated ear drums or chronic ear infection.
- C. A cardiac condition (heart trouble) or poor circulation.
- D. A history of having spat up blood or similar condition of the lung.
- E. Use of alcohol, causing a lack of coordination and mental alertness.

25. A normal meal may be eaten several hours before diving, but it should be high in carbohydrates with no gas-forming or heavy foods.

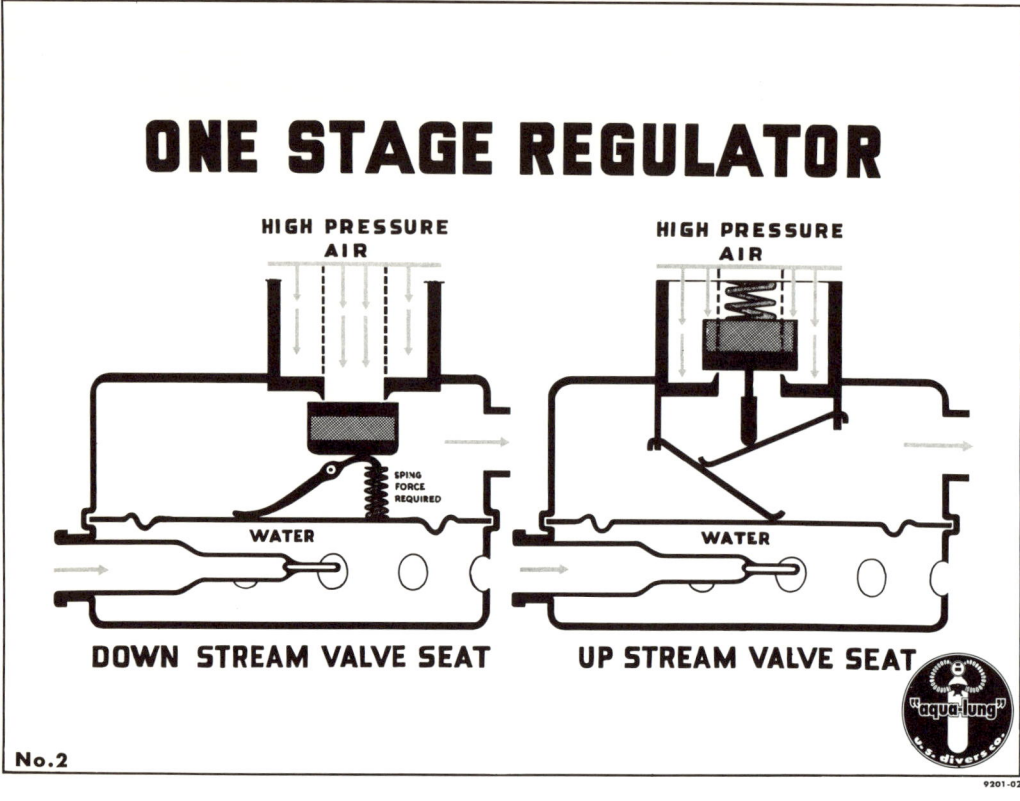

Fig.113. The Upstream and Downstream Single Stage
An engineer designing a regulator mechanism is immediately faced with the problem of variation of pressure from 2,000 psi to 200 psi in the cylinder. This cylinder pressure acts on the valve seat to either open or close the valve depending upon whether the valve opens "downstream" or "upstream" with the flow of air. Both types are illustrated in the drawing above.

In the "downstream" type it is clear that high pressure air entering through the orifice tends to *open the valve*. The force exerted is calculated by multiplying the area of the orifice times the pressure in the cylinder.

This opening force of high pressure air vitally affects the operation of the regulator. A mechanical force, such as a spring, must be balanced against the force of the cylinder air pressure. It is also clear that the opening force will vary with the pressure in the cylinder. A full cylinder of 2,000 lbs. pressure will exert more opening force than when its pressure has dropped to 500 lbs.

In the "upstream" type valve, the variation is exactly the opposite. The high pressure cylinder air acts as a *closing force* and tends to seat the valve. As cylinder pressure drops, this force becomes less, and breathing becomes easier. This is at low cylinder pressure—at the end of a dive. *Courtesy U. S. Divers Co.*

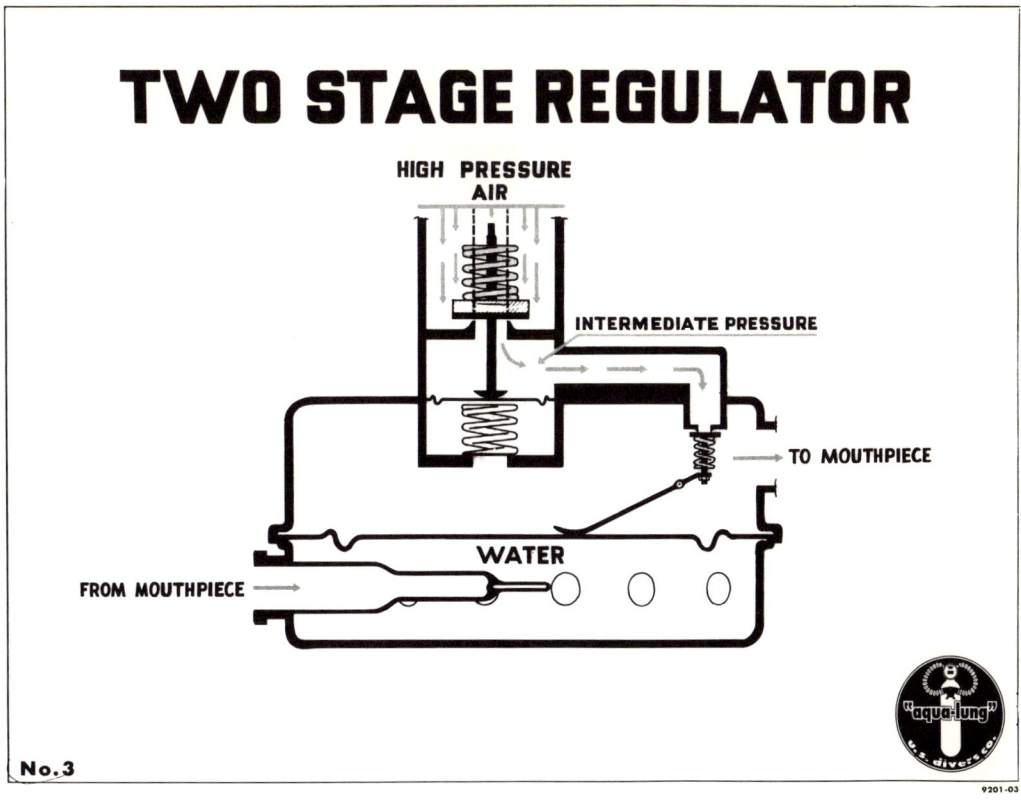

Fig. 113a. Two Stage—Two Hose Type

In this type, high pressure cylinder air is reduced to breathing pressure in two stages. The first stage valve reduces cylinder pressures to a lower predetermined pressure in the intermediate chamber leading to the second stage valve. The large diaphragm activating the second stage valve is then balanced against a much lower and more consistent intermediate pressure.

In the first stage, high pressure cylinder air acts as a closing force tending to push the valve through the orifice. Counteracting the closing force of the cylinder air is a large spring pressing against a small diaphragm with a stem attached to the valve. Movement of the diaphragm, up or down, moves the stem up and down, and opens or closes the valve.

In the second stage, a slight inhalation causes the large diaphragm to move. This opens the second stage valve and allows air to flow to the mouthpiece. In this case, the large diaphragm controls only the low, intermediate pressure leading to the second stage valve.

Since intermediate pressure increases as tank pressure falls, a two stage two hose regulator of this design will breathe easiest when cylinder pressure is low—at the end of a dive when fatigue is a factor. *Courtesy U. S. Divers Co.*

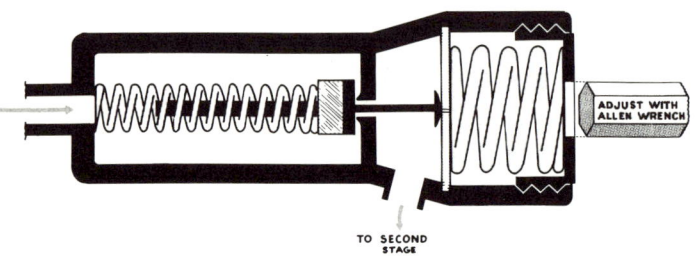

No. 4

Fig. 113b. Ordinary Single Hose First Stage
The standard first stage valve used with single hose regulators works very much the same as the first stage in two hose regulators. The hose leading to the second stage at the mouthpiece carries the intermediate pressure.

Here again, high pressure cylinder air acts as a closing force seating the first stage valve.

The single hose first stage is depth compensated by water pressure which enters the spring area, presses the diaphragm upward and opens the valve. The valve will remain open until air in the intermediate chamber is equal to surrounding water pressure plus the calculated, predetermined pressure.

But we have variation due to changing cylinder pressures. A low cylinder pressure exerts less closing force on the valve. The spring will hold the valve open until intermediate pressure in the hose increases sufficiently to depress the diaphragm and close the valve. In some regulators the increase in hose pressure is as great as 50 percent.

In single hose regulators the diaphragms are much smaller than in two hose regulators and are extremely sensitive to variations in pressure. The number of square inches of surface area in single hose diaphragms is so small that slight variations in hose pressure make a great difference in breathing effort. *Courtesy U. S. Divers Co.*

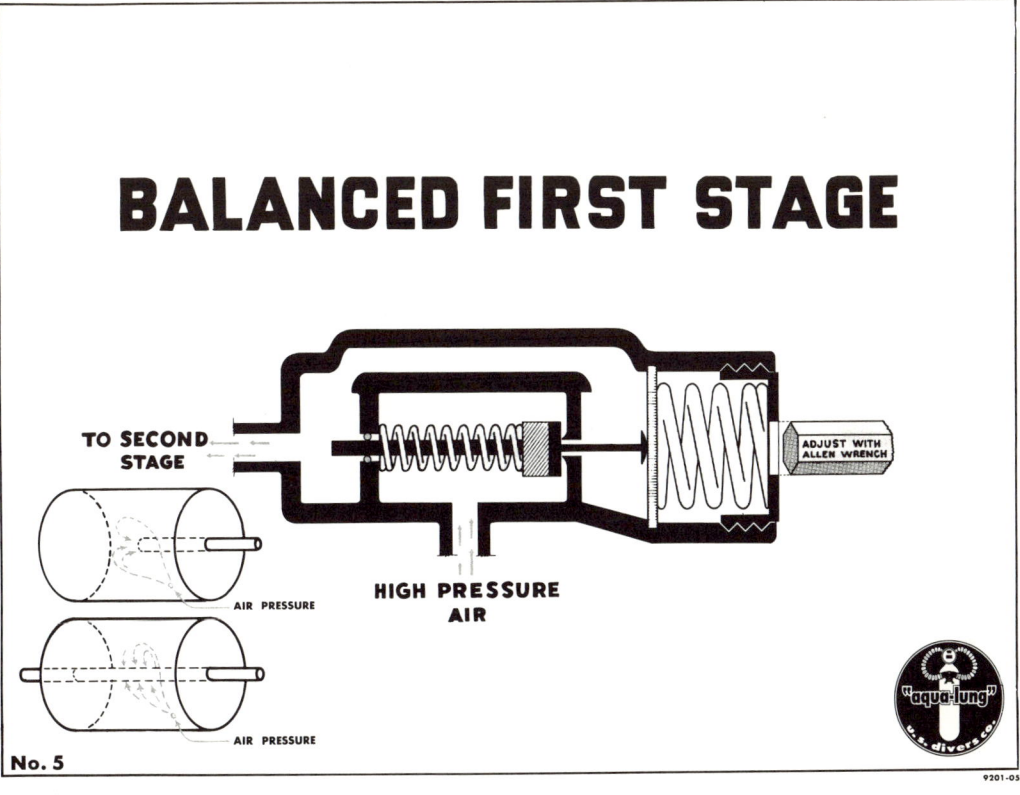

Fig. 114. Balanced First Stage
In the balanced first stage valve, cylinder air pressure has no effect in seating the valve.

The can with the end of the stick inside illustrates an unbalanced valve. Pressure applied to the can tends to drive the stick outside. The diameter of the stick determines the force with which it will be expelled.

The can with the stick completely through it illustrates a balanced valve. Pressure inside the can has no effect on the stick as it is neutralized in all directions. The diameter of the stick makes no difference.

In a balanced valve, a valve stem of exactly the same diameter as the orifice is extended *outside* the chamber. High pressure is not exerted on the end of the valve stem and we have the same result as the stick extended completely through the can.

With cylinder air pressure neutralized, only the mechanical forces of springs affect operation of the valve. These springs can be set to give exactly the desired intermediate pressure. And this pressure will remain the same over all stages of cylinder pressure. With the valve unaffected by variations in cylinder pressure, large orifice diameters can be used to give *large volumes of air flow with no increase in suction effort.*

The balanced valve is also depth compensated. *Courtesy U. S. Divers Co.*

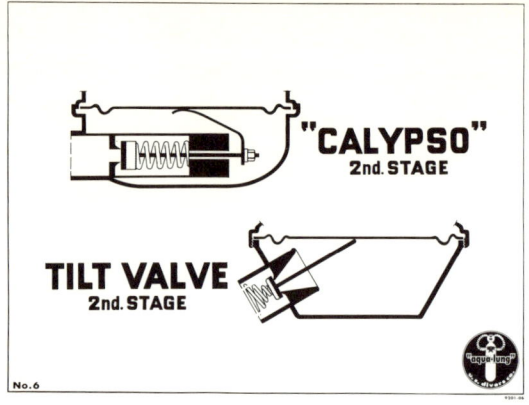

Fig. 114a. Single Hose Second Stages
Most widely used in the second stage of single hose regulators is the tilt valve outlined on the chart. The other second stage mechanism outlined on the chart is that of the Calypso. There are definite, positive advantages in the Calypso mechanism which more than justify its higher cost.

The most important feature is in the *upstream* or *downstream* opening of the valves. A tilt valve opens upstream, against the pressure of air in the hose. Any variation which produces an overpressure in the hose will tend to drive the valve seat against the orifice and increase resistance to breathing. The Calypso type second stage valve opens downstream with the flow of air. An overpressure in the hose tends to make the valve easier to open. Thus, with the variation of a standard first stage valve, this type second stage will breathe easier when cylinder pressure is low—at the end of a dive. *Courtesy U. S. Divers Co.*

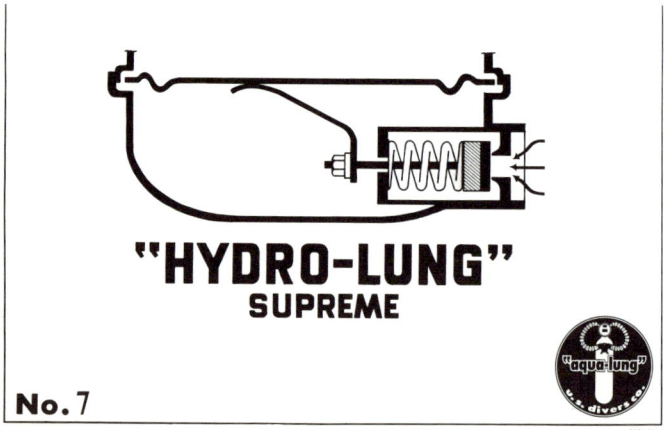

Fig. 114b. Hydro-Lung Supreme—Second Stage
The design of the Hydro-Lung Supreme second stage incorporates the same functional efficiency and Fail-Safe operation as the Calypso. The straight away opening valve gives full flow from the orifice with a slight movement of the lever. The downstream opening valve acts as a relief valve in case of overpressure in the hose. *Courtesy U. S. Divers Co.*

Fig. 115. Jane Russell shows the proper method for getting out of the water using a boarding ladder especially constructed for the use of divers wearing equipment. (Note the air reserve valve is in the down position.) *Courtesy, RKO Pictures*

V
Build It Yourself

Frequently accounts of the drowning of skin divers appear in *Skin Diver* magazine, the public press and periodicals. Most of these accidents have occurred when unsafe weight belts or home-made SCUBA units were used. Some divers may use dangerous home-made lungs and weight belts without safety-release buckles for many months without a mishap. However, such use of itself does not make an item safe. The real test is in an emergency where the improper functioning of a piece of equipment may cause a serious or even fatal accident. Underwater breathing devices are highly technical pieces of equipment on which manufacturers have spent millions of dollars in order to insure safe operation. The average diver does not have the technical skill to reproduce the equipment as well. It is

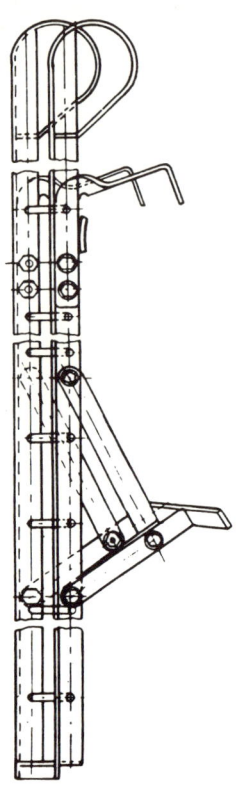

Fig. 116. The diving ladder can be made of wood, steel or aluminum. When using wood, select a good grade of clear white pine (if a hard wood is preferred, use ash or oak) for the side runners and use hardwood for the treads. Leather or rubber fenders can be attached to all the surfaces that touch the boat. The ladder when complete should be about 12 feet long and 3 feet wide. Either paint or varnish the finished product. All metal parts should be painted or made of galvanized steel. The struts that give the correct inclination of the ladder when in use may be folded against the frame after removing the securing bolts for stowing.

not worth the few dollars which may be saved by making an aquatic lung, when a small construction error may cost the diver his life. The price of the commercially made SCUBA units are fairly reasonable and, as more people become active in skin diving, the increase in equipment sales will undoubtedly lower the price even further.

Most of the items listed in this chapter (with the exception of the carbon dioxide gun) are the minor accessories which a diver may use. Therefore it is not completely essential that they be built with the same exacting standards required in the making of the aquatic lungs. In the case of the weight belt, a simple, safe version of a quick-release buckle is given.

As much care as possible should be exercised in their construction for, when carefully made, they will last for many seasons, and any well-built piece of equipment is a source of satisfaction to the diver who makes use of it.

Most of the projects listed here are made of materials that can be obtained at your local hardware store, plumbing supply house or hobby shop. Other materials like packing glands and "o" rings can be obtained from manufacturers.

Sounding Line

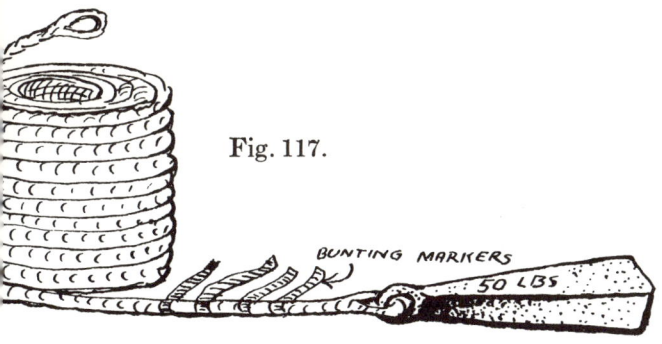

Fig. 117.

When diving deeper than 50 feet (Fig. 117), a sounding line is to be used to measure the depths the diver descends to and for decompression stages. A 1-inch (circumference) cable-laid (to prevent twisting) manila hemp rope is suitable. A 50-pound weight should be attached to the end of the rope to keep it taut when in use. If the tide or currents are too strong, more weight may be needed. The stages should be marked with colored bunting (1″ x 3″) and in 10-foot increments. The following scheme in foot-units is the one used by the United States Navy:

10—1 cloth tag, red	80—3 cloth tags, yellow
20—1 cloth tag, yellow	90—3 cloth tags, blue
30—1 cloth tag, blue	100—4 cloth tags, red
40—2 cloth tags, red	110—4 cloth tags, yellow
50—2 cloth tags, yellow	120—4 cloth tags, blue
60—2 cloth tags, blue	130—5 cloth tags, red
70—3 cloth tags, red	140—5 cloth tags, yellow
	150—5 cloth tags, blue

Underwater Knife

A strong serviceable underwater hunting knife can be made fairly simply in the following way. The diver may always elaborate on this job and produce a conversation piece. Intricate carving on the handle and etching on the blade can dress up this tool most effectively. The first step is in selecting a quality metal for the blade. Stainless,

Fig. 118a.

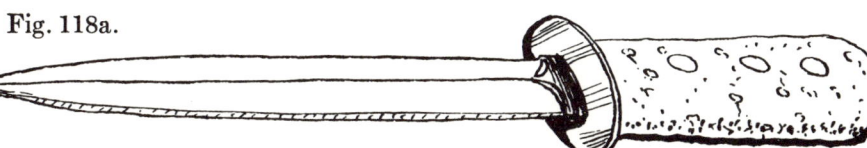

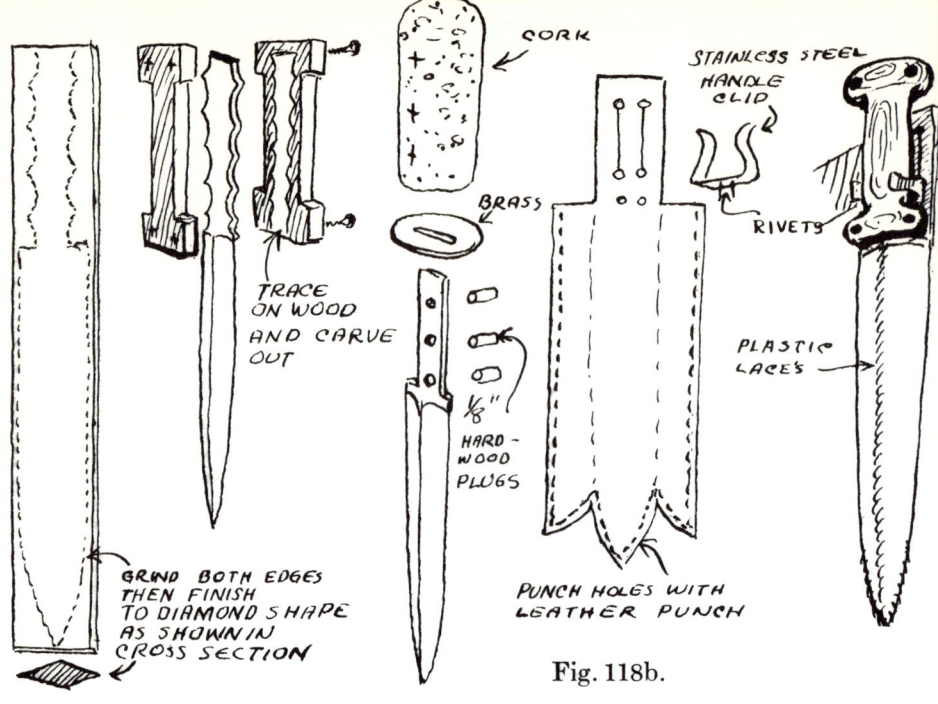

Fig. 118b.

nickel, or chrome steels will resist corrosion, but they do not hold an edge as well as regular steels. The latter metal must be kept well oiled or it will rust rapidly around salt water. For practical purposes, stainless steel is the best, and a piece 15″ by $3/16$″ by 1″ will be needed for the blade. Mahogany, cork, or walnut will work well for the handle. Heavy vinyl plastic is better than leather for the scabbard and can be obtained at most auto seat-cover stores. When gluing the wood together a good grade of waterproof cement must be used. Grind the blade to the shape in the drawing. Trim the handle wood to shape as in the drawing. Attach handles to blade with cement. Countersink and plug the screw holes before finishing with sandpaper. The wood handles should be soaked for about three days in linseed oil when finished. Trim the scabbard neatly out of the material selected, then punch the holes to accommodate the lacing and rivets. Attach the handle clip and cut the belt slits. If cork is being used for the handle, grind the blade square (drill 3 $3/16$″ holes in the handle end), then force the handle into the cork. Be careful to avoid splitting the cork during this operation. Measure the location of the holes on the handle and drill through the cork, making certain they line up so the dowel pins will fit, glue and place the dowels in position and plug the holes before finishing. The handle should then be painted yellow for locating if it should be lost while swimming, as yellow is the most visible color.

Underwater Recon Sled

Fig. 119a. The recon sled is being towed by a boat with a steel cable or nylon rope. The diver can submerge and stay under for as long as the air in the breathing unit will last. *Courtesy, R K O Pictures*

The recon sled is ideal for searching large areas of water quickly. A power boat is needed to tow it through the water. When used, great care should be exercised when near other boats or swimmers in order to prevent accidents. The "exploded view" should give a working idea of how it should be constructed.

The framework can be made of ordinary $3/4''$ pipe. If the joints are welded, make certain all seams are completely sealed, otherwise sea water will soon destroy the piping. Waterproof the threads with pipe-sealing compound at all joints.

The marine-plywood platform should have all the edges sealed with shellac, lacquer, or varnish. When attaching the foam rubber, make sure that all the edges are secure by screwing a furring strip along all edges. Use auto safety glass for the protecting shield. (The mechanic at the glass shop can build this assembly for you if desired.) When insulating the edge of the glass, use a good rubber-to-metal cement to seal the edges into the frame which can be obtained at most auto supply stores. The fore and aft planes and rudder assembly can be made of $1/16''$ sheet metal or marine plywood.

Fig. 119b.

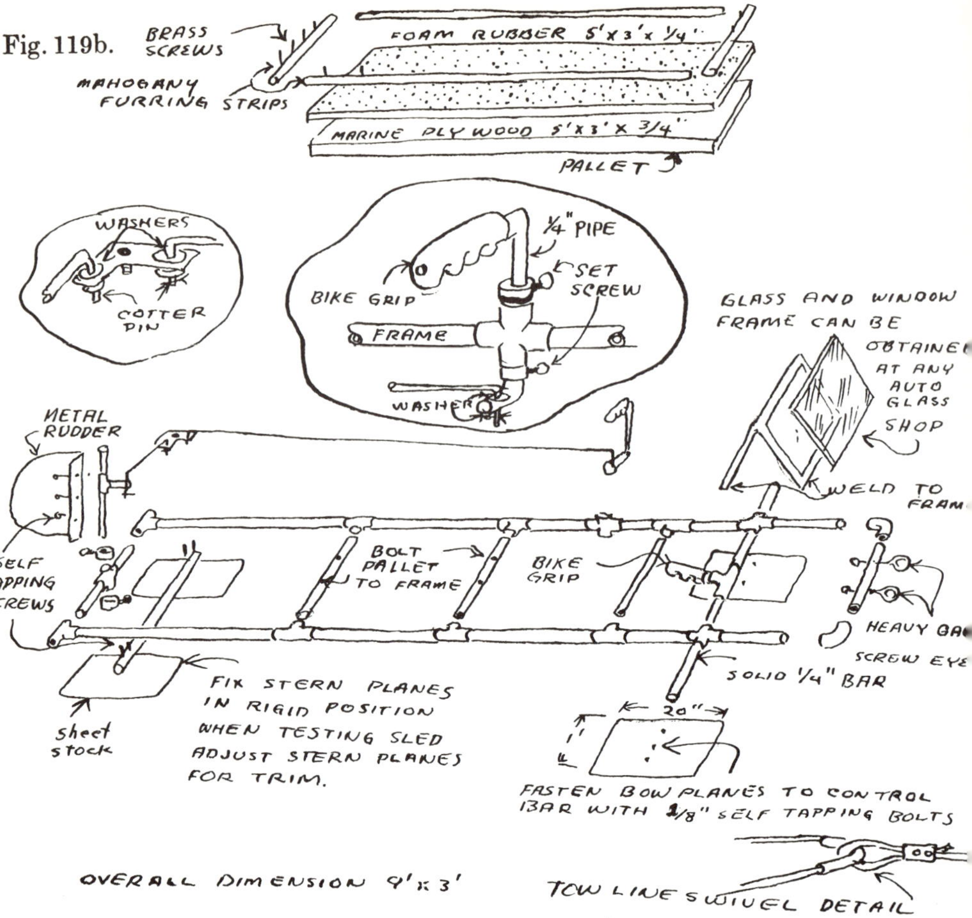

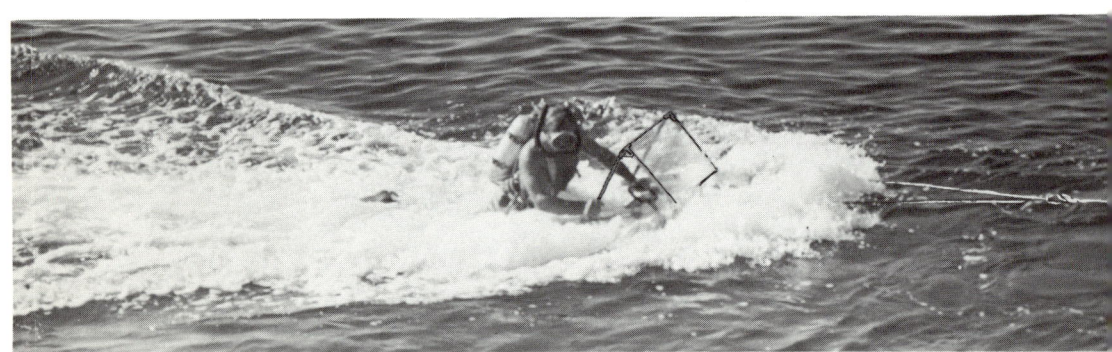

Fig. 119c. Notice the inclination of the window and its supports. The two guy lines that attach the sled to the tow cable are fastened by a heavy swivel. *Courtesy, R.K.O. Pictures*

Warning: If a rate of ascent is greater than 60′ per minute an air embolism may result. Regulate breathing to half breaths while using sled.

All lever arms should have washers on both sides and be kept well greased at all times. Before painting or lacquering the framework, clean all deposits of oil and dirt off the pipes and vanes with lacquer thinner. Then red-lead or yellow-chromite the complete sled before the final paint is applied.

List of materials (o.d.—outside dimension; i.d.—inside dimension):

16′ x 1″ x ⅛″ mahogany furring strips
31′ of ¾″ pipe o.d.
8′ of ¼″ pipe o.d.
4 cross pipe sections ¼″ i.d.
1 ¼″ T-section
4 90° elbows
12′ of ⅛″ steel rod
9 T-elbows
12 ¼″ washers
1 piece of ⅛″ steel plate 1′ square (for rudder)
1 piece of auto safety glass, 3′ x 2′
Assorted sizes of bolts, screw eyes (brass if possible), and wrench set

1 piece of ⅛″ sheet steel 20″ x 4″ (for control planes)
60′ of ¼″ nylon tow line
1 piece of marine plywood 5′ x 3′ x ¾″
1 piece of foam rubber 5′ x 3′ x ¼″ thick
1 quart of red lead paint
1 quart of marine paint, any color
1 tube or can of pipe sealing compound
1 pipe tapping set with ¾″ and ¼″ dies
2 bicycle grips
1 ¼″ drill and bits

Search Pattern

When planning to search a large area of water (Fig. 120a–e), the following layout can be used in conjunction with detailed charts of the area. The buoys can be made out of empty 5-gallon cans, painted and with numbers, and a line attached to a heavy cement weight will usually hold them in position. After the area has been marked off with the buoys, mark their exact position on the chart, making land observations wherever possible. This will simplify the relocation of the buoys if they have to be removed or if a storm destroys the layout.

Fig. 120a.

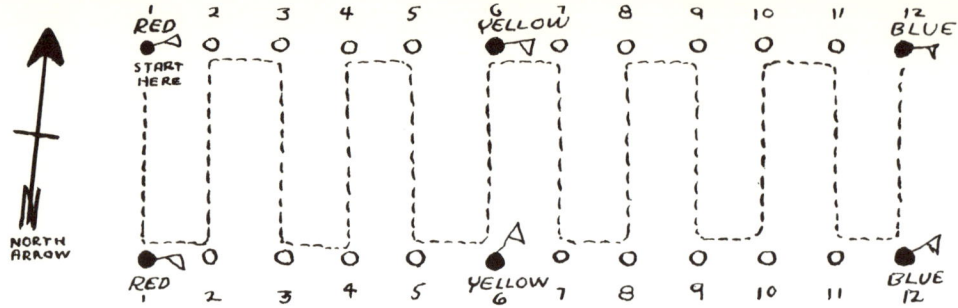

Fig. 120b. The distance between the buoys (*i.e.*, 1—2—3—4—etc.) should be twice the visible underwater distance. That is, the diver can see half the distance from marker 1 to the corner buoy and halfway to marker 2; and from 2 position everything can be observed halfway between 2 and 3, etc. To tighten this pattern, place the numbered buoys so that there is a visual overlap between each increment.

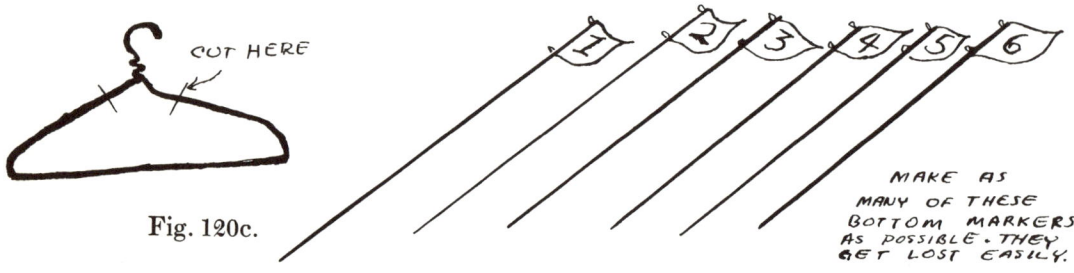

Fig. 120c.

BOTTOM MARKERS. The diver can make these helpful aids out of wire coat hangers with white or yellow markers attached. They can be used to mark areas that have been searched, when there is a possibility of an overlap.

Fig. 120d.

SMALL ITEMS. Nails, bolts, or screws can be carried easily if sandwiched between two long strips of scotch tape and then fastened to the diving belt. The Army engineers sometimes use rope to act as a carry-all similar to the sketch shown.

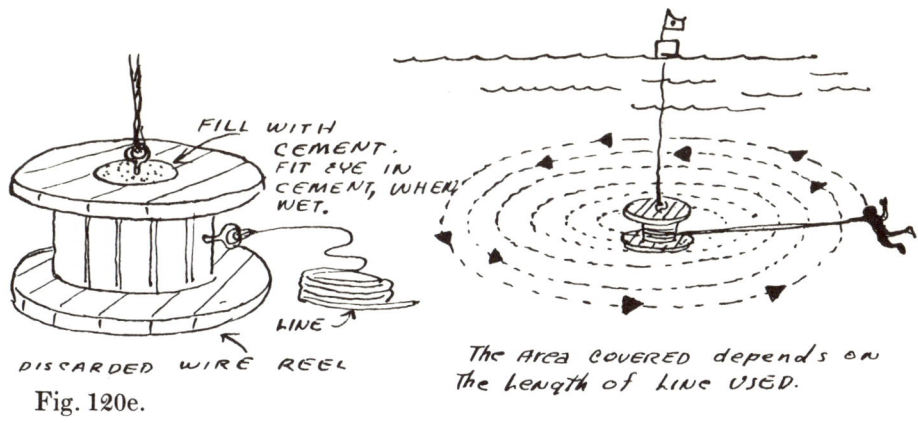

Fig. 120e.

THE CIRCULAR SEARCH. In order to make a thorough search of a circular area where the bottom is fairly level, an old discarded wire reel can be converted into a helpful tool. When it is weighted with cement, the diver by swimming in either direction will wind up his line on the drum.

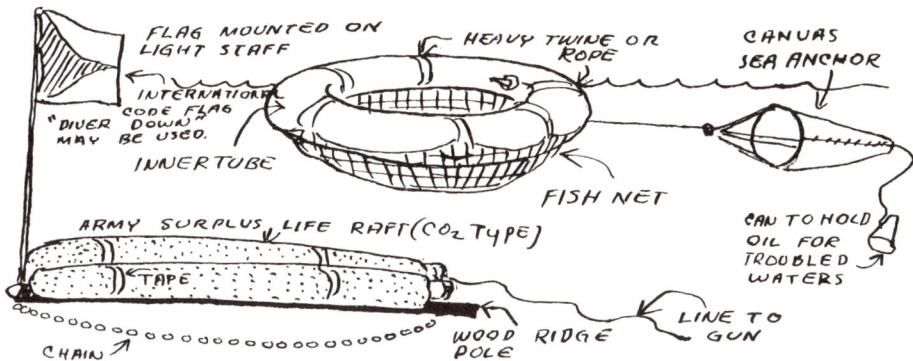

DIVING FLOAT. A belt life raft that can be obtained from most Army and Navy stores can be converted into a serviceable float. The addition of the flag may be necessary when diving in areas where there is a lot of boat activity, or when swimming in front of surf casters.

Fig. 121. Adapting a surf board for diving. *Photo by Mel Small*

Fig. 122. Camera case is a self-built plastic case for a Leica camera. The film transport, speed, and shutter release are all located on the outside of this case. This case costs about $15 to build. Fig. 122a (below) is a plastic Rolleiflex case which features outside manual controls and a synchronized flash attachment. Fig. 122b of the movie case (right) is built out of a Navy surplus pressure cooker and contains a battery powered Bolex movie camera. *Photos by George Knoblach*

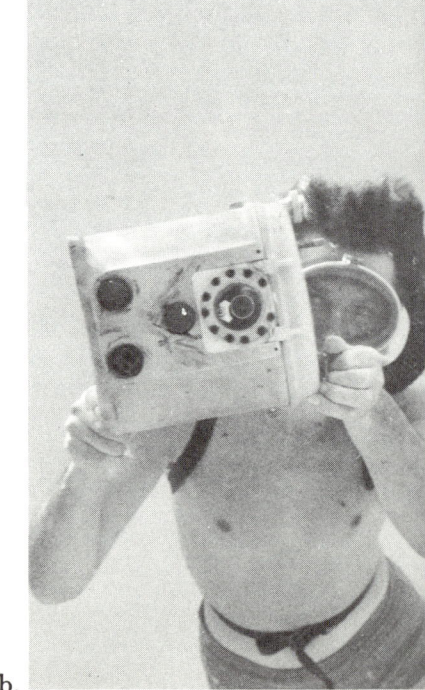

b.

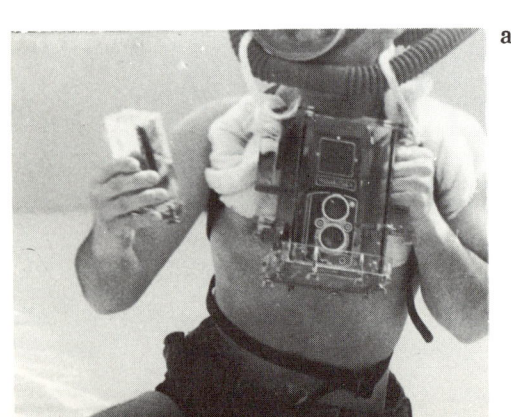

a.

Underwater Still Camera Housing

As there are many types, sizes, and styles of cameras which can be adapted for underwater use (see also Chapter VIII), only the basic principles will be given. From them the diver can adapt the couplings, lever arms, and glands to his own particular case design. When built properly the case should keep out all water; the joints of plastic can be sealed with plastic cement. Use at least ¼" plastic when this material is used. Wood is cheap and can be fashioned into a serviceable housing. In some instances a rubber bag can be used after a glass porthole has been installed. The main drawback with this type of arrangement is that the camera case must withstand the total pressure of the surrounding water which otherwise may crush the camera. This type of case must only be used in shallow water. Also the camera may shift inside the bag causing a distorted or faulty picture, or the rubber may tear resulting in expensive repairs. So if an expensive camera is to be used underwater, a suitable housing should be made for it. To test a housing for leaks after it has been built, simply lower it in the sea to the depth you plan to photograph.

Fig. 123a. Exploded view of camera.

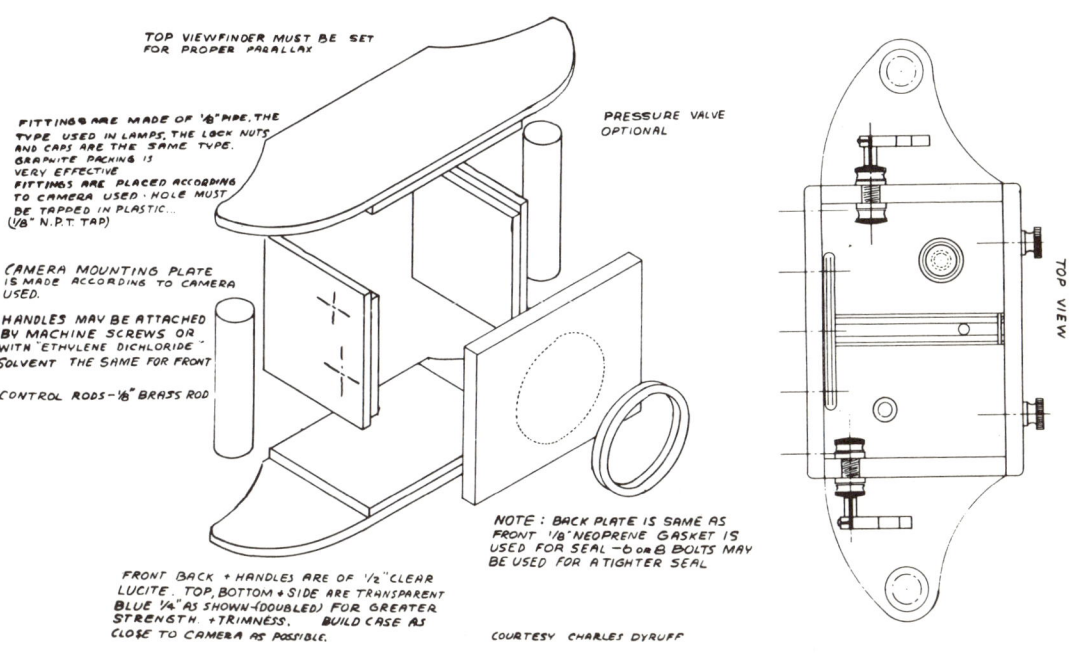

Fig. 123b. Shallow water case.

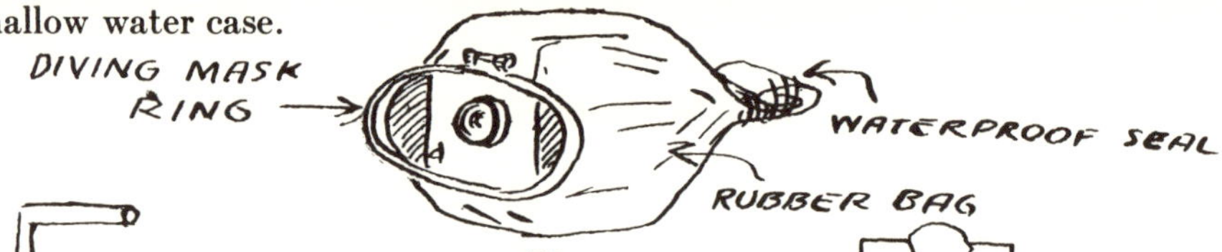

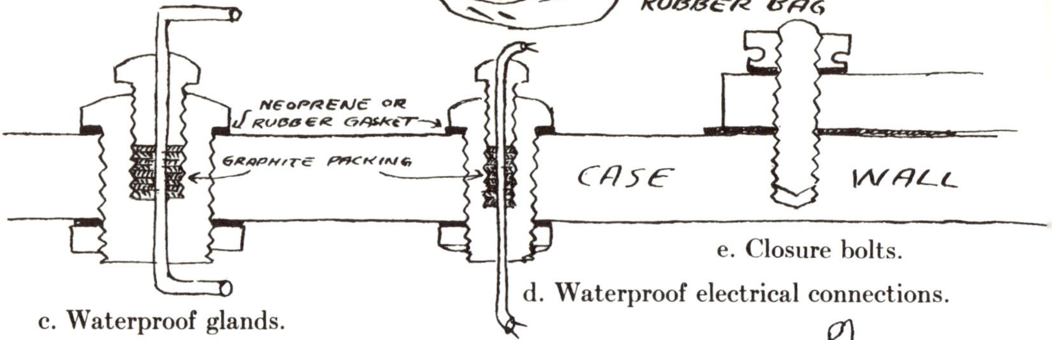

c. Waterproof glands.

d. Waterproof electrical connections.

e. Closure bolts.

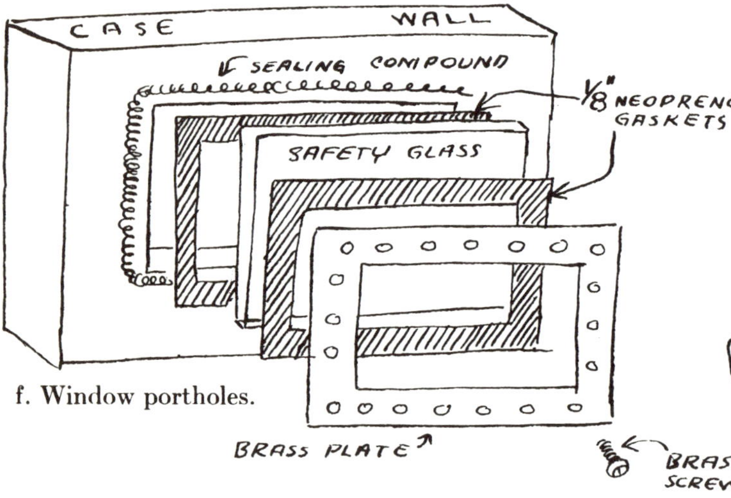

f. Window portholes.

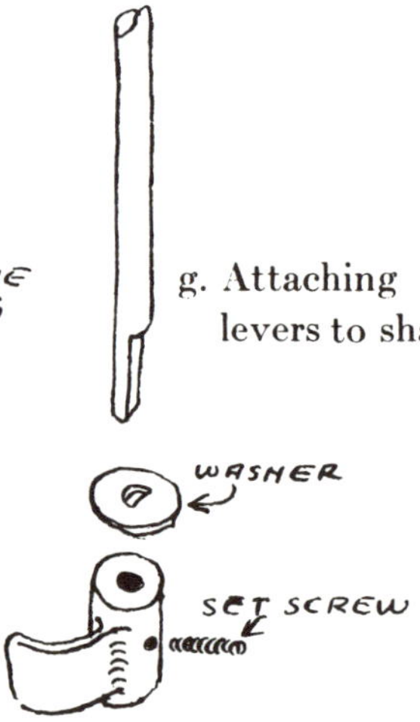

g. Attaching levers to shaft

Fig. 124. The Leica camera case shown is cast aluminum. This material is ideal for 35 mm. cameras as the housing, when designed properly, will withstand great pressures, and will endure hard knocks. To build a metal case requires considerable skill, as wood patterns must be fashioned first, then meticulous machining follows, in order to insure a completely watertight seal. This rig features the aquaphot porthole (see Chapter VIII), which can be adapted to most underwater housings if the manufacturer's instructions are followed. *Courtesy, ALPHA Photo, Inc.*

Weight Belt

The importance of having a weight belt has been mentioned in several places in this book. They can be simply made. Figure 125 shows several of the various types the diver can make and a few of the commercially available ones. Every weight belt must have a safety-release closure before it is worn in the water.

Use about 1½ yards of 1½-inch webbing. Now cut or bend out of heavy gauge brass a horseshoe ring. Attach this ring to the belt with a rubber band or a short piece of nylon line.

To make the mold to cast the lead weights, make two halves out of hard wood or ceramic clay. Have a wire ring to hold the mold together while the metal is being poured. Make extra weights and have them available on all diving trips. Remember, the weight belt is expendable.

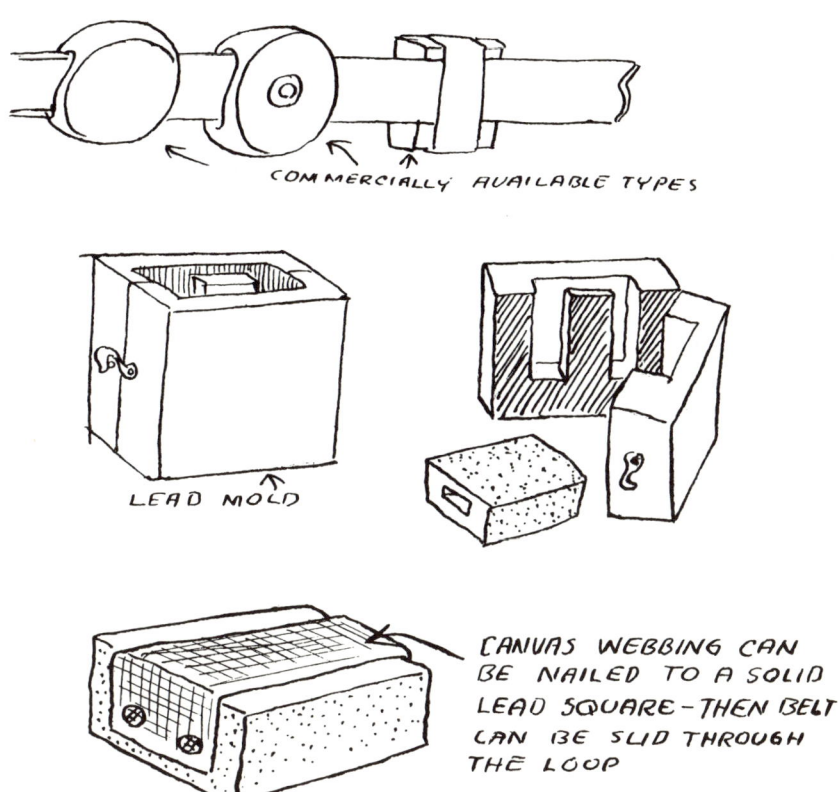

Fig. 125. Lead molds.

Safety-Release Buckles

Materials needed for the safety-release buckle:
$1/16''$ copper or brass plate $2'' \times 2''$. Drill $1/16''$ holes in each corner.

$3/4''$ brass or copper bar $1\frac{1}{4}''$ long. Drill $1/8''$ hole in bar $1/8''$ from end and silver-solder to brass plate in center. Rivet brass plate to belt at end of left side of webbing.

Put 5 grommets $1''$ apart on belt webbing right side and jock strap starting $1''$ from end of straps that have been rolled over $1/4''$ and riveted. Make a release pin of $1/8''$ brass and solder to a $2''$ brass ring. Attach to this ring a heavy rubber band about $4''$ long and then attach to belt.

When attaching tank to the harness, use the straps that come with the tank to lash it to the frame.

Be sure to have an inflatable life preserver attached to the frame and one to the diver whenever the SCUBA is used. Figure 126 shows other types of safety-release buckles.

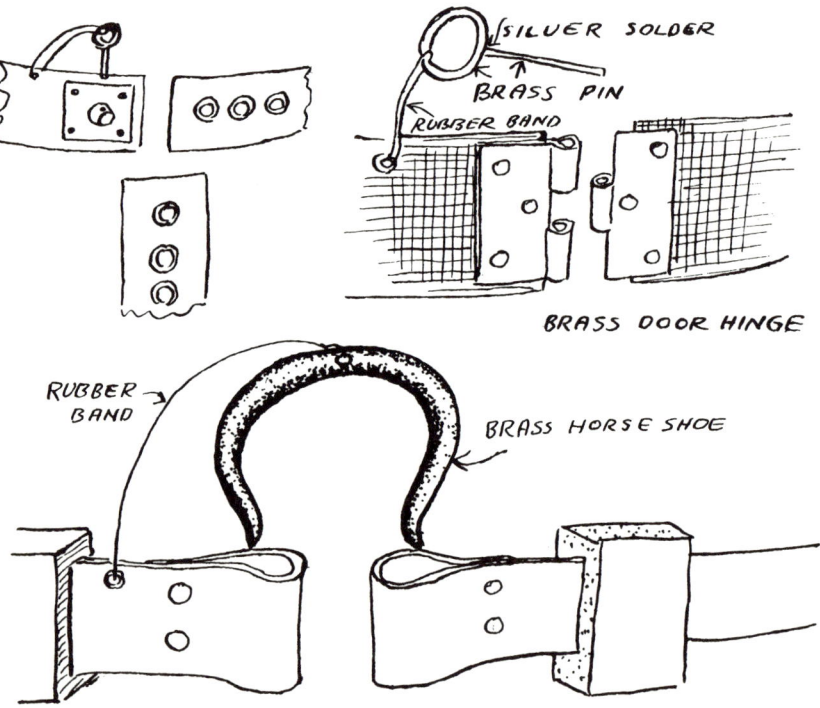

Fig. 126. Safety release buckles.

Salvage Balloons

The salvaging of boats or objects of considerable size, when block and tackle or salvage barges are not available, may be carried out by the use of gas-filled balloons which are often just as effective. The following chart gives an idea of the underwater lifting power of air balloons.

Lifting Capacity of Gas-Filled Balloons

Balloon Size in inches Diameter	Lifting Weight	Cubic Feet of Gas Required To Fill Balloons	
		(90 ft.)	(180 ft.)
20	140 (lbs.)	4.4	8.8
30	490 (lbs.)	15	30
40	1175 (lbs.)	41	82
60	3930 (lbs.)	90	247
80	9460 (lbs.)	280	565
120	14 (tons)	989	1977
160	33 (tons)	2366	4731
200	65 (tons)	4590	9231
240	113 (tons)	7985	15960
280	180 (tons)	12762	25423

Courtesy, Dmitri Rebikoff

The procedure to follow when salvaging a large boat can roughly be seen by considering the following factors. Salvage is not a simple job but it is interesting and at times a profitable one. However, the old maxim of "finders keepers" may not always be the case (see Chapter IX).

1. Make an accurate reconnaissance of the site.
2. Take pictures if you have the time (every compartment and the surrounding area).
3. Make a model of the wreck, for testing in a water tank.
4. Obtain plans of the boat from the builder.
5. If plans are unavailable, have divers measure every compartment.
6. Estimate how many balloons it will take to raise the boat, following the chart above.
7. Make paper pattern of the rooms that are to contain the balloons.

8. Fabricate the balloons following instructions furnished by the Du Pont Company, Wilmington, Delaware. The balloons should be made of heavy weight sheet vinyl.

9. Attach a high pressure fitting to each balloon.

10. All rooms that will contain air bags should have all sharp edges covered.

11. Fold the bags accordion-fashion and place in wreck.

12. Place a large nitrogen bottle beside each room with enough hose to attach to the inlet valve.

13. Have a diver operating each valve.

14. If the boat is resting in mud, a high-force water hose will be needed to loosen the mud as the balloons are inflated.

15. First try the salvage procedure on the model that has been constructed. Do this in a large aquarium tank. By following this procedure you will get an idea of how the boat will react when the balloons are filled.

16. Follow the lessons learned in raising the model, when raising the boat.

17. Every boat will have its own particular problems. The method here offered is a fairly simple technique for salvaging. Many other problems will arise at the site and require additional equipment and men.

Sea Anchor

When using inner tubes or surfboards, or other floating equipment as a base while spearfishing, have a sea anchor along to prevent the wind from blowing it away. It can be constructed simply as shown below.

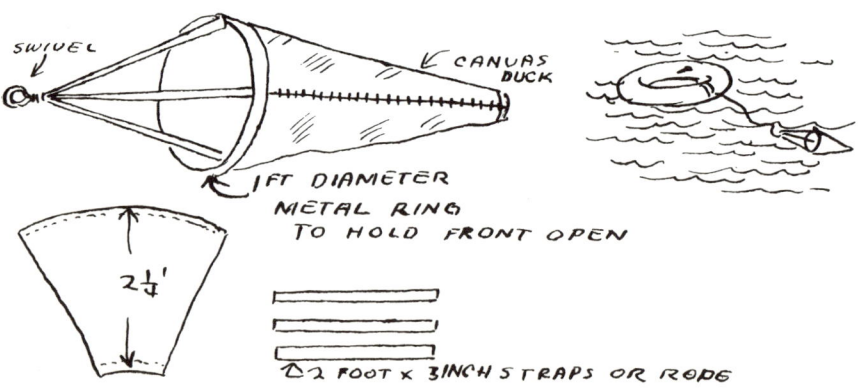

Fig. 127.

Hand Spear

The hand spear is the simplest of the many types of underwater weapons. Anyone with a little skill can make one of these versatile spears. The following is a description of the materials and method of making it:

1. Shaft of 10″ length, ¼″ diameter steel.
2. Winged barb spearhead with leader of cable and snap-on type swivel.
3. 15′ of 50-pound test, cotton or nylon line.
4. Rubber ring to secure line to pole. (See that steel shaft is slotted on end for holding the winged barb spearhead.)
5. Type of pole (recommended): Either a bamboo, or wooden pole of fir dowling, approximately ¾″ in diameter and from 8 to 10 feet long.

To assemble:

1. Drill hole in the end of the pole to about a 3″ depth. Be certain to get a perfectly centered alignment.
2. Drive steel shaft into hold so that it fits securely.
3. The line should be attached about 4″ from the shaft-end of the spear. The other end should be tied into a loop for attaching the snap-on spearhead.
4. Additional wrapping of copper wire is recommended. However, this is not absolutely necessary and is optional.

You now have completed for use a thrust-type spear.

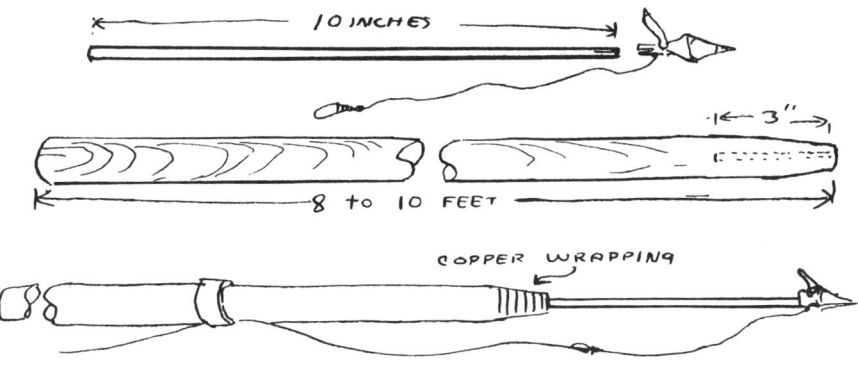

Fig. 128.

Hawaiian-Sling-Type Spear

To make this spear into a rubber-propelled type, use a length of heavy rubber, preferably 2 feet of surgical-type tubing available from Sea Net under stock number R-100 or at any machine supply store.

Drill a ⅛″ hole about ¾″ from the handle end of the shaft, looping and tying off both ends of the rubber band or tubing to make a sling.

To operate as a sling spear, loop the rubber sling between the forefinger and thumb, grip the pole and stretch the string until a comfortable tension can be felt. At this point, the spear should be tape wrapped to insure a good grip on the pole.

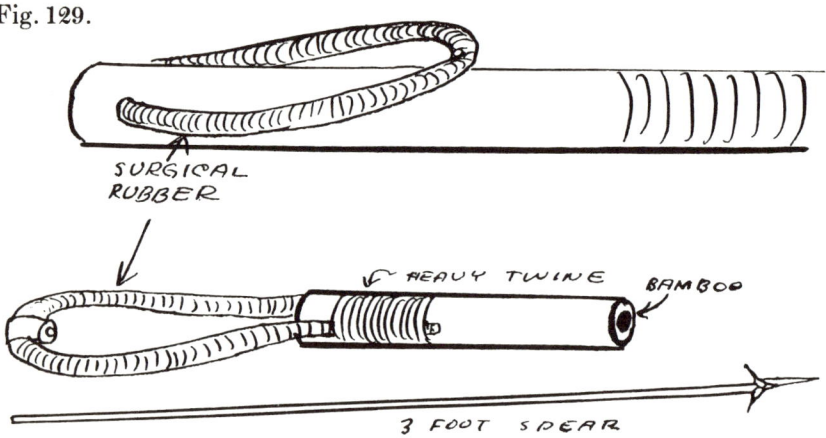

Fig. 129.

Spearheads

Figure 130 shows a few of the many types of spearheads you can make. Use a good grade of steel.

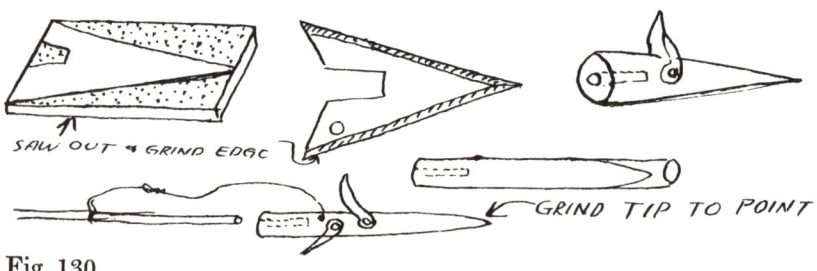

Fig. 130.

Gas-Powered Gun

The gas-type gun which we will discuss here contains a constant pressure of 849 pounds per square inch, at 70° F., so you can readily see the need for proper handling.

There are two models which can be constructed with few tools and a minimum of cost. One type may be completed in 30 minutes for about $2.00. This will be a little difficult to operate until you become accustomed to its use. Figure 131 (top) shows the above-mentioned type.

For type #1, we need a 211 size trigger-type carbon dioxide fire extinguisher; one 36″ length of aluminum tube, 3/8″ outside dimension, 1/4″ inside dimension, outside tapped to a 1/8 pipe thread; a solid aluminum 1/4″ rod, 36″ long; metal strapping; a piece of wood 6″ x 4″ x 1″.

The first step is to screw the tubing to the swivel on the fire extinguisher, then bend the tube without a sharp kink along the cylinder. The wood is then cut so that it fits the curve of the cylinder and forms a handle about 1″ wide. The metal strapping is then placed over the tubing and made fast to the handle. We are now ready to use the gun for an enjoyable sport. After the season is over, by removing the tubing and having the cylinder refilled, you can use the tank as a fire extinguisher until you are again ready for fishing.

For the second type we must expend a little more time and money, but still there is a saving over a commercial-type gun. Fig. 131 (bottom) shows us a gun much easier to use, but that can only be used as a gun, not again as a fire extinguisher, once adapted.

For type #2 we need a 2-pound size trigger-type carbon dioxide fire extinguisher, a 36″ length of aluminum tube, 3/8″ o.d., 1/4″ i.d., outside tapped to 1/8 pipe thread, a solid rod 36″ long as a spear, metal strapping, a piece of wood 6″ x 4″ x 1″. Also a 1/2″ (high pressure steel) close nipple, a 90° elbow 1/2″. The first few steps will have to be done by a carbonic repair or fire extinguisher recharge station, as they have special tools for this work. First the valve and siphon tube must be removed and the siphon cut to about 2″ from the valve. The nipple is then tightened into the cylinder with Expando or similar valve compound. The valve is now screwed into the elbow which is then tightened to the nipple again using compound. The steps that follow can be done by you the same as for type #1, except that you do not bend the tube.

The fire extinguisher used may be purchased at a fire extinguisher or Army surplus dealer. A used one is just as good as a new one and half the price. When purchasing the cylinder, look on the shoulder below the serial number for a marking such as this, 9–49, showing the date of last hydrostatic test, meaning that the tank was pressure tested to at least 3,000 pounds per square inch in September, 1949. If the mark is over five years old, which it may well be, it will be necessary to have it tested again as local and Federal laws deem it illegal to fill unless tested within a five-year period. This may cost about $3.50, but it is well worth it. For recharge, it should be sent to a reliable fire extinguisher dealer as they have the necessary repair parts, should a leak develop in the valve.

To lessen the recoil when using, it is a good idea to drill four small holes about 2″ from the end of the barrel; this will allow the gas to escape in all directions.

The reason for suggesting that the above work be done professionally is that the gas is under very high pressure and that in the home workshop you cannot ordinarily make the connections between the valve, elbow, and cylinder leakproof.

If desired you may attach a 50- to 75-foot nylon line to the spear by means of a screw eye. Caution should be exercised when using this device for if the line should snag, it may turn the spear back in your direction.

Fig. 131.

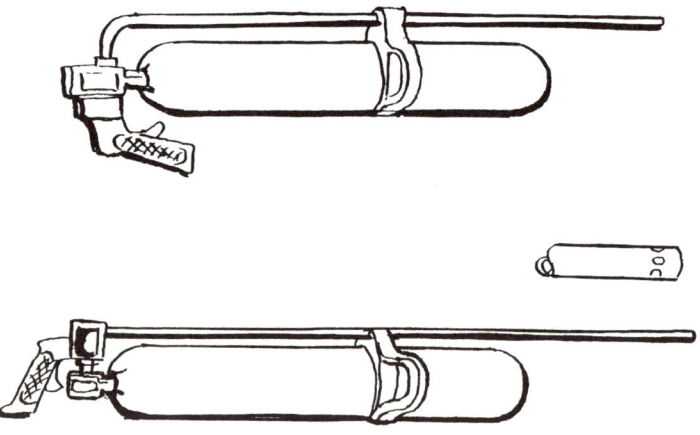

Tool Case

A tool case can be constructed simply and is ideal for carrying all the items the diver may need while on a trip. The pouch can be made of heavy canvas, plastic, or leather, 12" x 15", using 6 yards of plastic lacing and 1 foot of nylon or cotton line for the tie cord. All the items that are to be kept in the case should be well greased in order to prevent corrosion that occurs from salt water. If canvas duck is used, additional protection against corrosion can be achieved simply by impregnating the canvas with oil after the case is completed. Other items that may be included might be spare parts for spear guns, or tips, extra straps, loading bars, etc. The case can be made either larger or smaller simply by altering the dimensions shown on the sketch.

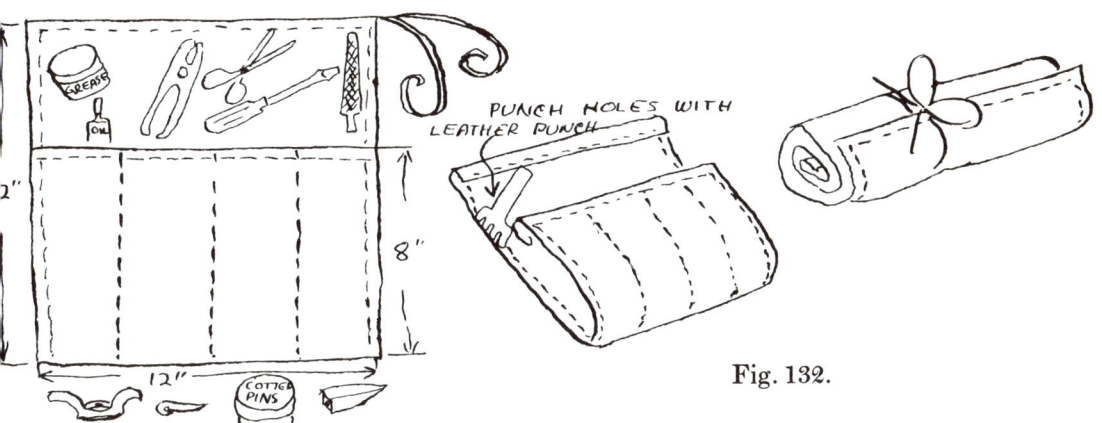

Fig. 132.

Skin Diving Belt

A serviceable yet safe underwater hunting belt is a welcome accessory for most skin divers. When completed the diver will have a handsome, rugged piece of equipment that will help him in organizing the many items he may need while underwater. All of the parts used in the construction of this belt can be purchased at a hobby or craft store. The pouch for spare spear tips can be either purchased (any small coin purse that has a closure than can be opened or closed with one hand) or made. No lines for fish or other items that may injure the diver should be attached to the eyes on this belt. The belt must have a safety-release catch if it is to be considered safe for diving (see Fig. 126).

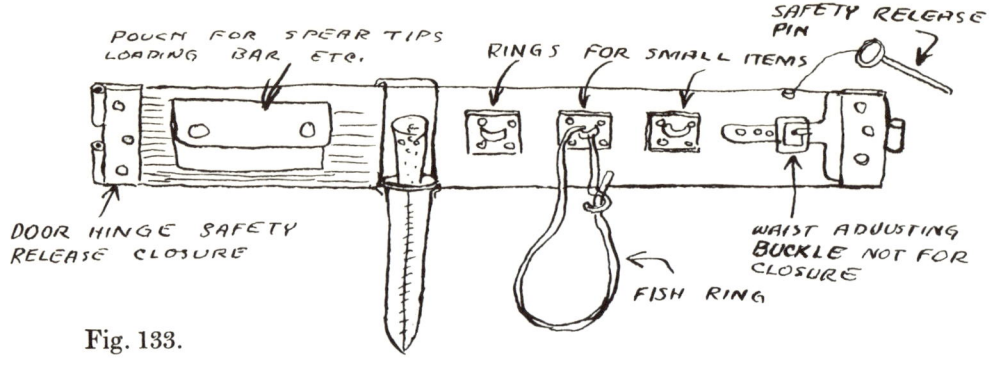

Fig. 133.

Marking Board

Underwater marking boards are ideal for the skin diver who wants to make sketches or keep records of the things seen or experienced below the surface. The crayon marks can easily be erased from the plastic board with a rag. A small chain or a rubber band can be used to attach the crayon to the board.

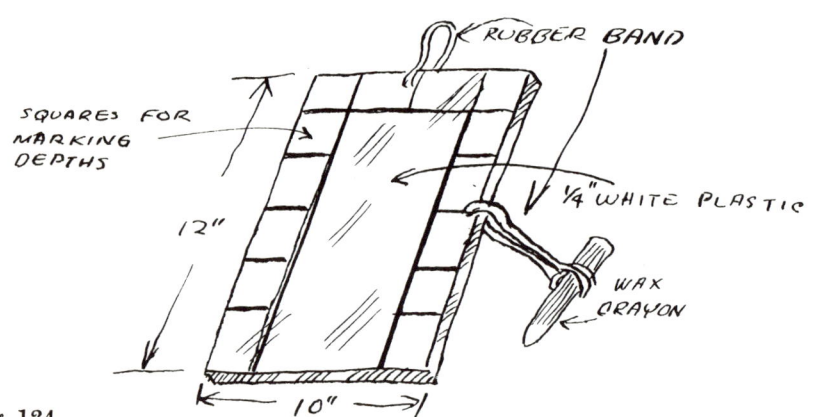

Fig. 134.

There are many things the diver can build that are not listed here. Among them are: carrying cases for **SCUBA** units, spearhead cases made out of wood, regulator cabinets, underwater flashlights, underwater speaking devices, diving platforms, and others.

As a note of caution about building underwater appliances, always consider the safety factor as of first importance in building any such equipment.

Photo by George Knoblach

VI The Techniques of Spearfishing

An aspect of skin diving which today attracts many sportsmen is the fast-growing sport of underwater spearfishing, recently formally recognized by the Amateur Athletic Union as a national amateur sport.

The idea of catching fish with spears is not new. Many primitive peoples speared fish for food, and wall paintings and statues show that the ancient Egyptians fished with spears. The major difference between spearfishing then and now is that the skin diver spears his fish while completely submerged in the water, a condition which was made possible by the development of the diving mask that permits the underwater swimmer to see what is around him.

The practice of spearing fish originally acquired a bad reputation, which is still reflected in the prohibiting laws of many states, for as practiced before the advent of underwater spearfishing, it in-

Fig. 135. The easy way—an Egyptian head of the family is supported by his wife and daughter as he spears fish from a boat. From a wall painting in an Egyptian tomb in Thebes.

volved spearing or gigging fish, often at night, using lights to attract them. Underwater spearfishing, however, is at least as sportsmanlike a procedure as rod and reel fishing, since the diver matches his wits and skill against the fish which have the advantages of speed and of being in their own element, while the diver must come up periodically for air. (No true underwater sportsman spears fish while wearing a SCUBA.) The real underwater sportsman only spears fish he intends to use for food, or occasionally, if he is highly skilled and accompanied by companions for safety, he may spear dangerous or difficult fish such as sharks, barracuda, moray eels, and large rays. But he never kills fish wantonly and wastefully, and ignores the merely decorative or the inedible fish. He never spears fish in order to sell them, and he obeys all laws of his state in regard to the purchase of a fishing license and the spearing of fish. (The "Maine" lobster must never be speared.) Many skin diving clubs work with conservation authorities and try to help preserve rare or overfished species. Underwater spearfishermen should also stay away from nets belonging to commercial fishermen and should avoid antagonizing commercial or rod and reel fishermen. The wise diver knows that by observing the above rules he will help to preserve the sport of spearfishing for the enjoyment of himself and others.

Spearfishing can be done using simple hand spears with rubber

Fig. 136. Ed Bair of the Sons of the Beaches Club with a 10-pound moray eel caught with a hand spear. This can be dangerous (see the Vernon Brock incident in Chapter II) and is definitely not for the amateur.

powered slings or with powerful spear guns. But probably the first problem of the underwater fisherman is learning where to find fish. Many a diver has gone hungry because he has picked the wrong area in which to fish and has found it puzzlingly empty of fish.

The characteristics of the water and of the bottom terrain have a great deal to do with whether or not an area will be populated with fish. Poor fishing areas are sand bottoms with sparse vegetation, unprotected beaches with strong surf, dirty, polluted water, and muddy bottoms. Charts which can be obtained from the United States Coast and Geodetic Survey (Washington 25, D.C.) may be helpful, since they indicate the type of bottom found in various localities. The color of the water is also an indication: deep blue or green water means the water is deep, in surf areas of white foam indicate submerged reefs, and brownish areas show sand bars. Waves which do not break until they reach shore mean a sloping beach with no reefs nor rocks.

The best areas for fish seem to be around irregularities of the bottom such as reefs, wrecks, or large underwater rocks. Also good are areas where shallow water drops off into the depths along the edge of a sandbar since here larger game fish often lie in wait for animal life which inhabits the shallows. In fresh water lakes the larger game fish seem to lurk near the bottom at twenty to thirty feet, at the line where the vegetation ends as you go out from shore. (In many states spearfishing in lakes is still forbidden.)

Certain times are also better for fishing than others. Many forms of marine life dislike and avoid strong light. During the daylight hours, certain species of fish will be found in the lower areas of light penetration, but at night they move upward toward the surface to

Fig. 137. Spearfisherman Phil Evans brings in a 47-pound striped bass. *Photo by Paul Tzimoulis*

feed. At night, also, tidal pools and beaches swarm with life that is hidden in the daytime. So, the spearfisherman is most likely to find fish near dawn or toward the last daylight hours when they will be feeding nearer the surface. More fish will also be found near shore at high tide than at low tide, and more when the tide is coming in than when it is receding.

Once a good fishing area has been located, the procedure followed depends on the type of fish sought and on the fisherman's choice of weapon. Many skilled spearfishermen have stated that the greatest sport lies in the skillful use of the hand spear (see Chapter IV for description of weapons), since with this primitive weapon the hunter's skill and endurance are all-important in catching fish. Rodney Jonklass, the well-known advocate of the hand spear, tells of spearfishermen catching an average of forty to sixty pounds of fish a day, using an eight-foot barbless brass and steel hand spear, including several types of fast-swimming fish, groupers up to forty pounds and a 120-pound shark.

The light hand spear is slender, flexible, well balanced, and is carried in one hand with great ease. The end may be merely sharpened to a point or have a barbless steel tip attached. Trident-like spear-tips with more than one point are generally suitable only for soft-fleshed bottom fish such as the flounder.

The spearfisherman swims slowly, usually on the surface or just below, breathing quietly through his snorkel and moving his hands and feet just enough to keep afloat. It often takes some time to accustom his eyes to the underwater dimness and to learn to spot fish. When he does spot a fish, he dives, either dropping fins first

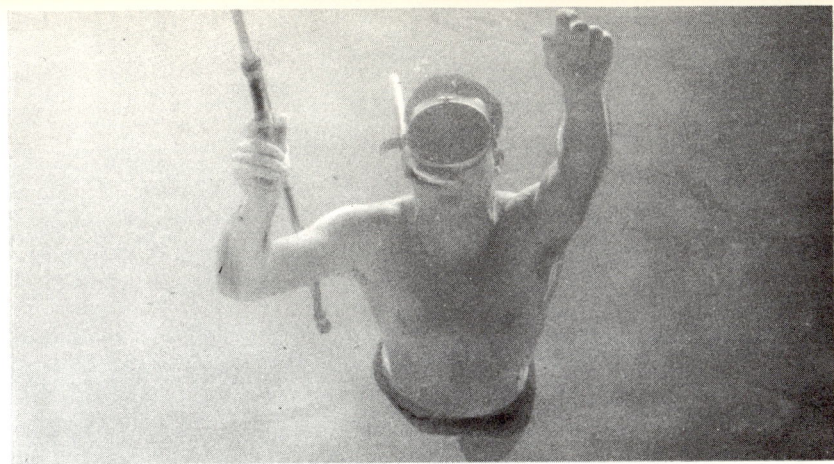

Fig. 138. The diver glides along, breathing quietly through his snorkel as he searches the water for fish, moving his hands and feet just enough to keep afloat without splashing. *Photo by George Knoblach*

with feet together (Fig. 139a) or surface diving by bending at the hip and swimming down, being careful not to splash or to kick his fins until his feet are completely submerged. He then tries to get in position to get a broadside thrust at the fish from as close range as possible, aiming just behind the gills and thrusting hard, swimming against the spear while gripping it firmly to push it completely through the fish. When the fish is impaled on the spear, it must be grasped with one hand on either side to prevent its escape and held in this manner or with the spear pointing up (after checking to make sure there are no other divers at the surface), while the diver kicks his way up to the surface for air. The fish should never be allowed to get into the air before it is completely subdued or it will flap violently. Because the fish must be held on the spear, the use of the hand spear is a strenuous sport and it is unwise to spear a fish which may turn out to be too big to handle. Once the fish is somewhat subdued, it can be attached to a fish ring by running the wire through the gills and out the mouth. The fish ring can be worn either at the diver's waist in waters where there are no sharks or other dangerous fish, or placed inside a waterproof bag in the float to prevent blood leaking in waters where it might attract unwelcome visitors.

The whole procedure, from the time the diver first sees the fish until it is impaled, must be carried through quickly and quietly to avoid frightening the fish, and to spear it and return to the surface before the diver's lungful of air is exhausted. This takes a great deal of practice before the spearfisherman can be fairly sure of getting the fish he goes after.

e.

Fig. 139. Methods of diving: a. Dropping fins first. The diver first lifts his body up slightly out of the water to get momentum for the downward plunge. b. Beginning a surface dive by bending at the waist. c. Next the diver swims down, being careful not to splash or kick with the fins until the feet are submerged. d. Leveling off and returning to the surface. e. The wrong method—splashing like this will scare all the fish away. *Photos by George Knoblach*

d.

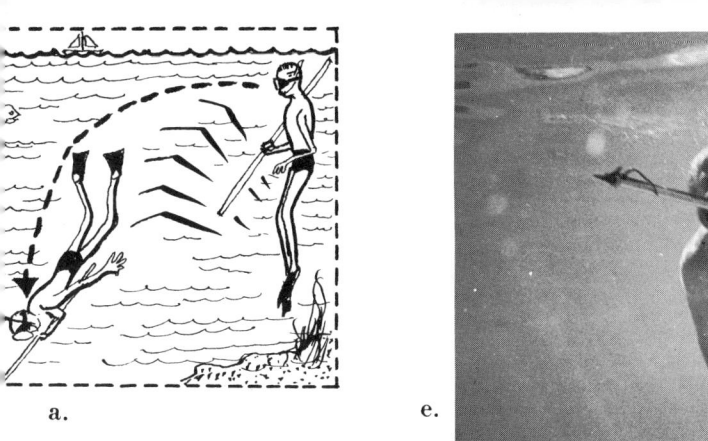

a.

e.

b.

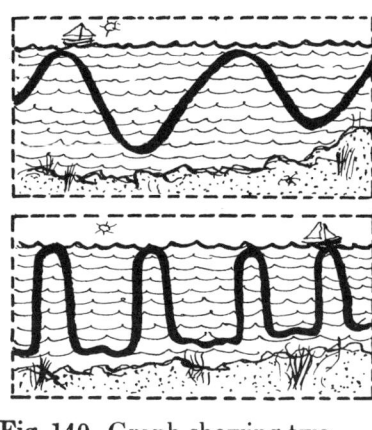

Fig. 140. Graph showing two different diving patterns:
a. General cruising;
b. Bottom searching.

One of the problems in spearing fish is that it is not always possible to get into position to spear them broadside on. The hand spear is often used in shallow water to spear fish from above while swimming along the surface. This is somewhat difficult since the back of the fish is the toughest spot, but the swimmer usually has time to maneuver for a favorable angle, preferably at a right angle from a flatter part of the fish's back on either side of the backbone. In most attack situations of this type, it is usually possible to get quite close to the fish, which makes for truer aim and better penetration. Once the spear is in the fish, the fisherman can then drop down on the shaft with his full weight, to allow the spear to penetrate the fish completely.

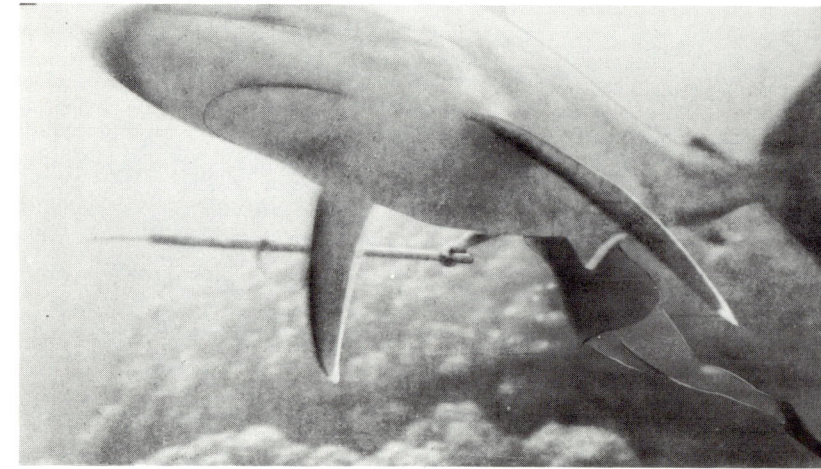

a.

b.

Fig. 141a. The heavy hand spear can be used by experts even against sharks. *Courtesy, RKO Radio Pictures.* b. Dropping down on the spear from above to push it through the fish, in this case a sting-ray. *Courtesy, Ben Holderness*

Heavier hand spears can be used to take larger fish. The light hand spear is a good choice for the beginner, since the use of it will help him develop a keen sense of tactics and accustom him to the visual distortion underwater, where everything appears slightly closer than it actually is. Once he becomes expert in hand spearing he can go on if he wishes to the more powerful and more dangerous spear guns which use a propellant such as rubber bands, springs, gas, or powder, to shoot the spear into the fish. Since laws have been proposed in some areas (a Bermuda law prohibits the use of spear guns) outlawing the taking of edible fish by any type of spear gun, it is probably wise to become expert with the hand spear first and then advance to the use of spear guns, wherever the law permits. By following this plan, the spearfisherman can enjoy his sport wherever he may be, and will not be completely at a loss if restrictive legislation should be enacted in his area. Another advantage of the hand spear is that it can be constructed simply and inexpensively by anyone (see Chapter V).

A device which is almost as simple as the hand spear, but gives slightly more propulsive power to the spear, is the Hawaiian sling, which consists of a small tube with a piece of rubber surgical tubing attached to one end. The procedure with this weapon is essentially the same as with the hand spear, except that the diver holds the tube in one hand and draws back the spear with the rubber band in the other, aims, and releases the spear toward the fish (Fig. 143). This device is usually suitable only for small fish, since the spear is small and the propulsive force not great, but divers working in groups have been successful in catching even sharks by using this weapon. Since no line is attached to the spear it is necessary to be extremely close to the fish before shooting, so as to be able to hold the spear within the tube or to grab it immediately afterward. This of necessity requires some knowledge of stalking tactics.

The hunter should swim along as previously described, peering about in all directions to search out fish (Fig. 146). When he spots a group of fish he must select one, aim at it, and keep his eyes on it while he dives, as silently as he can. If he is noisy or jerky in his movements, all the game will have scattered by the time he arrives. If he dives with the sun behind him, he is somewhat less likely to be observed by the fish. It is important to keep all movements deliberate, to move smoothly, as close to the fish as possible, and then release the spear without undue hesitation. If fish do scatter, they may pause curiously a little way off, and the diver can have another try. The

Fig. 142. It is wise to be cautious after spearing dangerous fish; even though they may appear to be dead. Gloves should also be worn when spearfishing. *Courtesy, Ben Holderness*

Fig. 143. The proper firing technique for the Hawaiian sling. *Photo by Paul Tzimoulis.*

Fig. 144. Nurse shark speared with a Hawaiian sling. Keeping a hold on the spear requires endurance, but the divers can spell each other. *Courtesy, Ben Holderness*

Fig. 145. The wrong way to stalk fish—splashing the feet like this will warn fish away. A slow steady flutter kick is best. *Photo by George Knoblach*

Fig. 146. While underwater, the diver should be on the alert at all times in order to spot fish or possible dangers. *Photo by George Knoblach*

important thing is to avoid alarming the fish since no diver is a match for a fast-swimming fish underwater if he tries to chase it. He can also try sneaking up on the fish from different directions or from behind rocks.

More powerful rubber powered guns are the two- and four-strand Arbaletes, as discussed in the chapter on equipment. The advantages of this type of weapon are that it propels the spear with more power; it can be cocked before approaching the fish (see Chapter IV for instructions on how to load) and fired with one hand, while the line attached to the spear permits playing the fish and lessens the possibility of losing the spear. The techniques of approach and stalking are the same with this gun except that, although the closer the diver is to the fish the better, it is not necessary to get as close to the fish as with the hand spear and the rubber-powered sling. In areas where there are a lot of spearfishermen, fish may become too wary to be approached closely enough to be taken with these simpler weapons.

With most spear guns a barbed spearhead with retractable wings is used. This means that the fish need not be completely impaled in order to prevent its wriggling off the spear, but it is still necessary to get a penetration of three or four inches to prevent the fish escaping. The line should be gripped immediately after spearing to prevent the fish from swimming into a cave or crevice where he may prove impossible to dislodge (especially groupers) and the spear may be bent or lost.

The spring gun, also discussed in the chapter on equipment, is somewhat more accurate than the rubber-powered guns since the spear is held on a true course by the barrel. This gun is aimed as shown in Fig. 148.

It is necessary to learn how to load both of these types of spear guns while in the water, since too much time and effort would be lost if the hunter returned to the beach or boat for each successive loading. Loading techniques are described in Chapter V. The spearhead should never be pointed at any part of the diver's or anyone else's body in loading it or after it is loaded. The diver always checks to be sure that no one is above before pointing it at the surface and, while stalking fish, he should swim with the spear pointing down or in a straight line with his body if no one is in front of him.

The underwater hunter should have his spear gun in attack position, loaded and ready at all times. There will be times when a big

Fig. 147. Jerry Bastian of the Sea Otters shows a world's record 42-pound halibut speared at Monterey Beach using the two-strand Arbalete. Rubber suits are a necessity in colder waters.

Fig. 148. Aiming the spring gun. The gun should be held in a straight line with the body, as shown. *Photo by George Knoblach*

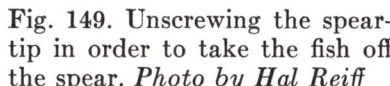

Fig. 149. Unscrewing the spear-tip in order to take the fish off the spear. *Photo by Hal Reiff*

Fig. 150. A man-eater shark shot with the Ben Holderness original Aqua-Gun. More powerful underwater weapons are justified for really large and dangerous fish. *Courtesy, Ben Holderness*

Fig. 151. Arthur Pinder with the sailfish he speared, the first ever taken by an underwater spearfisherman. *Courtesy, The Skin Diver*

Fig. 152. Hans Hass and friend with a pompano. This fish makes good eating. *Courtesy, RKO Pictures*

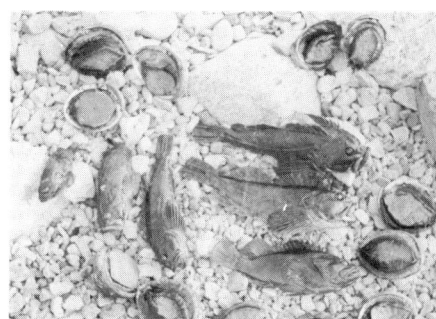

Fig. 153. Other sea food available to the diver:

a. Abalone, shown with cabezon and rock bass. These delicious shellfish, native to California, are pried off rocks with an "ab iron," inserting the iron under the edge and giving a quick flip to detach the abalone. Abalone steaks must be well pounded and then kept in a cool place for a while before serving so as to tenderize them. *Courtesy, Sons of the Beaches*

b. California clawless spiny lobster in its hole. *Courtesy, Ben Holderness.* These lobsters can be spotted by their long feelers sticking out of the hole. Various methods of catching them are advocated. One is to attract the lobster's attention with the face (a hypnotic stare?) while sneaking up on him with the hands on either side (heavy gloves must always be worn). If the lobster is too deep in the hole to be grasped, it can be enticed out by dangling a squid in front of the hole, and when the lobster comes out, the diver can clamp a gaff hook on it. Another method is to wiggle the tips of the fingers just above the entrance to the hole, and when the lobster comes out to investigate, the feelers can be grabbed gently but firmly; if it is grabbed too hard, the feelers will pull off. Then if the lobster is allowed to back into its cave slightly it will loosen its spines to go deeper into its hole, and the diver can then pull it out. Sometimes it is necessary to repeat this procedure several times, but the catch is well worth the trouble.

fish will appear suddenly and be gone in a few seconds. If for some reason a fish presents only his head, no matter how hard the diver tries to get a broadside shot, the diver then swims as close as possible, and aims into the fish's mouth and fires. The spearfisherman must try to anticipate the fish's moves. When within range, it may turn suddenly, presenting another angle. The diver must then shift his position slightly in order to have the spear strike the body at no less than a 45° angle, otherwise the spear may only knock off a few scales and not penetrate. On a long shot with any type of spear gun, it is necessary to aim slightly above the fish in order to compensate for gravitational pull and to prevent the spear from falling short. A good rule however is, if possible, not to fire when more than one spear length away. When a fish is moving, the hunter should lead the fish a few inches before firing. When a fish comes into range while the diver is in motion, he should stop before firing, otherwise he will probably miss.

Accurate aiming takes practice, and it is a good idea to carry on practice sessions in a secluded area or a strictly *private* swimming pool. A target of a fairly soft material which will not damage the spear can be set up underwater, and the diver can then practice diving down to it and firing in one continuous motion. This skill is necessary when fishing in deep water, since the diver must shoot and return to the surface before his air runs out.

Some divers secure the line to their float or to a carbon dioxide inflatable float to avoid having to play the fish while underwater and holding the line. However most spearfishermen feel it is more sportsmanlike to try to land the fish without this assistance, unless the fish is a very large one. With larger fish, divers often alternate, one going up for a breath of air while the other holds the line. Some quite large fish have been landed in this manner.

For really large fish it may be necessary to use carbon dioxide guns and spears with power heads. A stainless steel wire leader about three feet long must be attached to the spearhead to take up the initial shock and prevent the fish from snapping the line after it is speared. When rigging a gun for big game, it is necessary to attach a 150-pound test nylon line long enough (about 50 or 60 feet, coiled in the tube) to permit the diver to return to the surface for air, if being towed by the fish, and prevent the loss of his gear. Although some fishermen disdain power heads, others have found that, using them, they were able to shoot from distances of ten or even fifteen feet without the danger of merely wounding the fish and having it escape to die later. Needless to say, extreme care must be exercised when using power heads since these are quite lethal.

The choice of weapon, often hotly debated by partisans of various types, really depends on the individual fisherman, his skill, the area where he fishes, and the type of game he is after. The important thing in any case is usually not merely how powerful the weapon is, but the skill of the fisherman in approaching, aiming at, and landing the fish. Fish instinctively will try to outmaneuver the diver. Only experience will teach the best method of stalking various species.

There is not space here to describe all the game fish, since these vary according to the area, and most divers are aware of those in their own locality. Therefore, we will simply mention briefly some of the most sought-after species.

a.   b.

Fig. 154. a. Mel Small with his record striped bass. b. Black bass speared off Montauk. *Photo by George Knoblach*

The striped bass is a popular Atlantic Coast fish which has been successfully introduced on the West Coast, and which may run to over 100 pounds. These fish are found close to shore, in salty rivers and bays, in surf, tide rips, and off rocky shores, particularly in cooler waters, and can even adapt to fresh water. They are found closer to shore in the spring and fall since they move inshore during the winter. Since they feed at night, early morning or late evening hours are the best time to find them, and they can often be located by the sound of their tails slapping the water.

Sea bass are related to the jewfish and groupers, and are found around coral, rocks, wrecks or shellfish beds. The various species range from fish a few inches long to the giant black sea bass which runs to over 400 pounds. Black sea bass weighing over 300 pounds have been caught by spearfishermen. The white sea bass is not a true bass but a member of the croaker family. White sea bass weighing over 64 pounds have been speared. Channel bass, members of the drum family, run to over 80 pounds.

Popular with underwater spearfishermen are the groupers, which are common off the Florida Keys and off southern California, often around caves or wrecks. These are rather clumsy looking fish but are good eating, especially in fish chowder. When speared, they often wedge themselves into rock crevices with their spiny fins, which makes them almost impossible to dislodge. Most groupers do not run more than 50 pounds, but the jewfish, which is also called the black grouper, may run as large as 600 pounds.

The sailfish and the marlin are fast swimming, mackerel-like fish found in all warm seas, and are among the rod and reel fishermen's favorite game fish. Although these fish usually frequent waters too far offshore for the spearfisherman, Arthur Pinder, former "athlete of the year," became the first spearfisherman to land one (Fig. 151). Angered swordfish might attack divers (as they do fishing boats).

The tarpon, another popular game fish among rod and reel fishermen, is found particularly around Florida but occurs throughout the Atlantic from Long Island to Brazil. It may run to 350 pounds but is sought primarily for sport rather than as a food fish. Florida spearfishing clubs have agreements which prohibit spearing of tarpon, leaving them for the rod and reel fishermen.

The pompano is an excellent food fish found in tropical water near Florida and in the Pacific, along sandy shores. Recently a pompano weighing 127 pounds was speared near Honolulu.

Related to the pompano are the various jackfish or "jacks," members of the crevallé family which are usually found near coral reefs. The amberjack, an Atlantic Ocean fish which is occasionally found as far north as New England, may run to over 100 pounds. The yellowtail, a similar fish found in the Pacific, runs to about 90 pounds. These fish often try to flee into coral caves when speared.

A smaller fish popular among Atlantic Coast spearfishermen is the sheepshead, a member of the porgy family, found from New Jersey to the Gulf of Mexico. An excellent food fish, they run up to around 20 pounds and are found around pilings, rocks, bridge abutments and shellfish beds.

Another fish often caught in more northern waters along the East Coast is the blackfish or tautog, which is related to the wrasses of coral reefs. Running under 25 pounds, they are found near rocks, jetties, pilings and shellfish beds. The Blackfish Rocks off Montauk were named for this fish.

Other smaller fish such as red snappers and cobia found in warmer waters off the East Coast and the Gulf of Mexico, weakfish and croakers further north, cabezon and lingcod in waters of the northwestern states and jack salmon and baya off lower California, and the smaller species of bass common to many areas are also popular food and game fish among spearfishermen. The various species of bottom fish such as flounders and halibut, found in cooler waters along both coasts, are good food fish which can be taken by less experienced divers. The fish speared by skin divers are not always the same species as those generally caught by rod and reel fisher-

Fig. 155. Billie Colville of the Sea Nymphs with a halibut taken with a trident-type hand spear. This kind of spear is suitable only for soft-fleshed bottom fish like the halibut. *Photo by Lamar Boren*

men, since some inshore species are too large or too wary to be caught with a hook and line, and others range too far from shore to be accessible to the spearfisherman.

Certain areas have gained a reputation as a spearfisherman's paradise. Among the closest to the continental United States are the Florida Keys, the Bahamas, Bermuda, and, on the West Coast, Baja California and Guaymas, Mexico. Before planning a trip to any unfamiliar area, it is wise to check on local laws, dangers such as sharks or poisonous marine life, and what it is necessary to carry in the way of food and equipment (whether or not compressed air sources or diving equipment stores are available), as well as whether boats must be owned or rented to reach diving areas. Most of these facts can be learned from skin divers who have visited the area, from articles in the *Skin Diver* magazine, or by writing to the local Chamber of Commerce.

Before any spearfishing trip all equipment should be checked to make certain everything is in good working order. Every sharp item should be well protected, and all guns carried unloaded. On spear guns the line or cable release should be checked to be certain it will not foul, perhaps injuring the diver's hand and fingers or even turning the spear back toward the diver. Gloves should always be worn while spearfishing, and extra ones should be taken on a trip. A few minutes spent each evening of a trip looking over equipment and repairing the damages of the day's sport will enable the diver to enjoy himself the next day without being frustrated and unsuccessful due to faulty equipment.

Wherever the diver goes, he should behave as a true sportsman and take all precautions for his own safety and that of others. If these rules are followed, spearfishing can continue to be an exciting and challenging sport for many years to come.

a.

b.

Fig. 156. Safety precautions when spearfishing:

a. Be careful not to get tangled with kelp or eel grass when preoccupied with stalking a fish. *Courtesy, Ben Holderness*

b. All spear guns should be unloaded on the beach and when coming in and out of the water. The bright markings on the rubber helmet and suit of the diver in the foreground are a good precaution in order to make the diver more visible to surface craft. *Photo by Hal Reiff*

c. Never dive alone. The ocean is a large and lonely place. The diver should also have a float. *Photo by George Knoblach*

VII SCUBA Clubs and Activities

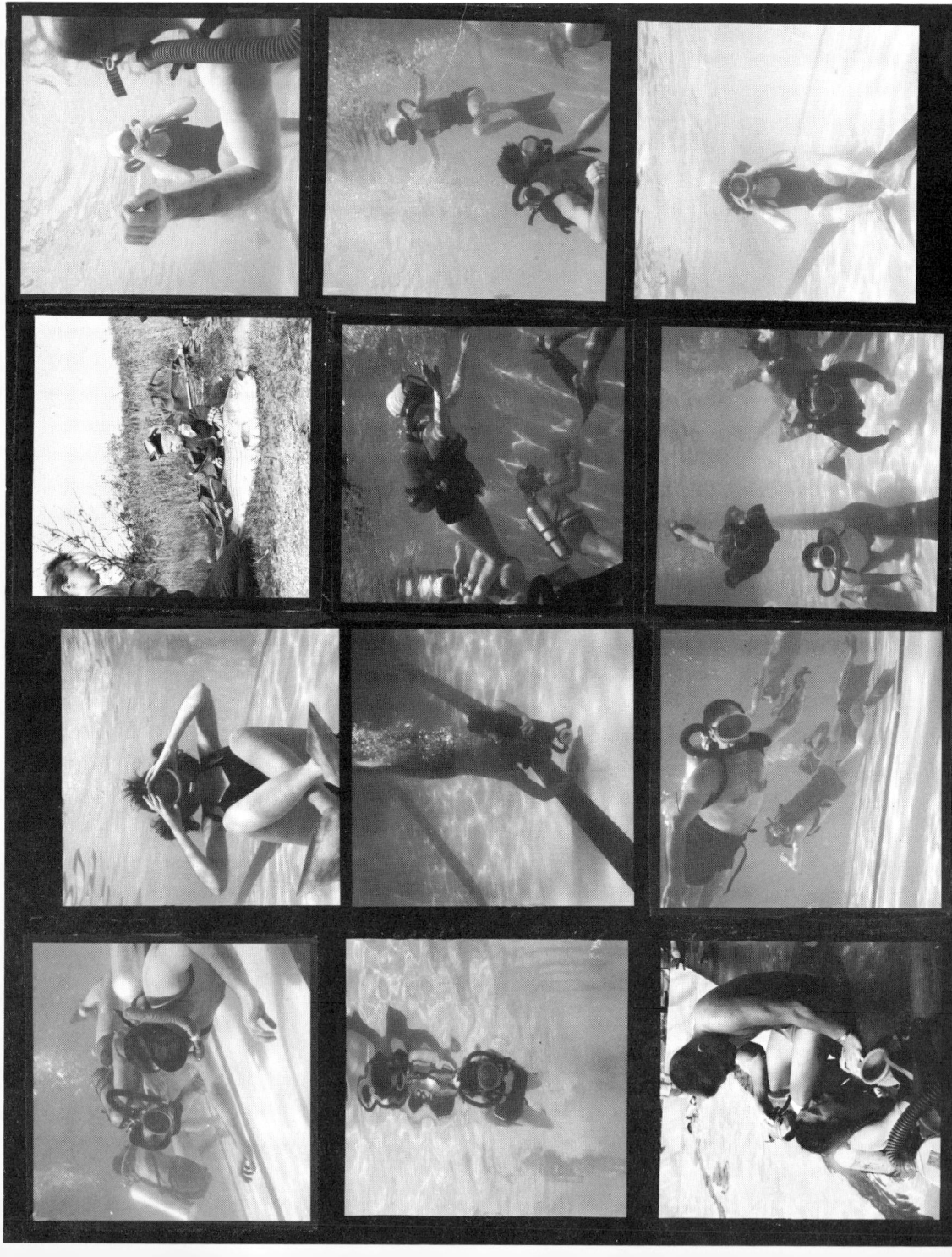

There are so many diving clubs springing up around the country that it would take an electronic computer to keep track of the number. Estimates run between 500 (an average of ten clubs per state) to as high as 1,500 throughout the United States. The majority of skin diving clubs are located, as one would expect, in Florida and California. A few clubs have turned to the serious business of search and recovery for police, sheriff's, and fire departments. Some do salvage work. Civil Defense Diver Units have been organized throughout the country. Most clubs, however, are dedicated to sport diving.

Obviously these clubs are popular. Just what does the diver get out of belonging to a club other than companionship, you may wonder, and why can't one get that just by diving with a friend or two without formally joining or aiding in organizing a club. The answer is that there are many advantages to belonging to a club besides the obvious ones.

Having someone available to dive with is, of course, important. Several divers who earlier disparaged the buddy-system report, on learning the hard way, that it is not safe to dive alone. Clubs also serve as a pool of available information on skin diving: new developments in equipment, new books on the subject, laws affecting the skin diver, detailed information on various diving areas, as well as diving records, record catches of fish, safety information, and so on.

The best way to obtain information about SCUBA diving in your area is to ask at your local skin diving store. Clubs can also chip in to buy air compressors, boats, and other equipment that the average individual could not afford, or to charter boats if necessary to reach certain diving areas.

Clubs may have meetings with speakers who are prominent in the sport and can arrange showings of underwater movies. They also aid in exposing false advertising and thus protect members from the purchase of inferior equipment, as the Sons of the Beaches Club of Long Beach, California, does. Many clubs give courses of instruction in safe diving and the use of breathing equipment.

Certain clubs organize courses of instruction in other aspects of diving. For example, a Connecticut club has an underwater-safety course which includes instruction in salvage methods, the use of spear guns, and spearfishing tactics, the theory and literature of skin diving, and popular oceanography. After the course is finished the members must pass tests on the material covered.

The Underwater Explorers' Club of England has discussion and

Fig. 157. Diving together is safer and more fun. *Photo by Hal Reiff*

practice groups covering underwater photography, cinematography, and underwater TV, marine sound recording, submarine archeology, geology, studies of marine life, oceanography, medical aspects of diving, and underwater exploration.

Probably one of the most important functions of the diving club is to work for legislation favorable to skin divers and combine to prevent the passage of unfavorable legislation. The California Council of Diving Clubs has done a great deal in preventing restrictive legislation there and in campaigning for more lenient laws where it seemed wise to do so. In Florida, quick action by a spearfishing club was able to prevent the State legislature from passing a so-called "seining" bill which could have outlawed ninety percent of the spearfishing ground in the club's county; a proposed measure to prohibit the use of spear guns was also defeated there. In Australia, the Underwater Spearfishermen's Association of Australia was able to prevent action on a proposal to ban the sport altogether. And in Louisiana, the State legislature was persuaded to pass a bill legalizing spearfishing in salt water.

Many States have pressure groups of rod and reel fishermen who resent the underwater spearfishermen and attempt to restrict the sport legally. Many of these efforts are due to unfounded jealousy; but certain abuses by a few skin divers, such as the Fishers Island incident a few years ago when spearfishermen left a large catch of fish to rot on the beach, have aroused justifiable resentment. Diving clubs, however, have not campaigned aggressively solely for their own interests; they have been quite conscientious in making and promoting rules regarding spearfishing and in working with conservation groups.

As part of their efforts in this direction, clubs have helped to bring the true situation to the attention of the public, particularly in regard to claims that spearfishermen are responsible for the shortage of fish in certain areas by scaring them away or by indiscriminate slaughter.

The Puget Sound Mudsharks relate an incident on the subject of "scaring fish away." It seems that they fish around a sunken ferry at Edmonds, Washington, which is located about eighty feet away from the ferry slip. They spear a variety of fish including lingcod, black bass, kelp bass, rock fish, perch, bull cod, and other small species, and have taken as much as two hundred pounds of fish at a time from around this wreck. When dredges and pile drivers began to work a few yards away on a new slip, the Mudsharks were a bit worried for fear the fish would leave. However, after four months of construction, the fish remained as abundant as ever. This and other similar stories seem to indicate that it takes considerably more than spearfishing to scare fish away from their favorite haunts.

Most experts agree that the simple appearance of skin divers, however grotesquely garbed, in their area, would not make fish change their feeding grounds, and that the reported disappearance of certain fish is more likely due to natural causes such as migration or to overfishing by commercial groups.

The California Council of Diving Clubs points out that all sport fishermen including skin divers are regulated by the Fish and Game Commission which insists that they purchase a fishing license, and their catch is restricted by specific bag limits on lobster, abalone, and certain fish. Also they may not sell their catch. Many states have local laws prohibiting the use of spears to take fish at all, particularly in fresh waters. California does not permit the spearing of mollusks, crustaceans, trout, salmon, striped bass or garibaldi, and

Bermuda has set strict limitations on the use of the Aqua-Lung for spearfishing up to local authorities, which may put any restrictions they choose on the use of diving equipment in their area. Montauk Point was closed despite protests.

However, commercial fishermen in most areas are controlled only by the State legislature which may make little attempt to restrain them. Due to the overfishing of sardines by commercial operators in California, marine biologists have warned that if these fish disappear, other fish which depend on them for food may disappear too. The California Council of Diving Clubs wrote letters to the Fish and Game Commission protesting the reduction of sardines (that is, the commercial conversion into oils and other products), which resulted in no reduction permits being granted. Diving clubs have worked closely with conservation groups, including cooperating in collecting data for them and in helping to clear out the starfish which menaced the mollusk population. In California they have campaigned against certain commercial fishermen who were habitually taking whole boatloads of illegal "short" lobsters. Many clubs themselves prohibit the use of underwater breathing devices for spearing fish.

Spearfishing clubs have, on the whole, taken a very responsible attitude in regard to conservation, to community assistance, and to enforcing safety regulations within their membership. Many clubs have entrance requirements which prospective members must pass. The constitution of the Kelptomaniacs of California states that in addition to diving and bringing up certain specified fish, a member must be able to: swim 200 yards without a mask or fins, swim 75 feet underwater without fins and without surfacing, remain afloat without fins or a float for ten minutes, demonstrate a Red Cross rescue tow, and pass a safety test. This group's constitution also provides that members may vote to suspend any member guilty of gross neglect of safety rules and regulations. The Kelptomaniacs also were responsible for organizing and printing an excellent pamphlet on safety used as a reference in preparing this book.

Recognizing that they have some adverse publicity to combat, as well as misunderstanding by the general public of certain aspects of diving, skin diving clubs have tried to be of assistance to the community in various ways. They have frequently offered to help in rescue work and body recovery. In Washington, the Beachcombers Club was called on to assist in the search for the body of a small boy

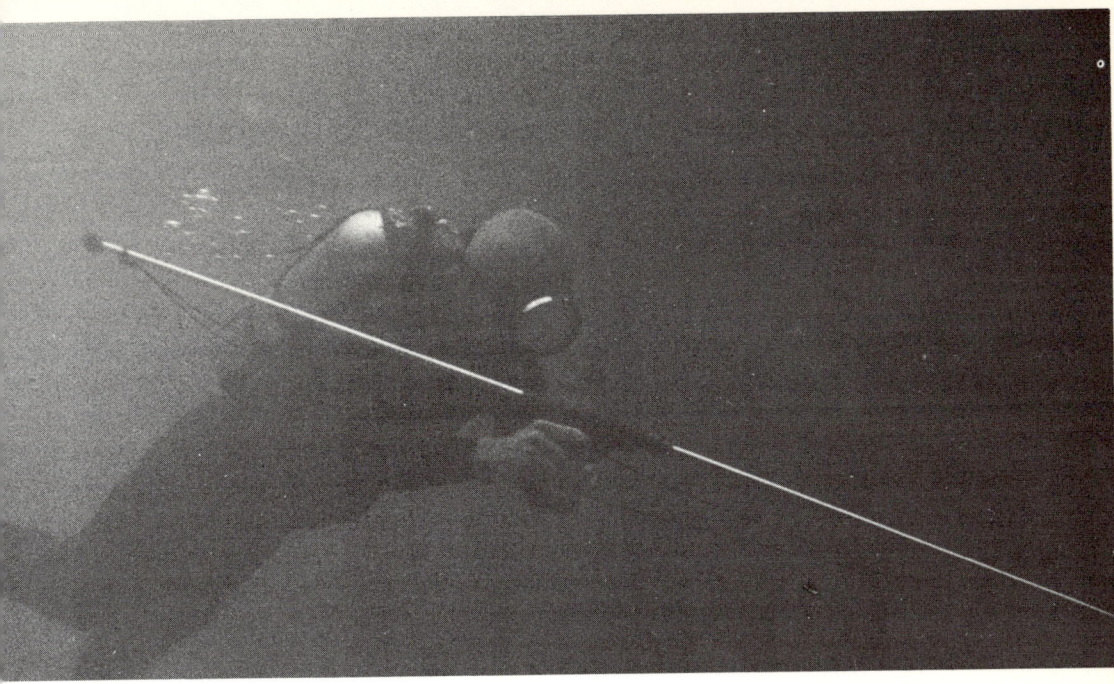

Fig. 158. Most clubs ban the use of SCUBA for spearfishing. *Photo by George Knoblach*

drowned in Hicks Lake when it was found that the efforts of an official helmet diver stirred up too much mud and impaired visibility. Jacksonville, Florida skin divers have formed an underwater rescue squad available and equipped to respond to emergency calls by the city. In California, the Northern California Skin Divers Club succeeded in recovering a body where the Coast Guard and a helicopter had failed. Also in California, members of the Sea Otters Club disregarded their own safety to rescue a boy who was attacked by a shark.

Many diving clubs have assisted their State conservation departments in surveys of fish and marine life. The Long Island Dolphins have been active in helping to supply data for the New York State Conservation Department which is attempting to find out why certain fish are dying out in some areas in its endeavor to make those areas habitable again. This club also voluntarily increased its minimum size limit of striped bass and blackfish, and is supporting the passage of a law prohibiting the netting of striped bass in New York waters. Members pledge to protect all rare species which are overfished or dying out, and never to use a SCUBA for fishing.

On both the East and West Coasts, clubs have assisted in "Opera-

Fig. 159. Divers and SCUBA clubs are frequently called upon to cooperate with police in the aid of retrieving objects, planes, cars, etc. from inland and coastal waters. Here, the Hartford Gillmen assist at a Civil Defense recovery demonstration. *Photo by Budney*

tion Starmop" which involved large-scale removal of the starfish which had been seriously depleting the mollusks in those areas. In an operation in the Los Angeles Federal Harbor, 225 skin divers removed an estimated twelve tons of starfish, many of which were more than two feet across. The California Council of Diving Clubs works with the Ocean Fish Protective Association there, and with the Scripps Institution of Oceanography in collecting and tabulating scientific data.

Foreign clubs such as the Club Alpin Sous-Marin and the Toulon Submarine Research Group have contributed a great deal in the field of underwater archeology and in experimental work with the French Navy.

More and more women are becoming interested in skin diving, despite Cousteau's comment about his wife, that women seem innately suspicious of the sport. Eugenie Clark, the skin diving ichthyologist of the Museum of Natural History, wrote an excellent book, *Lady with a Spear*, describing her experiences in the Pacific and in the Red Sea. Another experienced woman diver, Jane Crile, wrote a book, *Treasure Diving Holidays*, with her husband, Barney. And at Catalina Island, Rosalia Parry made a women's record dive of 209 feet. Certainly many of these women are at least as qualified as some of the male divers who enter the competitions, and it seems hardly fair that any team which can meet entrance requirements

Fig. 160. Woman spearfishing champion at a competition at Monaco. In the interest of conservation, awards are no longer judged as they used to be, by aggregate weight of fish, but by weight of individual fish speared. While SCUBA is, of course, not used in spearfishing competitions, extra weights (or even a specially weighted spear) furnish an added help to the diver, enabling him to stay down longer on a hunting dive. Too much weight, however, has sometimes proved fatal, and extra weighted divers have been found on the bottom together with the record fish they had speared before they blacked out. *Photo by Charvoz using Rebikoff gear*

Fig. 161. A primary target of interest and often of financial reward to diving clubs are undersea wrecks. Group participation is especially recommended in such circumstances, primarily because of the safety factor to the individual of having a number of divers present. *Courtesy, Établissement Cinématographique et Photographique des Armées*

should be disqualified on the basis of sex alone, since usual Amateur Athletic Union rules seem inapplicable here.

Skin diving clubs on the whole have shown a commendable awareness of their responsibilities to aid in the preservation and improvement of the sport, and to the community. They have shown an instinct for fair play and sportsmanship, have made efforts to improve equipment and enforce safety regulations, and have offered their services to the community whenever possible, in order to gain public acceptance for a not yet generally completely understood or accepted sport.

Skin Diver magazine periodically posts a list of clubs in the United States. Most club members are friendly and willing to help teach novices, and if their particular club is filled up, they will help others to form a club of their own.

a

b

c

d

e

Fig. 162. a. Diver finds anchor. Note white package attached to his belt. This package contains a folded underwater balloon called a "Port-A-Lift." b. The diver removes the balloon from his belt package. c. He ties the Port-A-Lift cord to the anchor. d. Air from the SCUBA mouthpiece inflates the balloon. e. Buoyancy of the inflated Port-A-Lift raises the anchor to the surface. *Photos by Gene Parker*

Fig. 163. SCUBA diver and undersea explorer Arnie Post equipped for a visit to the whale tank at an aquarium in order to "speak" to the occupants. He will record their sounds and play them back at different speeds in an attempt to make some sort of sound contact with them. His equipment enables him to talk to technicians above water who will relay the whales' sounds back to him for the whales to hear. It has been established that the squeals of whales and porpoises, when replayed at a slower speed, are really a series of grunts and groans which evidently are a form of communication among these deep-sea mammals. Researchers who have studied the matter are convinced that porpoises do possess a sort of "language" and that they, due to their relatively enormous brain capacity, may some day be able to understand ours. *Courtesy, Richards Aqualung Center*

Fig. 163a. The Bulow Seatow is a portable SCUBA diving propulsion unit. A 12-volt battery powers the electric motor propellor drive. The propellor is shielded to prevent injury to the diver. The Seatow will travel at speeds of 2½ to 3 knots to a depth of 100 feet. The Seatow "Guppy" model tows the diver. The "Minnow" is fastened to the diver's SCUBA tank and pushes the diver through the water. *Photo by Mozert*

b. T-14 "Pegasus" is a self-contained submarine vehicle for the SCUBA diver. The T-14 shown below carries lights, instruments, and camera. *Courtesy, Loral Electronics Corp.*

Fig. 164. a. Diver pulling starting cord on gasoline motor driven Sportsways Hookah compressor. Instead of wearing a tank on the back the diver trails an air hose. The compressor pumps air into the small tank at the left. Air travels through the hose to the regulator held by the man at the right. This is a very effective rig for gold divers or commercial divers since they do not have to transport tanks. b. (Below) The diver is ready for work. In this case the job is to clean the swimming pool. *Photographs by Paul Tzimoulis*

Fig. 165. a. Float flag by Seacraft. b. Seacraft's Marker Float is worn on belt or harness. Sinker drops to bottom as line unreels and float bobs on surface. c. Sirocco "Marc-A-Boy" is shown after CO_2 cartridge has inflated orange balloon. d. Healthways Diver's Utility Bag/Safety Float. e. Healthways Inflatable Divers Flag.

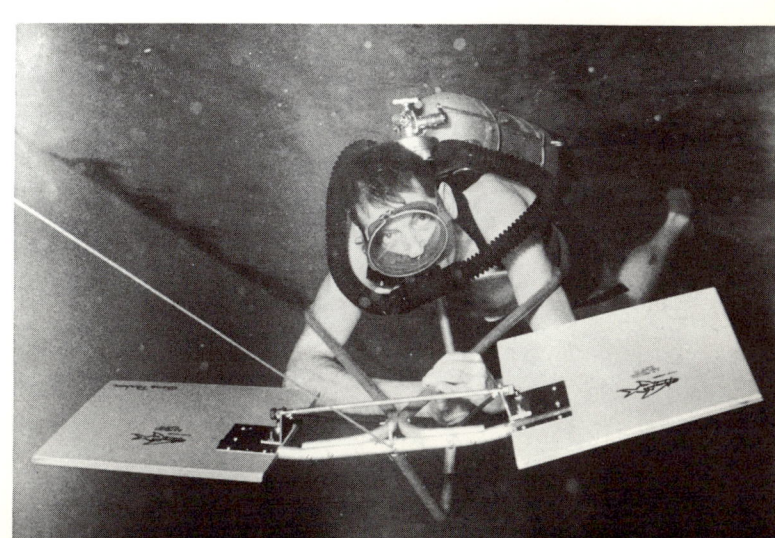

Fig. 166. Reploggle "Flying Fish" is a highly maneuverable towed diving plane. It is possible for a diver to search a swath fifteen feet wide and a mile long in a half hour. *Photo by Gene Parker*

VIII

Photography Under Water

Underwater still shots can be taken without the aid of breathing apparatus: a picture of George Knoblach taking training shots used in this book.
Photo by Bob Ferando

Naturally it is not possible to cover in this discussion such a complex and technical subject as underwater photography. All we shall attempt to do here is to summarize the basic information which might be of help to the amateur photographer or to the photographer attempting underwater photography for the first time. We will avoid such technical aspects as the physics of light refraction through water, involved exposure tables and formulas, and details of development and printing processes, as well as deep sea photography and television, both activities suitable only for professionals with expensive equipment. For those who are interested in a more detailed discussion of the subject, excellent references can be found in the back of this book.

Underwater photography involves so many problems of construction, waterproofing, lighting, etc. that it is only quite recently that equipment has been developed which is convenient and accurate enough to insure any degree of success for the nonprofessional photographer. From Boutan's first underwater stills to such recent refinements as Rebikoff's Torpedo, the remote control underwater TV camera, and cameras capable of taking pictures at the greatest ocean depths, has only been a matter of some sixty years.

Dr. Louis Boutan, the pioneer in underwater photography, was a French biologist who in 1893 succeeded in taking some recognizable underwater stills, using a large watertight copper box as an underwater camera case. He later experimented with artificial lighting underwater, using at first a complicated arrangement involving the blowing of powdered magnesium over an alcohol lamp, protected by a bell jar and mounted over an air-filled barrel.

In 1917, Dr. W. H. Longley developed a heavy brass underwater case on which the focus, and speed and trigger controls could be manipulated from outside the case. Several years later he achieved the first underwater color still pictures, again using magnesium powder as a light source, but by igniting a quantity of it on the surface of the water and using a reflector.

In 1927, Dr. Paul Bartsch of the Smithsonian Institution designed a motion picture camera which could be focused underwater. In the same year, a photographic diving bell was used to shoot *20,000 Leagues Under The Sea.* Commander Le Prieur, who also pioneered in the development of self-contained underwater breathing apparatus, made the first Kodachrome underwater movies in

1931, using a case of his own design in which the controls were operated through pieces of rubber hose.

Once the basic problems of underwater photography had been overcome and fairly successful stills and motion pictures had been achieved, speculation about the mysteries of the abyss inspired attempts to develop camera housings which would withstand and remain watertight in the tremendous pressures of these depths.

The Johnson-Smithsonian deep-sea camera housing, constructed in 1933 by E. R. Fenimore Johnson, proved watertight when lowered to a depth of 3,000 fathoms. Unfortunately, on the next lowering, the cable broke and the camera was lost.

In 1939, Dr. E. N. Harvey and Edward R. Baylor designed a pressure chamber containing a motion picture camera and a light source, with which they succeeded in taking pictures of undersea organisms at a depth of 700 fathoms. Then Dr. Maurice Ewing developed a camera rig which worked automatically on contact with the bottom and returned to the surface afterward, without being attached to the control ship by cables. With this camera he took many successful pictures of undersea terrain as deep as 18,000 feet.

Recently the British invented an underwater television camera with a movable turret with six interchangeable lenses which could be operated by remote control from the deck of a ship. With this sensitive camera they have been able to get pictures of marine life from tiny plankton up to large fish at depths to 80 fathoms.

However fascinating these deep-sea explorations may be, a development of more interest to the average diver-photographer is the Rebikoff Torpedo (discussed in greater detail later in the chapter), a self-propelled camera unit which carries its own light source. Also the increased availability of inexpensive, well-made, underwater camera housings has made underwater photography possible for a great many more people. Even after the problem of constructing watertight, pressure-proof housings was solved, however, several other problems still remain to be overcome if the diver is to get successful underwater pictures.

The main problems of underwater photography are the haze, resulting from the scattering of light by tiny particles in the water which largely reduces contrast, and the loss of light intensity and color values which increases with depth. These can be partially overcome by the use of filters, artificial lighting, a wide angle lens, and special printing processes.

Fig. 167. A smashed camera housing, showing the effects of water pressure on an unpressurized housing. The camera was ruined. *Courtesy, Cinefot*

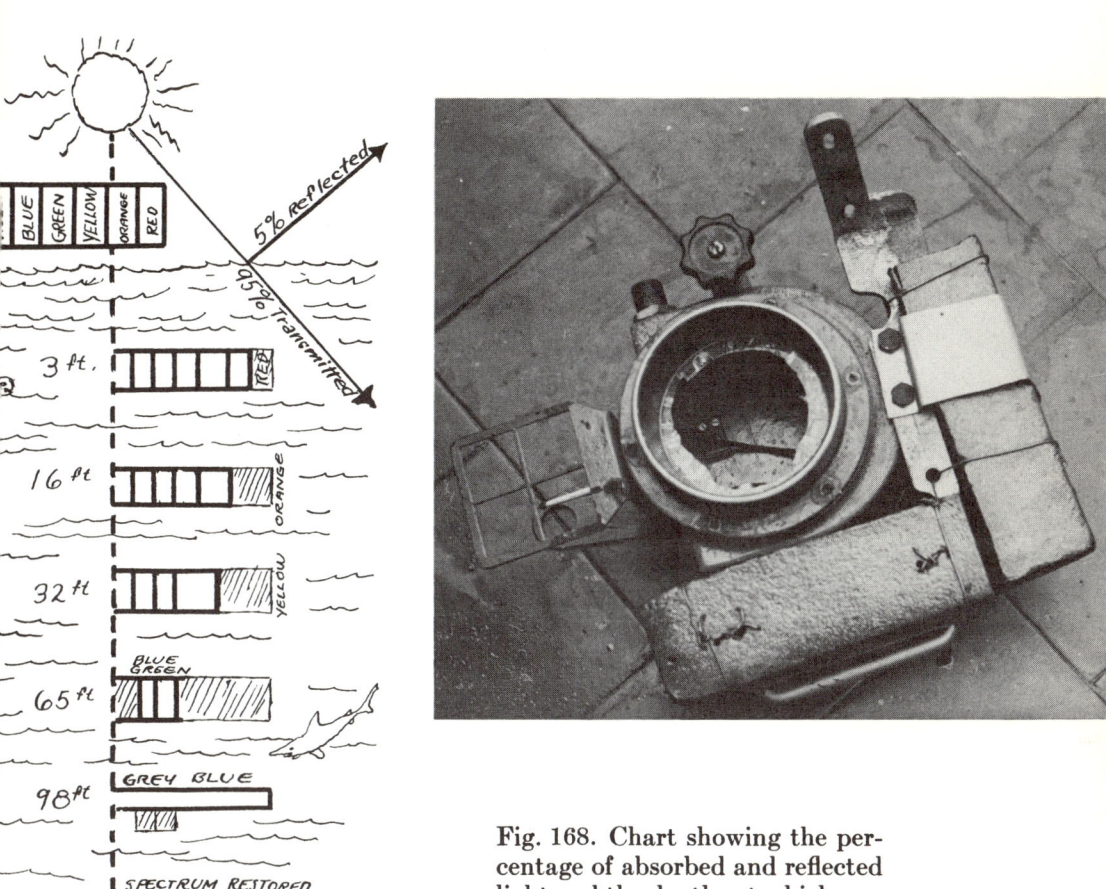

Fig. 168. Chart showing the percentage of absorbed and reflected light and the depths at which certain colors disappear. *Courtesy, Dmitri Rebikoff*

The best visibility is found in the clear blue waters of the open ocean, over rocky bottoms, off islands at some distance from the mainland, and during the cooler months, as the water then has fewer microscopic organisms and the winds are usually offshore with less suspended sediment in the water. Late morning and early afternoon are generally considered the best times for, with the sun directly overhead, light penetrates more deeply into the water. However, some photographers prefer more angled sunlight for modeling effects. Since choppy water cuts down light transmission and impairs visibility, a calm sea is best for photography.

A camera to be used in underwater work should have the following features: a short focal length for depth of field; a fast lens (at least F/3.5); as large a number of pictures as possible with one loading, and ease of operation, including accessibility of all controls, provision for ascertaining at a glance how the lens is set and focused without turning the camera around, and the easy removal of the housing back for quick reloading.

U.S. Diver's new Calypso 35mm camera needs no waterproof housing (see page 248). Most of the others are intended for land use and therefore must have a housing or blimp to make them watertight and pressure-proof. Not all land cameras are adaptable for underwater use since some have bellows, others have controls in awkward places, and some are too large and cumbersome for convenient handling.

The best still camera for amateur use under water is a 35 mm. box camera, of which there are several types available. A camera to be converted for underwater use should be rugged, have centrally located control knobs, interchangeable lenses, adaptor for synthronized flash, film transfer knob and cocking mechanism in one, easily accessible F stop, and easily accessible speed and shutter control. Since all these controls must be operated through a watertight case, the more openings necessary, the greater difficulty in waterproofing. Since most underwater pictures are shot at a fixed focus, a range finder is usually not necessary.

For commerical color work a reflex camera is desirable, since some publications will not accept 35 mm. color transparencies for reproduction. The advantage of this type of camera is that the photographer can keep his subject in view at all times in the ground glass, while operating the focus manually. Naturally, the housing for this type of camera must have an additional window over the ground glass. Its disadvantages are its size and bulk and the fact that it takes only 12 exposures before reloading is necessary.

The Rolleiflex is a good camera of this type, but its F/3.5 lens is a bit slow for color work in natural light. However, a new F/2.8 lens being designed should increase its range and versatility.

One of the most versatile and best cameras for underwater work is the Leica, since it can take 36 exposures with one loading, the film transport automatically sets the shutter, a variety of excellent lenses is available for it, and it is small, compact, and rugged.

Fig. 169. Underwater still camera housings: a. Inexpensive plastic Brownie housing; b. The Fenjohn "Goggler"—Fenjohn cast aluminum underwater flash; d. German Rolleiflex housing by Franke & Heidecke; c. New French Rolleiflex housing; e. French Leica housing; f. *Akustische* Hans Hass Leica housing showing easily removable back.

The Robot, another 35 mm. camera is frequently used in color work and has the advantage of a spring drive which resets the shutter and advances film with no winding control necessary. However, its negative size is somewhat smaller than the standard 35 mm. Some underwater photographers like the Stereo-Realist for its three-dimensional effect, but its slow lens may make artificial light necessary.

The Fenjohn Goggler, built especially for underwater work has the advantage of taking forty-five 70-mm. pictures without reloading, of all controls easily available to the diver, of using commercial color-size negatives, of having a synchronized flash attachment, of a focus calibrated in underwater distance, and of an easily opened housing, which is watertight to 300 feet without pressurizing, but that can be pressurized.

Although until quite recently only expensive custom-made underwater housings were available, a variety of housings is now on the market ranging from a plastic case complete with a Brownie camera at around $30 to a German Rolleiflex housing at $375. Many underwater photographers attempt to make their own cases from a variety of materials—from plastic and wood, to pressure cookers and even rubber gloves. Details on building your own camera case will be found in an earlier chapter.

A good underwater camera housing should be as simple and compact as possible, should render all control knobs easily available, should have a quickly and easily removable back for reloading, should be strong enough to resist pressure and shocks, should have rounded corners for safety, and should of course be completely watertight. Outlets for synchronized flash, pressurizing nozzles, and tripod attachments are other desirable but not essential features.

Plastic cases are among the least expensive, but are generally not dependable at depths over 10 to 15 feet. Plastic also has the disadvantage of scratching easily, although this can be partly prevented by a protective ring or removed by proper polishing. Plastic cases also usually require several bolts for watertight sealing, which makes quick film changes difficult.

With metal cases, measures must be taken to prevent corrosion, particularly with aluminum, and it is necessary to avoid combining metals which create an electrolytic action when used together, especially in salt water.

Different brands of housings have various advantages and disadvantages. The Ondiphot housing for the automatic Rolleiflex which is widely used for commercial work, especially color, was designed nearly twenty years ago and has the advantage of controls corresponding in shape and position to those of the camera itself. A recent French Rolleiflex housing is said to be an improved and simplified version of the Ondiphot. A German-made Rolleiflex housing designed by Hans Hass is perhaps the best but it is expensive.

A circular cast-aluminum housing for the Robot camera, in which the film advances automatically, takes 24 pictures in quick succession and has a port for synchronized flash attachment. However, it has only one outside control, the trigger, and this camera's negative size is small.

The greatest variety of housings is that made for the Leica, cases for this camera being made in France, Germany, and the United States. The most expensive and probably the best Leica housing is the German-made *Akustische* designed by Hans Hass (see Fig. 169f). The housing has the following advantages: speed, focus, wind, aperture, and trigger controls accessible to the diver; corrections to compensate for underwater distortion of distances; synchronized flash; pressurizing outlets; tripod mounting socket; sturdy but relatively lightweight construction; a handsome carrying case with enclosed kit for tools and spare parts; and a back removable with a flip of the finger. It is good without pressurizing down to 300 feet. A disadvantage has been that it would not take the extreme wide-angle lens, but an adapter is being made to overcome this difficulty. This case with the Leica camera was used to take all of the training pictures in this book.

For large cameras and when working at greater depths, the case should have a pressurizing outlet. The unit may then be attached to a demand regulator to achieve an inside pressure equal to that of the surrounding water. Most diving helmet exhaust valves can also be adapted for this purpose.

A good underwater movie camera should be compact and light in weight and should be one which will accommodate a wide-angle lens, which will take a long roll of film, preferably 100 feet, which has a variable frame speed, and which has controls which can be conveniently reached and adapted to an underwater housing without too many complications. Since an electric motor is virtually a necessity in underwater work, the camera should be one which will take such a motor without elaborate adjustments. A lens turret and a ground-glass viewer are superfluous here. Many divers have found the Bolex a good choice for underwater work; however, Dmitri

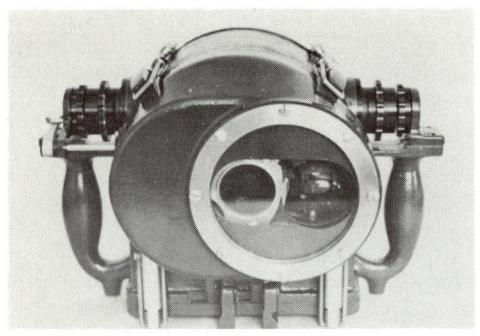

a.   b.

Fig. 170. Underwater movie camera housings: a. Fenjohn 16 mm. movie camera housing; b. Rebikoff 1200-volt torpedo with Aquaphot camera case with corrective porthole.

Rebikoff likes the French Beaulieu which he says is practical and economical and which can be bought with a specially designed underwater case. War surplus wing cameras can also be adapted for underwater use. Fenjohn sells a Bell & Howell 16 mm. movie camera complete with a specially designed underwater housing; however, it is quite expensive.

    Housings for underwater movie cameras should be lightweight and streamlined in design so that the diver can swim with the camera without being unnecessarily fatigued and hampered by excess weight and water resistance. However, excess weight can be partially counteracted by lashing empty bottles or floats to the camera. Several divers have made underwater housings from converted pressure cookers as noted earlier. Cousteau designed a "breathing box" which is pressurized by a small attached Aqua-Lung, but this presents possible danger of damage to camera and case through a faulty exhaust valve or accidental opening of the compressed air cylinder above water. Probably the best and most expensive underwater camera unit on the market is the Rebikoff Torpedo, a cylindrical box which contains its own light source and an electric motor for

Fig. 171. Movie cameras in action: a. Fenjohn 16 mm. movie camera; b. Rebikoff motion picture torpedo which propels the diver at a speed of two knots, *Photo Courtesy, Dmitri Rebikoff;* c. Housing for a Bolex made from a converted pressure cooker. *Photo by George Knoblach*

propelling the diver through the water, and to the back of which the camera is attached (Fig. 170b). This unit has self-sealing gaskets, the clamping of which is proportional to the water pressure, and is absolutely watertight to almost 200 ft., with no pressurizing necessary.

In taking underwater movies, it is important not to pan or swing the camera too quickly. This is a mistake often made by beginners and results in a nervous jerky effect which is difficult to follow and may make the audience seasick. Since the underwater world is an unfamiliar one to most people, it takes time to get one's bearings and identify objects seen on the screen; therefore, scenes should be longer than in ordinary movies. The action should be smooth with no breaks. It is very important to hold the camera steady while swimming, and stabilizing fins may be a help here. In order to allow the audience to catch details of fast-swimming fish which would otherwise photograph as a blur, the frame speed can be turned to slow motion. If the movie is intended for commercial showing, the minimum frame speed is 24 frames per second and the film must be at least 16 mm.

In underwater photography, both still and motion picture, a wide-angle lens should be used for best results. The advantages of this type of lens are that, since the camera can be closer to the subject, there is less water to shoot through, resulting in a clearer picture with better contrast, and the greater depth of field allows more latitude in focusing. With 16 mm. movie cameras, and usually with a 35 mm. still camera, the wide-angle lens will permit most pictures to be taken without having to change the focus. Since a wide aperture is necessary to admit light in the relatively dim underwater world, thus cutting down depth of field, the wide-angle lens is particularly helpful here and also, when the subject can be brought closer to the camera, less exposure time is necessary. With the extreme wide-angle lens, however, the physics of light transmission through the flat window of the housing may cause distortion and darkening at the edge of the print. (The extent of this can be determined by test shots in a swimming pool, which, incidentally, is an excellent place to practice using equipment and to test for leakage also.)

To overcome this problem, LeGrand, Cuvier, and Ivanoff developed a corrective porthole with two lenses, for greater depth of field and to eliminate aberrations due to water refraction (Fig. 173). This corrective porthole may be had to fit ten different cameras and is available through the Alpha Photo Corporation in New York.

Such lenses, however, are relatively expensive, and the amateur photographer who is not able to invest in expensive equipment can get adequate shots through experience in underwater focusing, and the use of fast panchromatic film, proper filters, high speed developers and contrast paper. A coated lens is a help, since it admits more light.

The housing lens is as important as the camera lens and should be of high quality optically flat ground plate glass, exactly parallel with the camera lens and as close to it as possible. Painting the inside of the housing dull black will help to eliminate light flashes on the print due to reflections or if a plastic housing is used, a lens shade will help.

Objects must be shot closer than normal under water. The maximum distance under ideal conditions is 60 feet and most shots should be no more distant than 8 to 10 feet. Underwater distances are deceptive; objects appear one fourth closer and one fourth larger than their actual distance and size. However, elaborate calculations to compensate for distance distortion often do more harm than good; since things appear to the camera the same way they do to the human eye, experience usually is the best aid in judging distances.

For black and white photography, either stills or cinematography, only panchromatic film is suitable for underwater. Due to the lack of light, a high speed film is generally used, such as Super XX or XXX. The difficulty here is that this film is larger grained and this may create problems when the pictures are enlarged. This can be partially controlled by developing slowly in a Microdol solution. Rebikoff, on the other hand, prefers Plus X with a paper developer.

Of the color films, Kodachrome is the most strongly saturated with color which helps to give a brighter picture in the underwater world, a world that tends to become monochromatic a few feet from the surface. Ansco color film is slightly more sensitive to red than other

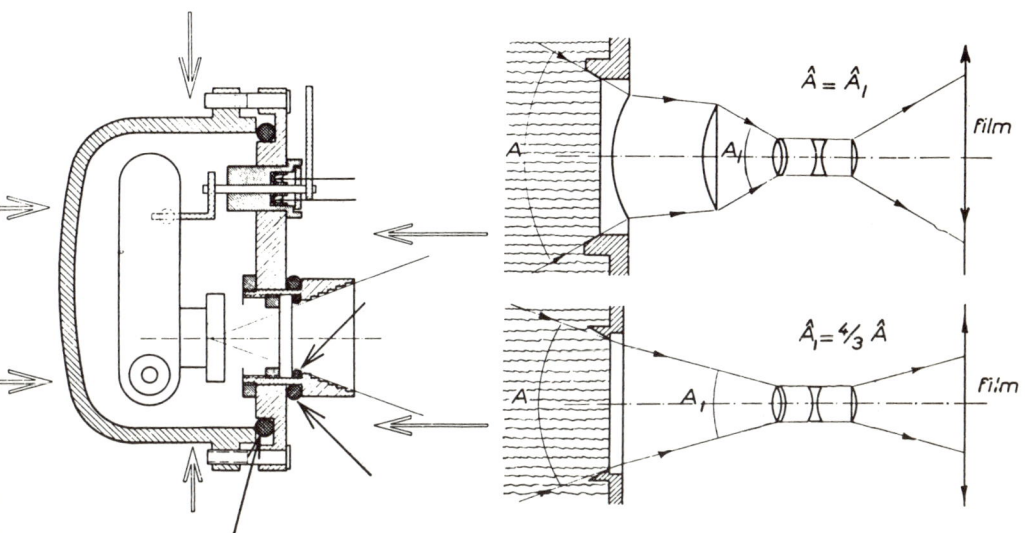

Fig. 172. Principle of the self-sealing "Aquaphot Robot." Section drawings *courtesy Aquaphot*.

Fig. 173. Principle of the Argus corrective porthole, showing its advantages over the flat porthole.

color films, and this is an advantage under water where the reds are filtered out after a few feet. For true color values, color film must be shot even closer to the subject than black and white—less than 5 feet; therefore, a wide-angle lens is a necessity.

Since color film is slower than black and white, a common difficulty is underexposure, causing a predominantly blue tone. However, with 16 mm. commercial Kodachrome the laboratory takes care of color correction. Kodachrome II is faster than regular Kodachrome but lacks color brightness under water. High speed Ektachrome has become a favorite underwater color film.

Figuring underwater exposure with an exposure meter is quite difficult due to reflections, light variations due to depth and distance of water to be shot through, and brightness of the sunlight above water. Best results seem to be achieved using a photoelectric meter, the best and most sensitive available. This meter can be placed in a clear glass jar with a screw top, or in a home-made or commercially designed case. Some cameras have a built-in meter.

The meter reading should be taken half-way between the camera and subject, with the meter angled slightly downward to eliminate surface reflections. Since meter readings under the best of conditions tend to be inaccurate underwater, it is wise always to take several exposures of a subject at stops above and below the meter reading. Experience with light conditions in various waters is the best guide. One well-known camera manufacturer now gives the following suggestions for work in clear water.

> Right under the surface . . . same exposure as above water.
> To a depth of 10 meters (30 ft.) . . . open up one stop.
> To a depth of 20 meters (60 ft.) . . . open up 2–3 stops.
> To a depth of 30 meters (90 ft.) . . . open up 3–4 stops.

If the bottom of the sea is sandy, light conditions can be compared with a snow landscape above water. The countless sand crystals with their reflecting power light up the shadows. Therefore, close your diaphragm by 1–2 stops.

There is some disagreement about the use of filters in underwater photography, but most photographers seem to feel that they are necessary for contrast and color correction below a few feet in depth.

In black and white photography, a K or G filter helps to eliminate blue haze. The exposure can then be calculated by using a filter over the light meter as well as over the lens. A yellow filter may be

Fig. 174. A sunken wreck conceals the elusive grouper. This skindiver is aiming a combination speargun-and-movie-camera. He not only catches the fish, but also records the complete action on movie film. *Photo by Paul Tzimoulis*

of some help in increasing visibility through really turbid water, and in bright shallow water a polarizing filter may help. Filters can also be used in black and white photography to increase contrast between subject and background or colors which would otherwise photograph as similar shades of grey. Fenjohn manufactures a set of plastic filters which can be mounted on the outside of the housing for changing underwater.

For color photography, color correcting filters are almost a necessity since at a few feet below the surface everything photographs as a uniform blue or green. The Wratten Color-Correcting Red Series are a help here (in yellowish waters near shore a magenta filter may be needed to admit blue as well). However, after a certain depth when reds have completely disappeared, a filter cannot restore them. The only solution here is artificial light.

Artificial lighting underwater is a complicated subject and many methods are too expensive and too technical for the amateur. Floodlights and electronic flash tubes can be very dangerous underwater if not properly insulated by an expert. Flash bulbs are the safest, the most economical and convenient source of light for the average diver-photographer. Only the batteries and the lead wire to the camera case require insulation, and bulbs may be changed underwater. Clear flash bulbs rather than blue should be used, as these are a source of additional red light. Larger bulbs are required than for above water, with a good reflector, and should be about three feet from the subject. Exposure can be calculated by using the numbers on the carton but placing the flash at one half the camera distance from the subject, and then doubling the flash distance number.

For underwater color movies, artificial light is necessary for true colors below a few feet from the surface. However, black and white films can be taken at a considerable depth using natural light only. Since underwater cinematography requires flat and uniform lighting, water-proofed floodlamps must be used. However, with DC current, which is preferred for safety, there may be a voltage drop through electrical leads which will affect the color temperature of the lamp. A slight loss would make a redder light that could help to replace reds lost underwater, though the light would not penetrate as far. The Rebikoff motion picture Torpedo, with a powerful lamp and enclosed battery is the safest and most convenient method of underwater cinematography, since the camera and light source are in one self-contained unit, and it can be used for scenes in small dark caves which the diver himself cannot enter.

Additional items of equipment such as tripods, mesh bags for carrying extra flash bulbs, a moisture absorbing cartridge of silica gel inside the housing are helpful. The housing should always be dried off before opening, with special care take to avoid scratching the lens. If the camera housing should become flooded, the camera should first be washed off in a fifty percent solution of clear water and alcohol, removing the lens if possible, and then bathed in light sewing machine or watch oil, manipulating the controls. It can then

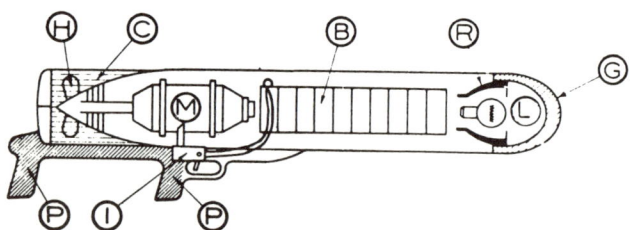

Fig. 175. Section drawing showing the principles of the Rebikoff "Dauphin Lux" torpedo: P—Handling and control handle; B—Storage battery; C—Propeller safety guard; H—Propeller; I—Sealed control switch; L—Incandescent lamp energized by battery B; G—Watertight window of the projector; R—Reflector; M—Electric motor.

be taken or mailed to the manufacturer for cleaning and repairs.

Careful records should be kept of various photographic data such as location, date, subject, depth, time of day, condition of water, distance of camera to subject, exposure, film, etc. Since experience is the best guide in achieving good results in underwater photography, much can be learned from such records.

Underwater photography is still a relatively new field, so exact and complete rules are still to be determined. It is becoming more and more widely used as a source of knowledge for various marine research groups, the Armed Forces, insurance companies investigating wrecks, marine engineers, archeologists, geologists, as well as for beautiful and evocative documentary films. Public interest has been such that even Hollywood movie companies have made several films recently in which much of the action takes place underwater. (Studio workers call these productions "wet westerns" and joke that any cameraman who wants to keep working had better learn how to use an Aqua-Lung.) Underwater photography is a fast-growing field and offers a potential source of pleasure and perhaps extra income for the diver who is interested. Commercial prints can often be sold to insurance companies, newspapers, magazines, advertising agencies, manufacturers of marine equipment or bathing suits, etc. Publications usually require 8" x 10" glossy prints, and they must be clear and sharp. Color transparencies should be preferably of a 2¼" x 2¼" minimum size. Although the field of underwater photography has so far been a limited one, and photographers have had to make an effort to sell their work, current interest is increasing so rapidly that good underwater photographers will soon become considerably in demand.

Fig. 176. Underwater photography—a fascinating hobby and means of recording the beauty of the underwater world. Photo from Hans Hass' *Under the Red Sea*. *Courtesy, RKO Pictures*

Fig. 177. There are many excellent underwater cameras on the market.

Of special note is a recently developed underwater housing that permits a diver to take an entire roll of Polaroid photographs while underwater, and to see the pictures while submerged! This housing was made by the Raymond Development Co. of Falmouth, Mass.

Fig. 178. Another remarkable development in the underwater photographic field is the U. S. Divers "Calypso" 35 mm. camera. The shell of the camera is the pressure-resistant housing. It is ready to submerge to 160 feet deep just as it is shown here. Wide-angle f3.5 lens. Speeds to 1/1000 second.

Fig. 179. A most unusual development in underwater photography. The Burton McNeely "up-down" camera permits a single photograph (through a level guideline on the front of the viewer) to be made of the surface *and* the underwater area so that both areas will appear on the same picture with only about 20% distortion or size increment of the underwater scene. *Courtesy, Parkway Fabricators*

Fig. 180. A compass becomes more than a convenience when the diver must find his way under heavy boat or ship traffic or under the ice. (Always use a safety line under the ice.) A compass is a useful tool for any SCUBA diver. a. Seawell compass as it would be viewed by the diver wearing it on his wrist. In this case it indicates the direction in which he is *looking*. b. U. S. Divers V-Z Navy compass. Spherical shape permits the diver to determine "North" from any position. c. Healthways submarine liquid compass. d. Taylor Instrument Co. compass has a floating dial card instead of a moving needle on a stationary card. For many divers this makes the compass easier to read.

Fig. 180a. Diver John Pritzlaff pauses for an underwater portrait. Note the compass on his wrist. *Photo by Gene Parker*

Fig. 181. Underwater housings can be made or bought ready-made for most cameras. The only absolutely waterproof underwater camera for 35mm film presently available is the Nikonos, which many photographers also use on land as well, especially when it is raining. *Courtesy, Parkway Fabricators*

Fig. 182. For underwater shots at night, shots in underwater caves, or at considerable depths, good lights are necessary, such as the Aqua-Lite, the Anderson Underwater Light, the Dynalite, Mity-Lite, and others. The Aqua-Lite has proved to be effective at a depth of up to 250 feet.

IX The Unexplored Sea

Its Legends and Its Secrets

Photo by George Knobl

Much of the fascination which the sea holds for us is due to its mystery; so much of the sea's depths is unknown and unexplored, so many things could exist hidden from our eyes in the eternal darkness of the abyss. Skimming the surface in his boats, man has always been uneasily conscious of the unfathomed depths reaching far below his sunlit world. Early mariners, contemplating the vast and seemingly endless sea, had no conception of its limits or its boundaries. And early divers, able to penetrate only a little way beneath the surface, and with distorted vision and limited air supply, caught only brief, blurred glimpses of the world below. Man, awed by that which he could not understand, envisioned symbolic perils, endowing the sea with a mist of myth and fantasy. In legends, he peopled it with mermaids and monsters; he told of fabulous sunken cities;

sometimes he thought that in its depths lay the other world where the souls of the dead gathered. In literature, the sea was often used as a symbol of the profound and the unknowable, of the dark and hidden depths beneath the surface of men's lives.

Many of the legends of sea monsters and other mythical creatures were attempts to explain the mysterious disappearance or wrecking of ships, or the crippling and death of pearl and sponge divers.

Thus Scylla and Charybdis, those terrible monsters of Greek mythology who destroyed the ships that were so rash as to venture near them, were actually symbolic descriptions of a whirlpool and rock on either side of the Strait of Messina which made navigation extremely perilous.

Later sailors told of enormous scaly sea serpents, and cuttlefish capable of crushing entire ships. Some of the sailors' reports of sighting sea monsters were probably based on encounters with the giant squid, which has been known to reach a length of fifty-five feet. And there is evidence that they may approach 70 feet. A ship's crew in 1875 told of seeing a sperm whale dragged to the bottom by an enormous serpent. Probably what they actually witnessed was the whale eating a giant squid.

Early divers who had no comprehension of divers' diseases invented their own explanations. The female Ama divers of Japan have a legend of a sea dragon which is their traditional explanation of how the women came to dive rather than the men. According to the legend, a terrible dragon, which lived in a beautiful palace at the bottom of a lagoon, killed pearl divers who dove in the lagoon by blowing poison at them. Prevented thus from diving, the people who depended on it for their livelihood were slowly starving. At last a

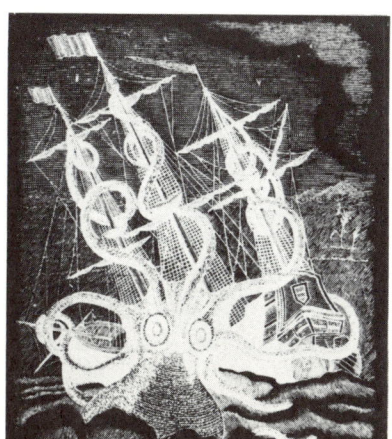

Fig. 183. Imaginative early print of a cuttlefish crushing a ship. *Courtesy, New York Public Library*

Fig. 184. Early German prints of sea monsters. *Courtesy, New York Public Library*

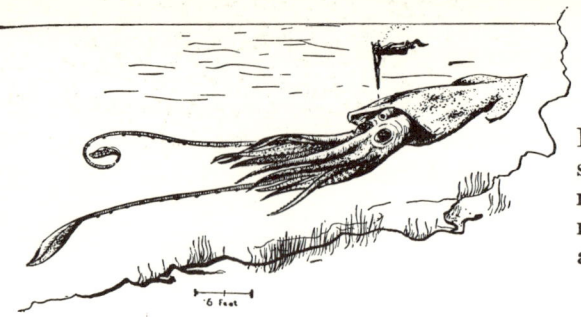

Fig. 185. A comparison of the giant squid which may run to sixty feet or more, which was probably the basis for many of the sea monster myths, with an average-sized diver.

young and beautiful princess of that region, who was an excellent swimmer, decided to dive down in the dark night to the dragon's palace and steal the huge white pearl, the symbol and source of his power, while he slept.

She succeeded in getting the pearl, but while she was swimming back up with it, the dragon awoke and pursued her. Since she could not swim fast enough to escape while carrying the pearl, she drew her knife (an essential item of diving equipment among Ama divers) and, making a slit under her bare breast, she inserted the pearl in her breast. With both hands now free for swimming, she reached the surface, but collapsed, dying on the beach. Her brother, who was waiting for her, then killed the dragon, and the community was saved.

Before she died, the princess revealed the hiding place of the pearl, and it was found that her blood had permanently stained the pearl a beautiful pink. Ama divers to this day dive bare-breasted, in tribute to the brave princess, and the pink pearl is considered the most valuable of pearls.

Other water-monster stories range from weird tales of deformed half-man, half-toadlike creatures brought up in nets, to enormous serpentlike monsters believed to inhabit inland lakes.

Probably the most famous of these is the Loch Ness monster of Scotland, said to have been sighted many times over the years. The latest report on this much-publicized creature, as reported by Richard Crosby in the *Skin Diver* magazine, came from the trawler *Rival*, which claimed that on December 6th, 1954, in Loch Ness, the entire crew had seen the outlne of a fifty-foot scorpionlike monster with eight legs traced on its sonic depth recorder used for locating schools of fish. Mr. Crosby notes that it seems unlikely that the sort of sonic recorder used in commercial fishing could graph such an exact shape, and concludes regretfully that since it was reported at a depth of five hundred forty feet, it is a bit out of reach of skin divers who might want to investigate.

The American Indians had many legends of water monsters. They believed that a sixty-foot monster with a dingy coat with bright yellow spots lived in Lake Manitou, Indiana, and would wreak his vengeance on anyone who disturbed the lake. They refused to fish or swim in it and were extremely disturbed when the Government wanted to build a dam there. Surveyors working near the lake also claimed to have seen this monster and described it as having a cowlike head and a long neck. (The Loch Ness monster has often been described in this way.) The Indians had apparently found the bones of a prehistoric creature near the lake whose teeth were 2 feet long, and this was probably the origin of the legend. Another Indian legend tells of a spotted, horned monster in a water basin near Forest Grove, Oregon, which had various objects tied around its body, and was followed by spotted dogs. It was believed to entice children and animals into the lake where they drowned and were changed into other forms. These Indian water monsters were at least extremely picturesque.

The concept of an ugly and frightening manlike water monster occurs throughout the folklore of many countries, as is shown by the accompanying illustration. Nor are all of these stories products of an earlier, less enlightened age. The *Skin Diver* magazine once carried the following account by the Sea Lancers Skin Diving Club of Santa Monica, California:

"The Sea Lancers have been diving frequently near the site of the coming SKIN DIVERS' JAMBOREE and on two occasions some strange reports came from some usually very sober and

Fig. 186. Manlike water monsters as visualized by: a. the French; b. the Germans; c. the Danes. *Courtesy, New York Public Library*

255

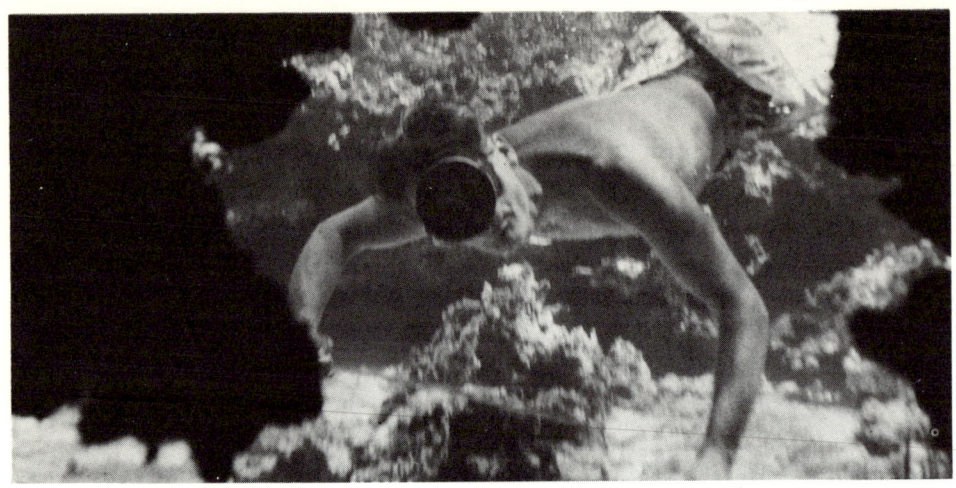

Fig. 187. Diver investigating a submarine cavern. *Courtesy, Ben Holderness*

reliable members. I hesitate to write this story as it reeks of sensationalism, but I feel it my duty as a club reporter to alert divers in the Palos Verdes area. Each report is basically the same. At a depth of about thirty feet in fairly murky water about dusk and nearly a quarter mile off shore, some type of an animal (?) approached each diver making menacing movements. Both club members made an outboard motor retreat into a kelp bed and then on to shore. What was the animal? A grotesque shape, more like a man than a fish, and nearly seven feet long! It swam rather clumsily as though it didn't live normally in the water. There is speculation in the club as to whether or not there is any connection with some flying saucer reports in the neighborhood at the same time. We feel this is a very serious matter and consequently made reports to the proper authorities and at that time learned that these were not the first reports of this kind. If any further sightings are made by any reader I would appreciate his contacting me."

This particular report later turned out to be a publicity stunt for the Skin Divers' Jamboree, with a diver dressed in a "gill-man" suit similar to the costume worn in the movie, *The Creature from the Black Lagoon*. However, it would seem to indicate that even today divers are not completely unconscious of or unaffected by the aura of fear and superstition which was for centuries associated with the waters of certain deep lakes and particularly with the vast and unexplored sea.

However rational and matter-of-fact the diver may be, he may suddenly find himself inexplicably afraid, alone in the depths of the unknown lonely sea, in a world without horizons, where vision is limited and dangers might approach suddenly, without forewarning by sight or sound, a silent world where he can talk to no one and is alone with his thoughts.

If he is a curious person, he will find enough which is strange and puzzling even in the lives of the sea creatures he sees, their intricate construction, their incompletely understood instincts and senses, and the mysterious way certain of their lives are linked with the moon and the tides, to make him wonder about the sea and its secrets. Gradually, as he overcomes his fears and begins to explore the undersea world, other things excite his curiosity—underwater caverns, or shipwrecks to be investigated; perhaps the finding of a rusted anchor, a few old coins or a fragment of pottery leads him to speculate about tales he has heard or read of sunken treasure, of lost continents, of remnants of vanished civilizations hidden beneath the sea.

The archaeological treasures and lost cities, known or suspected to be at the bottom of the ocean or inland seas, are valuable not only as works of art but also as "time capsules" of how the ancient peoples lived, for, unlike the surface of the earth, what has sunk beneath the waters is kept in a sort of maritime deep freeze.

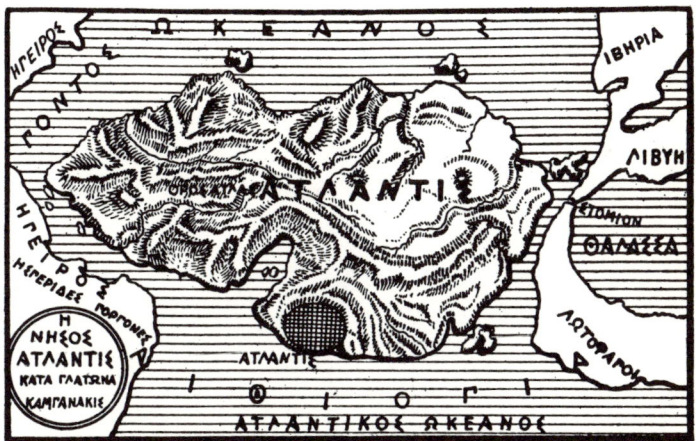

Fig. 188. Greek map purporting to show Atlantis situated between Spain, Africa, North and South America before the melting of the last glaciers caused a rising of the ocean's level. Note that the Sahara is shown as a lake and that the Mediterranean is closed between Spain and North Africa.

257

Remarkable discoveries have already been made, some of which have radically changed our concepts of the technological knowledge of antiquity. What was first thought to be a "child's toy," retrieved by divers from an ancient wreck at Antikythera in the Aegean Sea, proved, on a much later examination and cleaning, to be a sort of navigational "star computer," based on a system of interlocking gears, indicating that the ancient maritime peoples of the Aegean were much more advanced in navigation and probably sailed much further than originally supposed. Magnificent works of art, including the great statue of Poseidon, the Greek god of the sea, a copy of

Fig. 189. Diver excavating cargo and remnants of ancient galley (ship) under the Mediterranean, at a depth of 43 meters. He is holding an airlift, to clean mud and debris away from artifacts through air pressure. Piled amphorae and ancient jar containers, which usually indicate the presence of a sunken ship, can be discerned to the rear of the photo. *Courtesy, Établissement Cinématographique et Photographique des Armées*

which can be seen at the United Nations, have been recovered by divers from the sea bottom.

All over the world, on the continental shelves and still further down, fascinating archaeological discoveries are yet to be made. They will include the underwater Greek city of Helike, which fell into the gulf of Corinth in ancient times and was still visible from the surface in Roman times, the underwater cities and causeways off Yucatan and British Honduras, glimpsed from planes but not yet explored, the submarine "Atlantean" cyclopean walls and underwater pyramids on the Bahama Banks, underwater cities in the Caspian and Black Seas, sunken towns and ancient ports near the shores and around the islands of the Mediterranean, such as Caesarea, Tyre, Sidon, Baiae, parts of Carthage, and many others; roads on the sea bottom of the Caribbean and the Aegean leading to parts unknown, as well as massive ruins reported in the North Sea and in the Atlantic Ocean, off the coast of France, Morocco, and the Atlantic Islands.

The great fleets of antiquity lie preserved on the sea bottom, as do such modern (and valuable) giants as the *Titanic*, the *Lusitania*, and the *Andrea Doria*, all of which are at a distance now possible for divers to reach through special gas mixtures. Hundreds of ancient ships, some covered with thin gold plates, were sunk in the ancient sea battles near Salamis, Actium, and Sicily and presumably are still there. Thousands of ancient cargo ships, some carrying masterpieces of ancient art, were shipwrecked or sunk by pirates while only a few have been discovered. Even the arms of the Venus de Milo, known to have dropped into the sea within a hundred yards off the coast of the Greek island of Milos, are still awaiting a lucky discoverer.

But the greatest find of all would be the confirmation, by SCUBA research, of the world's most fascinating mystery—the existence of the lost continent of Atlantis which is believed by many to have been the first great civilization, a worldwide empire based on a continent in the Atlantic Ocean, a land of golden cities, mighty fleets and armies, struck down at the height of its power by a series of seismic catastrophes and now lying under the sea, with only the tops of its mountains protruding from the ocean floor.

There was a general belief in Atlantis in ancient times which lent credence to the theories of Columbus and other navigators and may well have contributed to the discovery of the New World. Plato dealt with the subject of Atlantis in great detail in his Dialogues,

Fig. 190. What many believe to be Phoenician, Maya, or even Atlantean underwater constructions have recently been found on the Bahama Banks, near Bimini, Andros, and other locations. As the Bahama Banks were above water approximately 12,000 years ago, they seem to indicate an extremely early civilization in the Americas. *Photo by Dimitri Rebikoff*

Timaeus and *Critias*, describing the cities, palaces, temples, the harbor works, irrigation systems, size of the population, and giving the distance from ancient Spain, almost as if he were writing a guidebook. Plato gave as his source Solon, the Athenian lawgiver, who had received the information from priests in Sais, Egypt, who had kept records of Atlantis written on temple columns.

He placed Atlantis in the Atlantic, in these words, making a curious allusion to what might be North America:

". . . in those days the Atlantic was navigable; and there was an island situated in front of the straits which you call the Columns of Heracles: the island was larger than Libya and Asia put together, and was the way to other islands, and from the islands you might pass through the whole of the opposite continent which surrounded the true ocean; for this sea which is within the Straits of Heracles is only a harbor, having a narrow entrance, but that other is a real sea, and the surrounding land may be most truly called a continent. Now, in the island of Atlantis there was a great and wonderful empire . . ."

Thousands of books have been written about the possibility of there having been a lost continent in the Atlantic based especially on the study of floods and other legends, animal and plant distribution on both sides of the Atlantic, lost land bridges connecting the continents, and surprising linguistic and cultural linkages between the ancient world and pre-Columbian America. Perhaps one of the most striking instances of linguistic coincidence, bearing on a common memory of Atlantis, is the fact that races living in a great circle around the Atlantic, with no apparent contact with one another, have preserved the common sound A-T-L-N to designate a lost paradise. The Greeks called it Atlantis, the Spanish and Portuguese —Antilla or Antilha, the Welsh—Avalon, and the ancient North Africans used the name Atlas, Atalanta, or Ataranta. The Egyptians referred to the western paradise as Aalu or Amenti. The Babylonians called it Arallu, while the Arabs thought the first civilization was in the western land of Ad. Even the name of Adam may also refer to a first race, Ad-am. The inhabitants of the Canary Islands, in the Atlantic, preserved the name Atalaya and thought, until their first contact with the outside world in the 1300's, that they were mankind's only survivors of the "sunken continent." On the other side of the ocean, in Mexico, the Aztecs said that their ancestors came from Aztlan, a great island in the sea, toward the rising sun. The Mayas called it Atlan and the Toltecs—Tlapallan, meaning "the land from which the gods came," bringing with them the arts of the first civilization. Despite many attempts to prove its nonexistence, Atlantis has proven to be an extremely long-lived legend and today, curiously, it is more lively than ever. It has recently been "discovered" again in at least two places. One is in Thera, one of the Cyclades islands in the Aegean, which exploded, losing much of its area beneath the sea about 1500 B.C. thereby giving rise, in the opinion of the supporters of this theory, to the story of the cataclysmic sinking of Atlantis. Another location suggested is around Bimini, in the Bahamas, where cyclopean ruins, apparently man-made, are being found on the Bahama Banks.

Plato, however, in giving a fairly exact date for the disappearance of Atlantis, 9000 years before *his* time (circa 427–347 B.C.), may have furnished us with a clue to the mystery. This date incidentally coincides with the melting of the last glaciers, which increased the level of the oceans and seas by about 800 feet, through a series of storms, rain, and tumultuous rising of the waters. This would tend to explain the worldwide legend of the Flood and the probable fate of Atlantis, as it is known that large parts of the ocean bottom, the Hudson and other river canyons, the Bahama Banks, the shoals off Yucatan, the North Sea, the American, European, and African continental shelves were *above* water about 12,000 years ago. The Azores are especially interesting with a history of violent earthquakes and the presence of deep-sunken sandy beaches found on the sea bottom around the islands. Divers who have dived deeply in the ocean know that the ocean bottom is *not* sand, sand being con-

Fig. 191. Jim Thorne, underwater archaeologist, making a deep dive on the acropolis of a sunken city near Milos, in the Aegean Sea. One of the building columns, still standing in place, protrudes from the rubble. *Photo by Jim Thorne*

centrated near the breaking waves of the shore. Also, a study of a depth chart of the Azores and Canary Islands clearly shows underwater plateaus which may be the vestiges of lost Atlantis, as well as the great underwater plateau of the West Atlantic Ocean. On some of the large modern maps, with undersea ridges and other features clearly indicated by sonar, one can practically trace an immense undersea land mass in the shape of a large island, or small continent, in the Atlantic, precisely where Plato said Atlantis existed.

With the new advances in depth diving, the development of underwater self-propelled reconnaissance vehicles and submarines, it will perhaps be the destiny of future SCUBA explorers to solve history's greatest mystery—that of lost Atlantis.

As Philippe Diolé says, more and more archeologists are discovering that they must become divers, since so many undiscovered remains of older civilizations still lie beneath the sea, and generally in a much better preserved state than those on land. Diolé laments the fact that divers unskilled in archeology have often missed important finds in ancient wrecks and have inadvertently ruined and injured things that they have found, and by taking objects out of the area where they were found, have destroyed all hope of discovering their function, relationship, or true age. Archeologists, he feels, must approach an underwater site with as much skill and patience as an excavation on land.

Several important archeological finds have been made recently by divers using self-contained equipment. Shipwrecks are particularly interesting from an archeological viewpoint, since they may contain a uniquely concentrated and varied collection of objects which give a fairly complete picture of the life of a vanished era. Since ancient ships stayed close to the coastline in their journeys, many wrecks are in water shallow enough to be reached by divers. In his *4000 Years Under the Sea*, Diolé describes the explorations of the Mahdia wreck lying off Tunisia at a depth of one hundred thirty feet, and said to be the most important archeological discovery since Pompeii and Herculaneum. First discovered by a Greek helmet diver in 1907, this ancient Roman ship was found to contain marble columns, statues, bronzes, urns, candelabra, etc., dating from the first century B.C. which now fill six rooms of a museum in Tunis.

Although the wreck had been several times examined by helmet divers, the French Undersea Research Group under Tailliez and

Cousteau felt that it might hold still further discoveries. In an expedition with the S.S. *Elie-Monnier* in 1948, they succeeded in raising four Greek columns, some lead anchors, an amphora, and one of the ship's copper nails, the analysis of which shed new light on the degree of skill in metallurgy which was possessed at that time. This group was able to remain at the site of the wreck for only eleven days, and both Tailliez and Diolé, as well as Alfred Merlin, the director of Tunisian Antiquities who was concerned with the earlier explorations, feel that a great many art treasures may still lie there to be discovered by divers working with the proper technical equipment. This would include dredges and suction devices for removing sand and mud without disturbing the site.

The French Undersea Research group has been involved in the exploration of other wrecks in the Mediterranean, notably Cousteau's exploration in 1952–53 of a third century B.C. Greco-Roman cargo ship off Marseille from which several thousand amphorae were recovered as well as samples of pottery.

The Club Alpin Sous-Marin of Cannes has also made several archeological discoveries beneath the Mediterranean, a veritable underwater museum, including a field of amphorae, the remains of a Greek port with jetty and part of a lighthouse, and of a Roman entry with marble columns, Roman and Phoenician lead anchors, and a head of Medusa in bas relief.

The Mediterranean, archeologists believe, still holds many discoveries, the further exploration of sites already known, as well as the discovery of new ones through research and in combination with archeological investigations on land. If, as some scientists believe, the level of the Mediterranean has been rising steadily for many years, as indicated by docks now lying many feet underwater off the coast of Crete and elsewhere, as well as the fact that both the Atlantic and the Mediterranean have risen measurably since 1890, all sorts of remains of vanished civilizations may lie beneath the Mediterranean mud still to be discovered.

In our own hemisphere, the Smithsonian Institution has been conducting for several years an exploration of historic shipwreck sites in Florida coastal waters, with funds provided by E. A. Link of the Link Aviation Corporation. Their ship, the *Sea Diver*, is equipped with magnetometers to detect iron beneath coral and sand several feet thick or through water up to forty feet deep, electronic detectors which locate the presence of an electrical conductor, sonar to define masses on the sea bottom, fathometers and navigational

Fig. 192. A sunken ship looms, intriguing and menacing at the same time. *Photo by Max Brandily*

aids to obtain exact fixes on shipwreck sites, as well as pumps and water jets to remove sand and debris from wrecks. When wrecks are encountered, the expedition's divers explore them, using shallow water diving gear, with face masks with attached hoses connected to built-in air compressors on deck.

These divers must be trained and observant to be able to detect the outlines of wrecks on the bottom, for, as M. L. Peterson, curator of the Department of History at the Smithsonian, says:

"The underwater shipwreck of popular fiction usually lies listing to one side, hull intact, masts erect, moss streaming from the rigging and perhaps even a skeleton at the wheel. In actuality, the wreck of a wooden ship over 100 years of age is marked only by coral- or sand-covered metal objects, all exposed timber having been destroyed by the *Teredo* shipworm. Metal remains that have lain in sea water in the southern areas of the Florida Straits are covered within a few years by a natural coral cement, which appears to be formed from the corrosion products of the iron object combined with the coral sand that abounds on the sea bottom in that area. Thus it is that a shipwreck site is camouflaged by nature and takes on the exact color of its natural surroundings."

Usually the most distinguishable remains of these wrecks are the outlines of the ship's cannon barrels, generally covered with coral and marine vegetation.

The Smithsonian Institution is primarily interested in the ships for their historical interest and uses the latest techniques for cleaning and preserving salvaged objects, which include pottery, old coins, tableware, swords, muskets, cannon barrels and cannon balls. All are of interest in identifying and dating the wreck, as well as in shedding new light on the life of bygone times.

Others, however, have long been interested in the Florida wreck sites for the treasure which many of the ships are said to have contained. The Spanish ships regularly passed through the Florida Straits on their voyages between Spain and Spanish America, and due to reefs and bad weather many of them were sunk. According to Mr. Peterson, in the years between 1520 and 1820, at least eight billion dollars' worth of gold and silver passed through these straits, and probably much more, since many of the shipowners concealed their actual wealth in order to avoid the heavy tax. It has been estimated that ships carrying a total of one hundred seventy million dollars' worth of treasure have been wrecked off the Florida coast alone.

In 1733, eight ships of a Spanish fleet carrying cochineal, mahogany, chests of silver and gold coins and ornaments, as well as most of the Mexico City mint's coinage of silver pieces-of-eight for two years, were sunk off the Florida Keys. One of these wrecks was discovered east of Key Largo by Arthur McKee who salvaged three seventy-pound silver ingots, and the Smithsonian Institution has subsequently investigated it and salvaged silver coins and figurines as well as weapons and other objects.

Tales of sunken treasure have fascinated divers for years. Jane and Barney Crile, authors of *Treasure Diving Holidays*, describe their search for sunken treasure in Florida waters, their discoveries of ivory tusks, coins, and uniform buttons, as well as a fabulous horde of "silver ingots" which turned out to be merely iron ballast.

In the past the salvage of sunken treasure, using hired professional divers, was difficult to accomplish without attracting the attention of the authorities. Now, with so many nonprofessional divers using self-contained equipment, it is possible that finds may be salvaged without being reported. Treasure hunters out only for gain may irreparably mar and destroy sites of archeological importance, through the use of dynamite and hurried and careless salvage methods. Diolé tells of treasure hunters looking for gold ornaments who blew up the Breton Megaliths with explosives, and of the galleys of Nemi in Italy which were stripped by treasure hunters who removed statues, bronzework, navigational gear, etc., which would have been of incalculable archeological value.

According to the laws of some countries the government owns any treasure discovered, but in the United States the Federal government makes no claim on any treasure found outside the three-mile limit. (On Federal property, the division depends on the cir-

Fig. 193. New voyages, where fish fly through a liquid sky. *Photo by H. Broussard*

cumstances, but the government has usually been very fair.) However, it must be brought in through customs, duty-free if over one hundred years old, and when converted to cash becomes taxable as income. All gold coins or bullion must be turned in to the Treasury Department, which will reimburse the finder for the full value of the gold.

Many sunken vessels known to contain treasure still lie unsalvaged in American coastal waters, particularly off Florida and in the Gulf of Mexico. Lt. Harry Rieseberg, diver and author of books on sunken treasure, lists the following: the Spanish galleon *Santa Margarita*, sunk on treacherous reefs off the east coast of Florida in 1595, carrying 7 million dollars' worth of silver bullion; a British frigate sunk off Soldiers Key with 2 million in treasure; fourteen Spanish vessels sunk off Carysfort Reef in 1715 carrying 65 million in treasure, of which $1\frac{1}{2}$ million was recovered the following year; an American vessel sunk off Gasparilla Island on the west coast of Florida with 1 million dollars in 1821; an American schooner sunk at the mouth of the Suwanee River in 1820, carrying 5 million in gold; the Spanish frigate *Santa Rosa*, sunk in Matagorda Bay, Texas, in 1816 with 2 million dollars lost; and three American steamers lost in the Gulf of Mexico just above the mouth of the Rio Grande River, carrying $\frac{1}{4}$ million in bullion. In Caribbean waters he lists many more, two of which he himself salvaged and recovered many thousands of dollars from. In Cuban waters, he lists a cache in an underwater cave in Cajun Bay, supposed to contain 3 million in treasure and the crown and jeweled robes of the "Virgin of Yucatan," an unidentified Spanish vessel in only 18 feet of water in Enseñada de la Liguanea Bay containing 14 tons of bar silver, and eleven Spanish galleons sunk in Matanzas Bay in 1628 with 30 million in treasure, as well as the *Santa Paula* off the Isle of Pines, from which he was able to salvage sixty thousand dollars of the $3\frac{1}{2}$ million it was said to contain.

Nor are Florida and Caribbean waters the only resting place of unsalvaged treasure ships. Thomas Penfield, author of *Lost Treasure Trails*, lists sunken ships known to have carried treasure, off California, Connecticut, Delaware, Massachusetts, Michigan, New Jersey, New York, Nebraska (in the Missouri River), North Carolina, Ohio, Oregon, Virginia, and Wisconsin (in the Wisconsin River) as well as off Florida and Texas.

Much treasure in ships of which the exact location is known has not been recovered due to the difficulties of salvaging it. The *De*

Braak, sunk off Lewes, Delaware, carrying 15 million dollars, including the jewels of Marie Antoinette, has several times been located and attempts at salvage made, but difficulties with winds and currents in the area have so far foiled every attempt. Another ship, the *Merida,* sunk in fifty-five feet of water off Cape Charles, Virginia, carrying 5 million has also defeated all efforts at salvage, although its exact location is known. Another treasure ship carrying 4 million in gold and silver, lies in New York City's Hell Gate passage in the East River, but the currents there, considered among the most treacherous in the world, have prevented it from being salvaged. It is now in fragments, buried under the shifting silt.

Many ships have not been salvaged because the cost of salvage operations, which might not even be successful, would amount to more than the possible gain. Salvage work is a difficult and often disappointing task, usually requiring thousands of dollars' worth of expensive equipment. Any extensive salvage of treasure by individual divers working alone without technical knowledge or proper equipment is highly unlikely. Most wrecks are covered by many feet of mud or shifting sands. However, a good bit of money has been recovered by individuals, probably more than will ever be known. Sunken treasure is a fascinating subject and one which will continue to intrigue divers for years to come. Chapter VII gives some hints on salvage work. It is to be hoped, however, that divers involved in such explorations will take the proper precautions for personal safety, and also report any finds of possible archeological value to the proper authorities before disturbing them.

Underwater exploration offers many interesting possibilities. Recently a Chicago diver found the ruins of a submerged city in the bottom of Lake Titicaca, while searching for Inca treasure. Although the Island of the Sun in the center of the lake was believed to have been the birthplace of the Inca civilization, he has so far found no treasure, but has brought up stone implements which have excited archeologists. Many sacrificial lakes or water basins which are recorded in legends and ancient records offer possibilities for recovery of treasure or archeological finds. Many investigations which would not have been practical for expensive professional salvage operations can be undertaken by individual divers using self-contained breathing equipment.

Naturally, really intensive exploration of the sea's depths—to investigate such mysteries as the "deep scattering layers," the possibilities of continental drift, or of land bridges which may have once existed between continents, of subterranean rock formations and sediment layers, which may reveal new knowledge of the earth's past and of areas which may once have been above water—can be undertaken only with equipment such as the bathyscaphe, the undersea coring devices (which now permit scientists to obtain cores or continuous sediment samples of the ocean bottom as deep as five miles beneath the surface and up to sixty-six feet long, covering a period of up to 200,000 years) and the sonic echo-sounding devices which not only register bottom contours but measure the depth of sediment in various areas.

However, explorations in water shallow enough for the diver may contribute considerably to knowledge of marine life, of the formation and resources of the continental shelves, and to archeological research in its attempts to uncover remnants of vanished civilizations and details of the history of man's past. Underwater exploration is a fascinating adventure which has really only just begun. Certainly it opens up potentialities for skin diving much more interesting and worthwhile than the mere enjoyment of underwater scenery or the sport of diving and spearing fish.

The sea waits . . . the possibilities . . . are infinite.

Bibliography

Books

Barnes, Harold, *Oceanography and Marine Biology*. London: Ruskin House, 1959
Beebe, William, *Half-Mile Down*. New York: Harcourt, 1934
Berlitz, Charles, *Mysteries from Forgotten Worlds*. New York: Doubleday, 1972
——— *The Mystery of Atlantis*. New York: Grosset & Dunlap, 1969
Carson, Rachel, *The Edge of the Sea*. New York: Mentor, 1959
——— *The Sea Around Us*. New York: Oxford, 1951
——— *Under the Sea Wind*. New York: Simon & Schuster, 1941
Cayford, John E., *Underwater Work*. Cambridge, Md.: Cornell Maritime Press, 1959
Clark, Eugenie, *Lady with a Spear*. New York: Harper, 1953
Condroyer, Emile, *Les Pionniers de la Plongée: histoire des machines plongeantes*. Paris: J. Peyronnet, 1948
Conference for National Co-operation in Aquatics, *The New Science of Skin and Scuba Diving*. New York: Association Press, 1962
Cousteau, J. Y., *The Silent World*. New York: Harper, 1953
Crawford, Carl, *Salvage Diver: The Lusty Story of U. S. Navy Salvage Divers at Work and Play in the European Theater of War*. New York: Wm. Frederick, 1946
Crile, Jane and Barney, *Treasure Diving Holidays*. New York: Viking, 1954
Cross, E. R., *Underwater Photography and Television*. New York: Exposition, 1955
Davis, Sir Robert H., *Deep Diving and Submarine Operations*. London: St. Catherine Press, 1935
Diolé, Philippe, *4000 Years Under the Sea*. New York: Messner, 1954
——— *The Undersea Adventure*. New York: Messner, 1953
Donnelly, Ignatius, *Atlantis, the Antediluvian World*. New York: Harper, 1949
Ellsberg, Edward, *Men Under the Sea*. New York: Dodd, Mead, 1939
Foëx, Jean-Albert, *Histoire Sous-Marine des Hommes*. Paris: Robert Laffont, 1964
Greuss, Robert, *Manual de l'homme sans poids*. Paris: Editions Maritimes et Coloniales, 1953
Grossett, Harry, *Down to the Ships in the Sea*. London: Hutchinson, 1953

Halstead, Bruce W., M. D., *Dangerous Marine Animals*. Cambridge, Md.: Cornell Maritime Press, 1959
Hass, Hans, *Diving to Adventure*. New York: Doubleday, 1951
——— *Men and Sharks*. New York: Doubleday, 1954
Idyll, C. P., *Exploring the Ocean World*. New York: Thomas Y. Crowell, 1972
Ivanovic, I. S., *Spearfishing*. New York: Barnes, 1951
MacGinitie, G. E., and MacGinitie, N., *Natural History of Marine Animals*. New York: McGraw-Hill, 1949
Nichols, J. T., and Bartsch, P., *Fishes and Shells of the Pacific World*. Washington: The Infantry Journal, 1945
Owen, David M., *A Manual for Free-Divers Using Compressed Air*. London-New York: Pergamon Press, 1955
Penfield, Thomas, *Lost Treasure Trails*. New York: Grosset and Dunlap, 1954
Petterson, Hans, *The Ocean Floor*. New Haven: Yale, 1955
Quilici, Folco, *The Blue Continent*. New York: Rinehart, 1954
Rackl, Hanns-Wolf, *Diving Into the Past*. New York: Scribners, 1968
Rebikoff, Dmitri, *Exploration Sous-Marine*. Paris: B. Arthaud, 1952
——— *L'Aviation Sous-Marine*. Paris: Flammarion, 1962
Ricketts, Edward F., *Between Pacific Tides*. San Francisco: Stanford, 1952
Rieseberg, Harry E., *I Dive for Treasure*. New York: McBride, 1942
Roberts, Fred M., *Basic Scuba*. London-New York: D. Van Nostrand Co., Ltd., 1960
Schenk, H. V., and Kendall, H. W., *Shallow Water Diving and Spearfishing*. Cambridge, Md.: Cornell Maritime Press, 1954
——— *Underwater Photography*. Cambridge, Md.: Cornell Maritime Press, 1954
Sears, Mary (ed.). *Oceanography*. Washington, D.C.: Publication No. 67 of the American Association for the Advancement of Science (Invited lectures presented at the International Oceanographic Congress, New York, 1959)
Siebe, Henry, *The Conquest of the Sea*. New York: Routledge, 1873
Steele, Frank R., *Bait Casting with a Thermometer*. Chicago: Richmond, 1947
Strykowski, Joe, *Diving for Fun*. Northfield, Ill.: Dacor Corporation, 1971
Sverdrup, H. U., Johnson, Martin W., and Fleming, Richard H., *The Oceans*. Englewood, New Jersey: Prentice-Hall, Inc., 1942
Tailliez, Philippe, *To Hidden Depths*. London: W. Kimber, 1954
Thorne, Jim, *The Underwater World*. New York: Thomas Y. Crowell Company, 1969
Von Arx, William S., *An Introduction to Physical Oceanography*. Reading, Mass.: Addison-Wesley Co. Inc., 1962
Waldron, Thomas John, *The Frogmen: The Story of the Wartime Underwater Operators*. London: Evans, 1951

Booklets

Bussoz, René, "Self-Contained Diving." Los Angeles: Nautilus, 1954
Cross, E. R., "Underwater Safety." Wilmington, Calif., Diving Research, 1954
"Guide for Sport Fishermen, Eastern Salt Water Annual." New York: Foster, 1954
Kelptomaniacs Diving Club, "Underwater Hunting Safety." Los Angeles, 1954
Jones, Max, "A Guide to Skin Diving and Underwater Spearfishing." Concord, Calif.: Universal Sales Co., 1953
Miner, Roy W., "Fragile Creatures of the Deep." New York: American Museum of Natural History, 1938
Peterson, Mendel L., "History Under the Sea." Washington: Smithsonian Institution, 1954
U. S. Navy, "Bureau of Ships Diving Manual." Washington: U. S. Navy Department, 1952

Articles

Bolin, Rolf L., "Report on a Fatal Attack by a Shark," *Pacific Science* Vol. VIII, No. 1, Jan. 1954
Martin, Robert, "Have They Found the Lost Continent?" *Mechanix Illustrated,* Nov. 1954
Moncrief, H. S., "Historical Developments in Underwater Photography," *PSA Journal,* Vol. 17, No. 11, Nov. 1951
Rebikoff, Dmitri, "Underwater Color Cinematography," *Journal of The Society of Motion Picture and Television Engineers,* 1954
Tassos, John, "Tourists in the Underwater World," New York *Times Magazine,* June 27, 1954.
Teruoka, Dr. Gito, "The Ama and Her Work, a Study of the Japanese Female Diver," *Japan Institute for Science and Labor, Report #5,* Tokyo, 1931

Periodicals

Skin Diver. 11220 Long Beach Blvd., Lynwood, California.
The Deep Sea Digest. Oceanic Research Associates, Box 333, Miami, Florida
Triton. (British Sub-Aqua Club) 25, Orchard Road, Kingston-on-Thames, Surrey.

Acknowledgments

The publishers wish to thank the following individuals, organizations, clubs, publications, and manufacturers for special assistance, suggestions, permissions, expertise, photographs, or the loan of equipment: Arnold Post, Richards Skin Diving Center; Paul Tzimoulis; Bill Vines; *Skin Diver* magazine; Ron Ribaudo; Robert Schaefer; Parkway Fabricators; Poseidon Systems U.S.A.; Farallon Industries; Jim Thorne; Dr. Manson Valentine; Dimitri Rebikoff, The Rebikoff Institute of Marine Technology; The French Ministry of the Navy; L'Etablissement Cinematographique et Photographique des Armées; M. L. Peterson; The Smithsonian Institution; Lee Pierino, *Time* magazine; George Knoblach; Ken Lore; U.S. Coast and Geodetic Survey; New York Public Library; H. Broussard; Lamar Boren; The Socony Mobil Oil Company, Inc.; Mel Small; La Squala di Milano; U.S. Divers Co.; Fran Gaar, The Aqualung School of New York; Alpha Photos Inc.; Ed Bair; Hal Reiff; Billie Colville; Phil Evans; Bob Ferrando; Aquaphot; Max Brandily; Burton McNeely; George Coggin, Alginier Industries; Dr. Fred Kornbacher, Aquavision; R. L. Bulow, Bulow Electric Co.; Jack Callahan, Burleigh Brooks Inc.; Paul Cherney, Cinefot; Sam Davison, Jr., Dacor Corp.; J. Harold Prather, Estwing Mfg. Co.; Ed Hansen, Evinrude; Norman Bates; Randy Stone; Healthways; Kimex; Kiekhaeffer Corp.; Loral Electronics Corp.; J. E. Barrett, Mity-Lite; Jim Cahill, Frank Sanger, New England Divers; Sam Raymond, Raymond Development Co.; Rolex; Safety Float Corp.; E. H. Repogle; T. F. Roche, Roflan Co.; Seamless Rubber Co.; Jack Glatt, Seawell; I. Robertshaw, Sirocco Products; I. F. Brownson, Superior Sport Specialties; Mark Haller, N. A. Taylor Co. Inc.; Fawn Scheffel, Taylor Instrument Co.; Henry Burnet, Underwater Electronics Corp.; H. F. Larson, W. J. Voit Rubber Corp.; Kenneth White, White's Electronics; Zodiac Watch Co.; Ambrose Gaines III, Florida's Cypress Gardens; Jerry Greenberg; Len Jones; Ken Crosby; Ron Higgins, Bob McComb, Schenectady Search and Recovery Unit; Leonard Maggiore; John Mahoney, N.Y. State Aquatic Director, YMCA; Dr. John McMullin, Pittsburgh YMCA SCUBA Instructor; Dow Nye, Sam Stack, Sam Stack, Jr., The Schenectady Aqua Addicts; Lee Prettyman, The Hartford Gillmen; Jack Sullivan, The Saratoga C. D. Divers; Milt Van Sant; U. S. Navy Dept.; Albert Stern, Norman Poller, RKO Pictures; Ben Holderness; Rene Bussoz; Twila Bratcher; U.S. Divers Co., and Diving Equipment & Supply Co.; Carolyn Tyson, artist; David Tyson, marine biologist.

Index

Note: Italic numbers indicate illustrations.

abalones, 26, 38, 57, 59, *210*
abyss, 19-22
accidents, *80*, 86-91, 138, 140
air (*see also* compressed air):
   alveolar, 71, 73, 75, 81
   component gases of, 71, 73-74
   partial pressures of components of, 74-75, *76, 77*
air bladder, 6, *6*, 7
air compressor:
   carbon monoxide poisoning caused by, 77
   gasoline motor-driven type of, *230*
   portable, 152, *153*
air embolism, 79, *80*, 86-88, 114
air pressure:
   adjustment of, 13
   on body, 67
air supply:
   early use of, 6, *6*, 11, 68
   compressed, *see* compressed air
   contamination of, 77, *167*
   experimental mixtures in, 79-80
   helium in, 79-80
   hydrogen in, 80
   water pressure on body and, 68
air tube and float, early use of, 7, 8, *8*, 94-95
Alexander the Great, 6-7
algae, 58
alveolar air, *see* air
alveoli, 71, 75
Ama divers, 72-73, 132, 253-254
amphibians, 53
anoxia, 72, 73, 77
antiquity, discoveries from, 257-259, 263, 264
Aqua-Lung (*see also* SCUBA), 4, *13*, 31
   ascent with, 84
   cylinders of, 13, 146, 148, *150-151*, 152, 153
   as "demand type," principle of, 146, 148
   diagram of, *147*
   diaphragm of, 148, 171, 172
   harness of, 149
   invention of, 13-14
   mobility in use of, 13-14

Aqua-Lung—*cont'd*
   mouthpiece of, 148, 152
   regulator of, *see* regulators
   rules for diving with, 168-169
   safety reserve valve of, 152
aquatic insects, respiration of, 93
Arbaletes, 135, *136*, 208, *209*
   loading of, 137
   schematic diagram of, *138*
   types of, 137
archaeological research and discoveries, 18, *21*, 224, 257-264, *258, 260, 262*, 266
Archimedes' principle, 70
argon, 80
Aristotle, diving mentioned by, 6-7
artificial respiration, 76, 77
   mouth-to-mouth, *87*, 89-91
art works, recovery of, 258-259, 264
ascent:
   accidents during, *80*, 88
   holding breath during, *80*, 88
   rate of, 79, *80*, 81, 84, 88
asphyxia, 77
Atlantic (East) Coast, 28, 35, 60, 61, 213, 214
Atlantis, 259-263
   map of, *257*
atmosphere, 67
atmospheric pressure
   components of air at, 74
   water pressure and, 67
Australia, coast of, 31, 40, 53, 54

baleen, 55
barnacles, 51, 60
barracuda, 36-37, 198
Bartsch, Dr. Paul, 233
bass, *200, 210*, 213, *213*, 214, 223
bathometer, *119*
Baylor, Edward R., 234
belt, skin diving, construction of, 195, *196*
belt weights, *see* weight belts

277

"bends," 6, 73, 80-86
  causes of, 80-82
  symptoms of, 81
  treatment of, 82
  whales and, 54-55
Bert, Paul, 81-82
binocular, 97
bivalves, 51, 57-59, *57, 59*
black bass, 213, *213*
blackfish, 214, 223
blackout, in anoxia, 73
blood, nitrogen in, 81
blood circulation, 75-76, *75*
boarding ladder, 102, *103, 175*
boats, loading of, 122, *123*
body, human, air spaces in, 67, 69-70, *69*, 71, *71*
Borelli, Giovanni, 8-10
Boutan, Dr. Louis, 233
Boyle's Law, 68-69, 74, *74*, 118, 148
breaker zone, 25, 26
Brock, Vernon, 38
"buddy breathing" system, 91
Bulow Seatow, *229*
buoyancy, 70, *72*, 73, 113, 114, 127, 154
buoys, construction of, 181, *181*
Byzantine divers, 4-5

caisson disease, *see* "bends"
California Council of Diving Clubs, 220, 221, 222, 224
cameras, underwater (*see also* photography, underwater), *145, 184, 186, 232,* 233-247, *248, 250, 251*
  filters of, 234, 244-245
  housings for, *see* housings, camera
  lenses for, *see* lenses
  movie, 233-234, 239-240
  remote-control, 22
  still, 233, 234, 236
  "up-down," *249*
carbon dioxide, 80, 93
  in air, 71
  increased partial pressure of, 76
  as waste product, 71, 73
carbon dioxide absorbents, 12
  malfunction of, 76, 146
carbon dioxide guns, *139*, 140, 144
carbon dioxide inflation, 114, *121*, 127
carbon dioxide poisoning, 73, 76, 77, 146
carbon monoxide poisoning, 76-77

cetaceans, 54-56
Challenger Trench, 19
children, precautions with, 102-104
civilizations, vanished, 259-263, 264, 269
clams, 57, 58, *59*
Clark, Eugenie, 51, **224**
clubs, diving, 29-31, 198, *218,* 219-226, *220, 226*
  archaeological finds of, 224, 264
  conservation role of, 59, 198, 221-222, 223-224
  improvement of sport by, 226
  informational role of, 29-31, 219
  instruction by, 219-220
  legislation and, 220-221, 222, 223
  requirements of, 26, 89, 114, 222
  rescue and retrieval work by, 223, *224*
coelacanth, 53-54
coelenterates, 38-41, 51
cold symptoms, diving with, 70
cold water, diving in, 129, *130, 131, 132, 209*
cold water survival, 118-124
colors, in diving attire, *132*
colors, underwater, 234, *235*
compass, underwater, 118, *119, 128,* 250
compass-depth gauges, 118, *119*
compressed air:
  in "demand type" SCUBA, 146, 148, 152
  early use of, in SCUBA, 11, 12-13
  outside water pressure and, 69
  vs. oxygen, 12, 146
compressed air illness, 72, 86
continental shelves, 19, 22
continental slope, 19
copepods, 23, 34, 40, *63*
coral reefs, 40-41
  marine life in area of, 46, 49, 52, *52*, 214
corals, 38-41, *40*
Cousteau, J. Y., 2, 5, 13, 14, 32, 48, 49-50, 56, 77, 127, 224, 240, 264
crabs, 40, 59, 60, 61
Cretan civilization, 4
Crile, Jane and Barney, 224-225, 266
Crosby, Richard, 254
Cross, E. R., 88
crustaceans, 40, 50, 55, 59-62
Cuatros Ojos, 51
currents, ocean, *see* ocean currents
currents, rip, *see* rip currents
current tables, 28
cuttlefish, 47

cylinder pressure indicator, *157*
cylinders, *see* Aqua-Lung

Dacor SCUBA, *156, 164*
Dalton's Law, 73-74
Davis, R. H., 12
decompression:
   explanation of, 81
   gradual, 81-82
   Navy Standard Table for, 82
decompression sickness, *see* "bends"
Decompression Tables, U.S. Navy, 82, 83-83f, 84-86
depth gauges, 118, *128*
   types of, *119*
depths, *see* water depths
Desco SCUBA, 152-154, *157*
devilfish, 42-46
diatoms, 22, 23, 29, 62
Diolé, Philippe, 14, 29, 48, 263, 264, 267
Dipterous fly, 93
diving (*see also* skin diving):
   ancient accounts of, 4-5, 6-7
   entanglement during, 113-114, *216*
   fears aroused by, 256
   in groups, *79, 85, 226*
   history of, 2-15
   husband-and-wife, *164*
   natural, 4-6, 71-72
   ocean zones favorable to, 22
   physiological problems of, 67-91
   sensations of, 13-15
diving bells, 22
   early use of, 7, 10, *10, 11*, 93
   photographic, 233
diving equipment (*see also* Aqua-Lung; SCUBA), 93-174
   abandonment of, 88
   early attempts at, 6-12, *6, 7, 8, 9, 10, 11, 12*
   home construction of, 175-196
   loading and securing of, 122, *123*
diving ladder, construction of, *176*
diving plane, towed, *231*
diving suits (*see also* rubber suits):
   closed, development of, 11-12
   early types of, 10-11
diving techniques:
   in entering water, 102, *104, 202-203*
   in surf, 24-26, *27, 85*, 118, *123*
diving watch, 118, *120, 128*
dolphins, 55, 56
drowning, 89, 175

Dryopidae, 93
dry suits (*see also* rubber suits), 124
   types and relative merits of, 127, 129-131
dugong, 54

ear, inner, 69, *69*
eardrum, 69-70, *69*, 127, 131
ear plugs, 70, 114
ears, equalizing pressure in, 69-70, 114-118, *128*, 131
East Coast, *see* Atlantic Coast
Egyptians, ancient, spearfishing by, 197, *198*
Eustachian tube, 69, *69*
Evans, Phil, *200*
Ewing, Dr. Maurice, 234
exhaustion, 102, 118
exploration, underwater, 18, 234, 269-270

fins, *see* swim fins
first aid kit, waterproof, 91
fish (*see also* marine life), 18, 31-54
   at abysmal depths, 20-22
   color changes in, 37, 52-53
   dangerous species of, 31-50
   food supply of, 22-23, 34, *63*
   game, species of, 212-215
   habitats of, 199-200, 213, 214, 215
   poisonous, 31, 38, 41, 91
   as poisonous to eat, 46-47
   strange forms of, 53-54
   temperatures of, and environment, 23
   tropical, 53
   vision of, 51
flashlight, underwater, *128*
Fleuss, H. A., 12
flippers, *see* swim fins
float flag, *231*
floats:
   CO_2 self-inflating, 114, *121*, 127, 212, *231*
   construction of, 118, *183*
   function and use of, 118, *122*, 127, 212
   types of, *121, 231*
   vest type of, 114, *121*
Flood legend, 262
Florida coastal waters, shipwreck sites in, 264-266, 268
Florida Keys, 48, 213, 215, 266
flounders, 51, 53, 214
free diving, *see* natural diving
French Undersea Research Group, 263-264
"froggles," 104
frogmen, Navy, 2, 5, 36, 146

gage pressure, 67
gases:
    laws of behavior of, 68-69, 73-75
    partial pressures of, at varying depths, 74-75, *76*, *77*
geoducks, 58
goggles, 13, 97, 104, 114
    Squale, 104-105
Great Barrier Reef, 40, 41
Greeks, ancient, 4
groupers, 208, 213
grunion, 56
Gulf Stream, 24

Haldane, J. S., 54-55
halibut, *209*, 214, *215*
Halley, Edward, 10, 93
harbor defenses, 4-5, 6
harnesses, 149, *156*, *158*, *160*, *161*, *162*
harpoons (*see also* spears), 137
Harvey, Dr. E. N., 234
Hass, Hans, 2, 31-32, *210*, 239
Hawaiian sling, 133, 135, *135*, *142*
    construction of, 192, *192*
    spearfishing with, 205, *206*
heart urchin, 42
Heathways SCUBA, 146, *158*
helicopter, recovery of diver by, *165*
helium, oil-water solubility ratio of, 79-80
helium-oxygen mixture, 79, 80
helmets, 7, *9*, 11, 68, 89
    with rubber suits, 127
    ventilation of, 76
hemoglobin, 75-76
Henry's Law, 74, 75
hermit crab, 40, 61
Herodotus, 4
Holderness, Ben, 133
Homer, diving mentioned by, 4
hood, for rubber suit, 127
horseshoe crab, 62
housings, camera, *125*, *184*, *251*
    construction of, 185-186, *185*, *186*, 238, *241*
    corrective porthole in, 242, *243*
    deep sea, 234
    maintenance of, 246-247
    movie, types of, 240-241, *240*, *241*
    plastic vs. metal, 238
    self-propelled, 234, 240-241, *240*, *241*
    still, types of, *237*, 238-239, *248*
    water pressure and, 234, *235*, 236, 241
hybroids, 38, 40, *63*
hydrogen-oxygen mixture, 80

ice, diving under, 129, *130*, *131*
ichthyotoxism, 46-47
immersion time, 5-6, 76, 77
    breathing and, 72-73, 105
    decompression for, 82-86, 118
Indian water monsters, 254-255
insects, aquatic, 93
intestinal organs, overexpansion of, *80*, 88

jackfish, 214
James, W. H., 11
Japan Current, 23-24
jellyfish, 38, 40, 50, 51, 53
jewfish, 213
Johnson, R. E. Fenimore, 234
Jonklass, Rodney, 200

kelp, 118
    entanglement in, 113-14, 216
killer whales, 55-56
King crab, 62
knives, underwater, 113, *114*, *177*
    construction of, 177-178, *178*
    types of, 115
Knoblach, George, *232*

larvae, 22, 23, 51, 93, 94
Le Corlieu, Commander, 13, 112
lenses, 236
    for camera housing, 242-243, *243*
    corrective porthole, 242, *243*
    wide-angle, 234, 239, 242
Le Prieur, Commander, 12-13, 233-234
life preservers, 114, *121*, 145
life-saving rescue techniques, *87*, 89
light refraction, 97, 102
Link, E. A., 264
lobsters, 59, 60-61, *61*, *211*
Loch Ness monster, 254, 255
Long Island Sound, 51
Longley, Dr. W. H., 233
lungfish, 53, *55*
lungs, 68, 69, 71, 73, 81

manta rays, 42-46
marine canyons and caverns, 19, 20, *256*, 257
marine life (*see also* fish):
    color changes in, 37, 49, 52-53
    coral-reef species of, 46, 49, 52, *52*, 56, 214
    edible, 56-62
    egg-laying of, 53, 56
    food sources of, 22-23, 34, 40, 55, 57, 63
    hostile, 31-50

marine life—*cont'd*
  luminosity in, 50-51
  mammalian, 54-56, 228
  observation of, 18, *20*
  ocean currents and, 23, 24
  ocean zones and, 21-23
  photographing of, 234, *241*
  as poisonous and stinging, 38-46, 215
  sexual activity of, 48, 50, 53, 61
  vision in, 51, 58
marking board, construction of, 196, *196*
marlin, 214
masks, 2, 8, 13, 94, 95, *145*, 152, *157*, 197
  care of, 106
  children's use of, 102-104
  clearing of, *100-101*, 152
  design of, 104
  development of, 97
  with eyeglasses, 104-106
  fogging of, 102
  "free-flow button" for, 152
  glass in, 97
  "nose squeeze" type of, *96*, 114, *128*
  parts of, 97, *98*, *100*
  precautions with, 102-104, *105*
  testing of, 97-102, *98-99*
  types of, *95*, *96*
  underwater distortion and, 97, 102
Mediterranean Sea, 29, 50
  exploration in, 264
  skin diving in, 2
Merlin, Alfred, 264
mermaid legends, 54
microscopic organisms, 29
Middle Ages, diving in, 5
mola mola, 53
mollusks, 56-59, *57*, 223-224
  diving for, 4, *21*, *59*
moray eels, 37-38, *37*, 49, 198, *199*
mourgons, 5
mouthpieces, 13
  of Aqua-Lung, 148, 152
  "buddy breathing" system with, *91*
  vs. full face mask, 152
  non-return valves in, 152, 155
  of snorkel, 106
mussels, 57, 58

natural diving:
  history of, 4-5
  limitations of, 5-6, 68-69, 71-72, 95
  oxygen consumption in, 72-73
nautilus, 47

naval warfare, 2, 4-5
nitrogen:
  in "bends," 55, 81, 82
  as component of air, 71
  vs. helium, 79-80
  partial pressure of, 74-75, *76*, 77, 81
nitrogen narcosis, 73, 77-80
nose clips, 114
nutrient salts, 29

ocean:
  "deep scattering layer" of, 50, 269
  depths of, 19, 20-22
  edible vegetation in, 62
  as food source, 18, 19, 22, 56-62
  marine life in, *see* marine life
  natural resources of, 62-65, *64*, *65*
  study of, 18, *20*, *21*, 224
  temperatures of, 19, 22, 23, 24, 118-124
  waves of, *see* waves
  zones of, 19-22
ocean currents, 29, 31
  causes and motions of, 23-24
ocean sunfish, 53
octopus, 38, 47-50, *48*, *49*, 51, 53, 57
  inky ejection of, 49-50
oil, undersea, 62-65, *64*, *65*
"Operation Starmop," 223-224
oxygen:
  in air, 71
  consumption of, 72, *73*, 75
  need for, 71-72
  in ocean abyss, 22
  partial pressure of, 74-75, *76*, 77
  self-valving of, 146
  toxic effects of, 12, 73, 75-76, 146
oxygen recirculating equipment, 12, 76, *147*
  hazards of, 146
  principle of, 146
oysters, 57, 58

Pacific (West) Coast, 24, 28, 42, 53, 56, 58, 60, 61, 213, 215
palolo worm, 56
Parry, Rosalia, 225
pearl diving, 5, 6, 70, 132, 253-254
pearls, creation of, 57
Penfield, Thomas, 268
Persians, ancient, 4
Peterson, M. L., 265, 266
photography, underwater (*see also* cameras, underwater), 97, 145, *145*, 232, 233-247, *245*, *247*, *248*, *249*, *250*, *251*

281

photography—*cont'd*
  artificial lighting in, 245-246, 251
  black-and-white, 243, 244, 245
  color work in, *235*, 236, 238, 243-244, 245, 246
  development of, 233-234
  distances in, 243
  exposure time and meter in, 242, 244
  film used in, 243-244
  importance of, growth in, 247
  movie, techniques of, 241-242, 246
  Polaroid, *248*
  problems of, 234-236, 242, 243
  still, 233, 234, 236, 243
Pinder, Arthur, *210*, 214
pipefish, 53
plankton, 22, 34, 40, 55, 57, 63
plant life, 18, 19, 22
plastron, 93
Plato, on Atlantis, 259-262, 263
Plutarch, 5
pollution, 29
pompano, *210*, 214
porcupine blowfish, 46, *47*
porpoises, 55, 56
  "language" of, 228
"Port-A-Lift," *227*
Portuguese man-of-war, 38, 39, 40
Poseidon Cyklon 300 Regulator, *155*
Post, Arnie, *228*
prehistoric diving, 4
pressure (*see also* air pressure; water pressure):
  atmospheric, 67, 74
  effects of changes in, 67-69, *68*
  equalization of, 13, 68-70, 114-118, *128*, 131
  positive vs. absolute, 67
  water depth and increase in, 68-69
Pritzlaff, John, *145*, *250*
propulsion unit, SCUBA, *229*
Puerto Rico Trench, 19
pufferfish, 46, 53

quick-release buckles (*see also* safety-release buckles), 89, 113, 116, *117*, 154, 176

rafts, in surf, 122, *123*
"rapture of the depths," 77-80
"rat-tailed maggots," 93
rays, 36, 42-46
  family tree of, *44-45*
Rebikoff, Dmitri, 239-240

Rebikoff Torpedo, 234, 240-241, *240*, *241*
  motion-picture, 246, *246*
rebreathing apparatus:
  early, 9-10
  modern, *see* oxygen recirculating equipment
recompression chamber, 82, 86
recon sled, construction of, 179-181, *179*, *180*
recovery methods, *165*, *224*
reeds, as breathing apparatus, 7, 94
regulators, 13, 146, *155*
  air flow requirements of, *163*
  balanced first stage valve in, 173
  Hydro-Lung Supreme, second stage of, 174
  installation of, on tank, 148-149, *150-151*
  single-hose, *125*, 152, 155, *156*, *158*, *159*, *161*, *164*, *170*, *172*
  single-hose, second stage of, *174*
  single-stage, upstream vs. downstream, *170*
  standard single hose first stage valve in, 172
  two-hose, *147*, 148, 152, 155, *159*, *161*, *164*, *171*
  two-stage, *147*, 148, *158*, *171*
Repetitive Decompression Tables, U.S. Navy, 83-83f, 84-86
Rieseberg, Harry, 268
rip currents, 26-28
rivers, underocean, 20
rock jetties, 26, *27*
rubber equipment, care in purchase of, 112
rubber suits, 112, 124-131, *125*, *126*, *128*, *145*, 154
  getting in and out of, 124, 127, 131
  helmet with, 127
  for ice divers, 129, *130*, *131*
  kits for construction of, 124-127
  maintenance of, 129
  need for, 114-124, 127-129, *209*
  principles of, 124, 127
  Unisuit type of, *see* Unisuits
  water pressure and, 131
  "wet" vs. "dry," 124-131

safety line, *130*
safety-release buckles, 89, 113, 116, *117*, 149, 154, 176, 195
  construction of, 188, *188*
sailfish, *210*, 215
salt water, buoyancy of, 70
salvage, 97, 219, *226*, *258*
  early methods of, 4, 6, 8, 10-11

salvage—cont'd
  economics of, 269
  procedures for, 189-190, 227
  of treasure, 266-269
salvage balloons, 189
scallops, 58
scorpion fish, 41-42, 43
SCUBA (self-contained underwater breathing apparatus), 4, 5, 145-174
  air supply of, see air supply
  air-supply contamination in, 77
  ascent with, 79, 80, 81, 84, 88
  basic rules for diving with, 168-169
  compressed air in, introduction of, 11, 12-13
  cryogenic, 149
  "demand type" of, see Aqua-Lung
  history and development of, 8-14, 12
  home-made, dangers of, 175-176
  mouthpiece vs. full face mask in, 152-154
  oxygen in, see oxygen recirculating equipment
  regulators for, see regulators
  safety precautions for, 167, 168-169
  spearfishing with, rules against, 95-97, 198, 222, 223, 226
  training needed for use of, 154
SCUBA clubs, see clubs, diving
Scylla and Charybdis, 253
Scyllias, legends of, 4
sea, see ocean
sea anchor, 118
  construction of, 190, 190
sea anemones, 38, 40, 41
sea bass, 213
seafood, 56-62, 210, 211
sea-horse, 53
sea monsters, 253-256, 253, 254, 255
search patterns, equipment for, 181, 181, 182-183
sea scooter, underwater, 165
sea snake, 41
Seatow, 229
sea urchins, 42, 43
sea water, chemicals in, 62
seaweed, 113
  edible, 62
self-inflating floats, see floats
"shark billy," 32-34
shark cage, 30
"sharkchaser," 32
Shark Dart, 30, 133

sharks, 22, 30, 31-36, 133
  blue, 35
  cooking of, 34
  ground, 34
  hammerhead, 33, 34, 35
  mako, 32-33, 35
  nurse, 36, 206
  porpoises and, 56
  protection against, 32-34
  spearfishing and, 198, 201, 204, 206, 210, 215
  species of, 32-33, 34-36
  thresher, 35
  tiger, 34-35
  whale, 33, 34
  white (man-eater), 32-33, 35-36
sheepshead, 214
shell collecting, 21
shells, mollusk, 57, 59
shipwrecks, 258, 263, 264-269, 265, 267
shrimp, 51, 59, 60
shrimp fishing, 60
Siebe, Augustus, 11
signals, hand, 90
sinuses, 67, 69, 71
  pressure equalization in, 70
sinus trouble, diving with, 104
skates, 36
  family tree of, 44-45
Skin Diver magazine, 95, 129, 175, 215, 226, 254, 255-256
skin diving (see also diving):
  age differences in, 132
  depth limits of, without breathing apparatus, 68-69, 71-72, 95
  experience and sensations of, 13-15
  growth of, as sport, 2-4
  women in, see women divers
skin-diving contests, 114
Smithsonian Institution, 264-266
snails, 57, 59
snorkels, 2, 3, 68, 94, 96, 97, 98, 102, 103, 145
  ball attachment for, 106-107
  design and function of, 106
  early concepts of, 94
  in pool, 105
  types of, 107, 108
sounding line, 177, 177
spearfishing, 2, 18, 27, 95, 118, 137, 197-216, 197, 198, 200, 201, 206, 210, 217, 245
  accidents in, 91, 226
  attacking game in, 204, 204, 208-212, 209

283

spearfishing—*cont'd*
  competitions in, *226*
  favorable areas and times for, 199-200
  hand spear in, use of, 198-199, *199*, 200, 201, 204-205, *204*, 215
  impaling fish in, 201, 204, *204*, 208, 211-212
  laws and regulations for, 95-97, 197-198, 205, 214, 221-222, 223, *223*
  poisonous fish and, 46-47
  with powered guns, 144, 199, 208, 212
  safety precautions for, 140, 208, 212, 215, *216*, 226
  stalking tactics in, 200-201, *201*, 205-208, *207*, 211-212
  techniques of, 197-216
spear guns, 135-144
  aiming with, *209*, 211-212
  Arbalete, *see* Arbaletes
  carbon dioxide, *30*, *139*, 140, 144, 212
  explosive-powered, 144
  gas and powder types of, 138, 140, 144, 205
  gas-type, construction of, 193-194, *194*
  Hawaiian sling, 133, 135, *135*, *142*, 192, *192*, 205
  laws against, 144, 205
  loading of, 137, 141, *143*, 208
  pistol grip on, 141
  power types of, 138-144, *139*, *142*
  rubber-powered, 135, *135*, *136*, 137-138, 140, 205, 208
  safety precautions for, 138, 140, 208, 212, 215, *216*
  spring, 138, *140-141*, 141-144, 205, 208
  spring, types of, 141, 142
spearheads:
  barbed, 208
  construction of, 192, *192*
  for hand spears, 133
  power-head, 140, 144, 212
  types of, *134*
spears, 26, 138, 140
  hand, 133, 198-199, *199*, 200, 201, 204-205, *204*, 215
  hand, construction of, 191
speartips, *138*, 144, 200
sponges, 51
  diving for, 4, 5, 6, 70
spontaneous pneumothorax, *80*, 88
Sportsways Hookah compressor, *230*
Sportsways waterlung, 146, *162*
"squeeze," 69

squid, 47, 50, 51, 57
  giant, 50, 55
starfish, 59, 223-224
sting-ray, 42, *43*
stonefish, 41-42
storm waves, 24, 25
striped bass, *200*, 213, *213*, 223
stunts, 5-6
submarine caverns, *256*, 257
submarine vehicle (T-14 "Pegasus"), *229*
suits, diving, *see* diving suits; dry suits; rubber suits; wet suits
"suit squeeze," 131
surf, *25*
  carrying gear in, *126*
  entering into, 24-26, *27*, *85*, 118, 122, *123*
  use of float with, 118
surge, 26
swellfish, 46
swells, 24
swim fins, 2, 8, *13*, 94, 95
  development of, *12*, 13, 107-112
  types of, *109*, *110*
  use and function of, *111*, *112*
swimming, 112
  distances between divers in, *122*
  skill in, 89, 222

Taillez, Philippe, 14, 124, 263-264
tarpon, 214
television camera, underwater, 234
temperature, body response to, 72, 89, 118-124, 127-129
Thorne, Jim, *262*
tidal forces, 23, 28
tidal zone, 19, 22
tides, 177, 256
  causes and types of, 28
  sea life and, 56
tide tables, 28
timekeeper, 82, 86
tool case, construction of, 195, *195*
treasure, sunken, 266-269
treasure hunters, damage done by, 266-267
Tridacna, 58
tridents (*see also* spears), 137

undersea labs, 65
undersea zones, 19-22
Unisuits, *131*, 166
  regulator attachments for, *155*
  with valved air control, *165*

U.S. Divers SCUBA, *160*
   regulators for, *159*

ventilation, 76, 80
Vinci, Leonardo da, diving appliances designed by, 8, *94*, 107
visibility, underwater, 28-29, 36, 235-236, 245
visual distortion, 97, 102
visual signals, *90*
Voit SCUBA, *161*

warfare, diving and, 4-5, 6-7, *9*
watch, watertight, 118, *128*
   types of, *120*
water:
   buoyant effect of, 70, *72*, *73*
   salinity of, 23, 67, 70
water depths:
   decompression and, 82-86
   increases in pressure and, 68-69, 131
   partial pressure of gases and, 74-75, *76*, 77
   range of, in diving, 5, 22, 68-69, 71-72, 79, 80, 95, 97, 225
water pressure (*see also* pressure), 4, 6, 7, 20
   camera housings and, *see* housings, camera
   effect of, on body, 67-70, 73-86, *74*, *76*, 77, 80
   effect of, on rubber suits, 131
   measurement of, 67
   partial pressures of gases affected by, 73-74
water spider, 93
waves (*see also* surf):
   approach to, in diving, 25-26

waves—*cont'd*
   power of, 24-25
   types of, 24
weakfish, 214
weapons, underwater (*see also* spear guns; spears), 133-145
weight belts, 14, 118
   construction of, 187, *187*
   dangers of, 89, 113, *117*, 175
   quick-release buckles with, 89, 113, *116*, *117*, 176
   types of, *116*, *117*
   use of, 70, 127
weighted shoes, 70, 89
West Coast, *see* Pacific Coast
wet suits (*see also* rubber suits), 103, 126, 145
   principle of, 124
   relative merits of, 129-131
   types of, 124, *125*
whales, 50, 54-56
   blue, 55
   communication with, *228*
   killer, 55-56
   sperm, 50, 55
   toothed, 55-56
   whalebone, 22, 55
women divers, 72-73, *132*, 224-226, *226*
   Ama legend of, 253-254
work, underwater, 6, *64*, *65*, *166*
   air consumption in, 163
   early equipment for, 10-11
World War II, diving in, 5

Zetterstrom, Arne, 80